The Future of work and Employment

Edited by

Adrian Wilkinson

Professor, Department of Employment Relations and Human Resources, Griffith University, Australia

Michael Barry

Professor, Department of Employment Relations and Human Resources, Griffith University, Australia

Edward Elgar
PUBLISHING

Cheltenham, UK • Northampton, MA, USA

Published by
Edward Elgar Publishing Limited
The Lypiatts
15 Lansdown Road
Cheltenham
Glos GL50 2JA
UK

Edward Elgar Publishing, Inc.
William Pratt House
9 Dewey Court
Northampton
Massachusetts 01060
USA

Paperback edition 2021

A catalogue record for this book
is available from the British Library

Library of Congress Control Number: 2019952343

This book is available electronically in the **Elgar**online
Business subject collection
DOI 10.4337/9781786438256

ISBN 978 1 78643 824 9 (cased)
ISBN 978 1 78643 825 6 (eBook)
ISBN 978 1 80088 243 0 (paperback)

Typeset by Servis Filmsetting Ltd, Stockport, Cheshire

Printed and bound by CPI Group (UK) Ltd, Croydon, CR0 4YY

Contents

About the editors

Adrian Wilkinson is Professor in the Department of Employment Relations and Human Resources at Griffith University, Australia. He has been short-listed by *HR* magazine for the award of HR Most Influential International Thinker. Adrian has authored, co-authored or edited thirty books and over one hundred and fifty articles in academic journals. Recent books include *HRM at Work: People Management and Development*, 6th edition (CIPD, 2016); *Contemporary Human Resource Management* (Pearson, 2016); *The Oxford Handbook of Employment Relations* (OUP, 2014); *Handbook of Research on Employee Voice* (Edward Elgar Publishing, 2014); and *The Oxford Handbook of Management* (OUP, 2017). Adrian has served on the Australian Research Council College of Experts. He is Fellow and Accredited Examiner of the Chartered Institute of Personnel and Development in the UK and Fellow of the Australian Human Resources Institute. He is Academician (Fellow) of the Academy of Social Sciences in the UK as well as Fellow of the Academy of Social Sciences in Australia.

Michael Barry is Professor in the Department of Employment Relations and Human Resources at Griffith University, Australia. His main research interests are in the areas of employee voice and engagement, international and comparative employment relations, and employer associations. He has published in leading employment relations and human resources journals, including *British Journal of Industrial Relations, Industrial and Labor Relations Review* and *Human Resource Management Review*, and has co-edited *Research Handbook of Employment Relations in Sport* (Edward Elgar Publishing, 2016), and *Research Handbook of Comparative Employment Relations* (Edward Elgar Publishing, 2011).

Contributors

Catherine Bailey, Professor of Work and Employment, King's College London

Michael Barry, Professor of Employment Relations, Centre for Work, Organisation and Wellbeing, Griffith University

Chris Brewster, Professor of Human Resources Management, Henley Business School, University of Reading

Jean Cushen, Lecturer and Director of Postgraduate Teaching and Learning, Business School, Maynooth University

Frances Flanagan is a postdoctoral research fellow at the University of Sydney in the Discipline of Work and Organisational Studies

David Foden, Advisor, Industrial Relations, European Foundation for the Improvement of Living and Working Conditions

Victor Gekara, Associate Professor of Logistics and Supply Chain Management, School of Business IT and Logistics, RMIT University

Rafael Gomez, Professor of Employment Relations, University of Toronto

Deanna Grant-Smith, Associate Professor, QUT Business School, Queensland University of Technology

Joshua Healy, Senior Research Fellow, Centre for Workplace Leadership, Faculty of Business and Economics, University of Melbourne

Peter Holland, Professor of Human Resource Management, Swinburne University of Technology

Sarah Kaine, Associate Professor of Management Discipline Group, Centre for Business and Social Innovation, University of Technology Sydney

Bruce E. Kaufman, Alumni Distinguished Professor of Economics, Andrew Young School of Policy Studies, Georgia State University and Griffith University

Gill Kirton, Professor of Employment Relations, School of Business and Management, Queen Mary University of London

Adrian Madden, Associate Professor of Human Resources and Organisational Behaviour, University of Greenwich

Paula McDonald, Professor of Work and Organisation, QUT Business School, Queensland University of Technology

Georgina Murray, Associate Professor in Humanities, Griffith University

David Peetz, Professor of Employment Relations, Centre for Work, Organisation and Wellbeing, Griffith University

Andreas Pekarek, Lecturer in Human Resource Management and Industrial Relations, Department of Management and Marketing, Faculty of Business and Economics, University of Melbourne

Katherine Ravenswood, Associate Professor of Employment Relations, Faculty of Business, Economics and Law, Auckland University of Technology

Darryn Snell, Associate Professor of Business Management, RMIT University

Huw Thomas, Lecturer in Management, School of Management, University of Bristol

Edwin Trevor-Roberts, Career and Leadership Expert, Chief Executive Officer of Trevor-Roberts Consulting

Adrian Wilkinson, Professor of Employment Relations and Human Resource Management, Griffith University, and Visiting Professor, University of Sheffield

PART I

The changing context

1.   Understanding the future of work

Adrian Wilkinson and Michael Barry*

A CASE OF COMPETING GRAND NARRATIVES

According to Yogi Berra, 'the future ain't what it used to be' (Scott 2019). Indeed, this is one of his better observations. The future of work is not a new topic despite the current acres of newsprint that suggest it is. We can go back to Alvin Toffler in 1970 – 'too much change in too short a period of time' – but, also, many others, from Jeremy Rifkin, who in 1995 predicted the end of work, to more recent publications that claim to be able to predict future trends (e.g. Gratton 2011; Ross 2016; McKinsey 2017).

Moreover, for many years we saw two grand narratives. One offered a utopian perspective of the leisure society (Keynes thought 15 hours of work would be enough for a good living by 2030), where for those at work, they existed as empowered knowledge workers. The other narrative envisaged a darker future, featuring intensification, surveillance, casualisation, austerity, financialisation, low pay, long hours, the platform economy and digital technology. In short, in the latter narrative, working life is portrayed as nasty, brutish and long. We see considerable debate at present in both the academic world and the wider community about the direction of work and the desirability of developments both for work and life outside work. A major part of this debate is also influenced by the globalisation of work, the impact of new technologies, and the shift of skills and knowledge development to low-cost labour countries (Howcroft and Taylor 2014). However, these stylised accounts lack granularity and are not based on interrogating the evidence so much as putting together a picture by using a series of often bold predictions, or by using one or two case studies to make generalisations about the future of work. Indeed, prediction is often mixed with prescription and description.

Too much of the literature on the future of work favours broad brush strokes in which the world is one of paradigm shifts. Variously, we are told we are in the midst of the fourth industrial revolution, the second machine age, the new economy (Ross 2016). These new, often shaky, assumptions are favoured over notions of contestation, unevenness and choice. It is as if there is a tsunami of change that cannot be shaped in any way and which delivers outcomes that cannot be negotiated. Of course, this suits global elites, those who may shape developments but can then attribute such developments to immutable external forces. Thomas Piketty's (2014) work shows how unbridled capitalism was earlier tamed with regulations that 'de-commodified' labour by providing social welfare and labour market support arrangements to redistribute wealth, and that social contracts were embedded in society until neo-liberalism eroded these structures.

Today, the positive grand narrative is downplayed, with the new vision rather more alarmist and also in receipt of considerably more air time – perhaps bad news sells? 'The robot ate my job' is perhaps the most common headline fitting with this narrative (see Table 1.1). McKinsey (2017) predicted that half of all jobs would be automated in the near future (for a different view, see Agrawal et al. 2018). Job losses through technology are of course not new. The Luddites were alarmed before they smashed machines, and the knocker-up profession lost its rationale when alarm clocks became affordable and reliable. While job losses are inevitable, new technology also creates jobs for IT specialists and gamers, among others. Moreover, as Fleming (2019) points out, robots might not destroy jobs as quickly or as extensively as expected. Instead, in a somewhat similar vein to the dystopian vision of the future portrayed in Shriver's book *The Mandibles*, the logic for retaining human labour will be that it might often prove cheaper than robots. Among other examples, Fleming cites the fact that sewer cleaners in India are cheaper than technology-based solutions in the UK. It is also worth bearing in mind that unemployment rates are similar to those of the 18th century (Bank of England KnowledgeBank 2019). Here again, our contention is that we need to analyse the future of work by drilling below the alarmist headlines about jobs, to see the importance of issues such as underemployment and poor wage growth (see Blanchflower 2019).

While scholarly research produces less exciting headlines than futurology, it also leads to more sober and nuanced assessments. Research, such as that presented in this volume, points to elements of continuity that always appear less dramatic than paradigm shifts and revolution. There are more people working in fast food franchises such as McDonald's than in leading technology firms such as Google, despite contentions surrounding the growth of the knowledge economy (Alvesson 2013). Moreover, the new economy has elements that look very much like the old. Briken and Taylor (2018, p. 455) describe a work process at the Amazon fulfilment centre in which employees are on the end of a 'bastardized, technologically driven, cost-obsessed form of lean working'.

In assessing these competing narratives, our aim in this book is to chart a forward-looking agenda for employment relations research. The brief for

Table 1.1   The end of work?

Title	Source/quotes
Artificial Intelligence WARNING: Can intelligent robots replace human jobs by 2025?	• S. Kettley (2018, 17 September). Artificial Intelligence WARNING: Can intelligent robots replace human jobs by 2025? *Express.* Retrieved from https://www.express.co.uk/news/science/1018786/Artificial-intelligence-AI-robots-replace-humans-machines-take-over-jobs
The Future of Jobs Report 2018	• WEF (2018). *The Future of Jobs Report 2018.* Insight Report. Cologny/Geneva: World Economic Forum • 'One set of estimates indicates that 75 million jobs may be displaced by a shift in the division of labour between humans and machines, while 133 million new roles may emerge that are more adapted to the new division of labour between humans, machines and algorithms.' (p. viii)
With His Job Gone, an Autoworker Wonders, 'What Am I as a Man?' You Will Lose Your Job to a Robot—and Sooner Than You Think	• S. Tavernise (2019). With His Job Gone, an Autoworker Wonders, 'What Am I as a Man?' *New York Times* • K. Drum (2017, November/December). You Will Lose Your Job to a Robot—and Sooner Than You Think. *Mother Jones.* Retrieved from https://www.motherjones.com/politics/2017/10/you-will-lose-your-job-to-a-robot-and-sooner-than-you-think/ • 'When robots become as smart and capable as human beings, there will be nothing left for people to do because machines will be both stronger and smarter than humans. Even if AI creates lots of new jobs, it's of no consequence. No matter what job you name, robots will be able to do it.' • 'Mass unemployment is closer than we feared—in fact, it may be starting already.'
Five Million Jobs by 2020: The Real Challenge of the Fourth Industrial Revolution	• O. Cann (2016, 18 January). Five Million Jobs by 2020: The Real Challenge of the Fourth Industrial Revolution. World Economic Forum. Retrieved from https://www.weforum.org/press/2016/01/five-million-jobs-by-2020-the-real-challenge-of-the-fourth-industrial-revolution/ • 'In terms of overall impact, the report indicates that the nature of change over the next five years is such that as many as 7.1 million jobs could be lost through redundancy, automation or

Table 1.1   (continued)

Title	Source/quotes
	disintermediation, with the greatest losses in white-collar office and administrative roles.'
Will Democracy Survive Big Data and Artificial Intelligence?	● D. Helbing, B. Frey, G. Gigerenzer, E. Hafen, M. Hagner, Y. Hofstetter . . . A. Zwitter (2017, 25 February). Will Democracy Survive Big Data and Artificial Intelligence? *Scientific American.* Retrieved from https://www.scientificamerican.com/article/will-democracy-survive-big-data-and-artificial-intelligence/?redirect=1
	● 'Today 70% of all financial transactions are performed by algorithms. News content is, in part, automatically generated. This all has radical economic consequences: in the coming 10 to 20 years around half of today's jobs will be threatened by algorithms. 40% of today's top 500 companies will have vanished in a decade.'
Robot automation will 'take 800 million jobs by 2030' – report	● BBC (2017, 29 November). Robot automation will 'take 800 million jobs by 2030' – report. BBC News. Retrieved from https://www.bbc.com/news/world-us-canada-42170100
	● 'Up to 800 million global workers will lose their jobs by 2030 and be replaced by robotic automation, a new report from a consultancy has found.'
800 Million Jobs To Be Lost By 2030 Due To Automation	● T. Frl (2019, 7 January). McKinsey: 800 Million Jobs To Be Lost By 2030 Due To Automation. *The Incomer.* Retrieved from https://www.theincomer.com/2019/01/07/mckinse-800-million-jobs-to-be-lost-by-2030-due-to-automation/
	● '800 million jobs are expected to be lost by 2030 due to automation and robotic labor, according to a study by the McKinsey Global Institute.'
The Future of Work: Could Automation be Positive?	● City News (2018). The Future of Work: Could Automation be Positive? (N. Ranson, ed.) *City News* (28), pp. 8–9. Retrieved from https://issuu.com/cityuniversitylondon/docs/city_news_issue_28
	● 'Automation could be a positive development if it is directed in a liberating way. Unfortunately, the history of automation in industry has tended toward deskilling the workforce, lowering pay and eroding conditions.' (P. Fleming as quoted on p. 8)

Table 1.1   (continued)

Title	Source/quotes
The Future of Work: Could Automation be Positive? Workforce of the Future: The Competing Forces Shaping 2030	• 'According to auditor PwC's recent Workforce of the Future report, 37 per cent of us are concerned we might lose our jobs to automation.' (p. 18) • PwC (2017). Workforce of the Future: The Competing Forces Shaping 2030. London: PwC • '37% are worried about automation putting jobs at risk – up from 33% in 2014.' (p. 8)
Jobs Lost, Jobs Gained: Workforce Transitions in a Time of Automation	• McKinsey (2017). Jobs Lost, Jobs Gained: Workforce Transitions in a Time of Automation. McKinsey Global Institute. New York: McKinsey and Company • 'We estimate that between 400 million and 800 million individuals could be displaced by automation and need to find new jobs by 2030 around the world.' (p. 11)

authors was as follows: map out the important intellectual boundaries for their field of research, outline the key research needs and link this research agenda back to how it should inform practice. We look first at current research topics, such as the rise of the gig economy and the role of platform companies. We examine the implications of such developments for key employment relations research agendas, such as (in)security of employment, equity, fairness, wellbeing and voice. Second, we asked contributors to take a view, or position, on the likely developments in work and employment to identify interesting areas of research that seem to address this future positioning. Our aim here is to explore interfaces between the field of employment relations (ER) and cognate disciplines so that our research agenda includes broader issues around innovation, globalisation and a new social contract. Our volume seeks both to review the extant literature on the future of work and to explore the big issues facing the modern workforce. While acknowledging that, and analysing how, the world of work is changing in important ways, we argue for a research base that allows more sober reflections on grand claims that surround the future of work. A base of research that is firmly grounded in evidence is also important to guide policy makers and practitioners who must tackle the issues raised in this volume.

In addition, we need a lens on the future of work that is neither reduced to a robots-or-jobs dichotomy nor polarised by assessments of lousy and lovely jobs (Goos and Manning 2007). In the UK, quality of work has become a major public policy issue, with the 2017 Taylor review outlining that work should not only be fair and decent, but also have realistic scope for development and fulfilment. If the following excerpt, comprising three of the five reasons why good work matters, gives a flavour of the ambitious nature of the project, it also provides a sense of the challenge confronting its achievement in the future:

> Because, despite the important contribution of the living wage and the benefit system, fairness demands that we ensure people, particularly those on lower incomes, have routes to progress in work, have the opportunity to boost their earning power, and are treated with respect and decency at work. Because, while having employment is itself vital to people's health and well-being, the quality of people's work is also a major factor in helping people to stay healthy and happy, something which benefits them and serves the wider public interest.
>
> Because we should, as a matter of principle, want the experience of work to match the aspirations we have for modern citizenship; that people feel they are respected, trusted and enabled and expected to take responsibility.
>
> Because the pace of change in the modern economy, and particularly in technology and the development of new business models, means we need a concerted approach to work which is both up to date and responsive and based on enduring principles of fairness (Taylor 2017: 6).

UNDERSTANDING THE FUTURE OF WORK

If understanding how the disruptive nature of technology will impact current work processes and employment arrangements is key to predicting the future, what is also important for ER research is seeing how disruption will impact the balance of power within, and the ongoing contestation of, the employment relationship (Dundon et al. 2017). As Quiggin notes (2020), when the balance of power favours management, disruption works against worker interests.

The changes examined in this volume are set against a backdrop in which organisations (and employees) are having to deal with the rise of highly competitive markets, financial crises, increasingly fast-paced technological change, the emergence of a finance-driven business model and the globalisation of markets. In addition, we see increased female participation, an ageing workforce, increased casualisation and greater employment insecurity (Batt 2018; Milkman 2018). Accompanying this has been a proliferation of different guises of employment, bringing into sharp focus the growth of new corporate arrangements and work practices, such as subcontracting, franchising, home-working and the use of illegal labour. These arrangements place increasing numbers of workers outside the reach of traditional regulatory institutions that provide core protections such as minimum wages, Occupational Health and Safety (OHS) standards, and workers' compensation (Wilkinson et al. 2018). David Weil (2014) points out that laws that regulate employment assume an employee/employer relationship and make presumptions about responsibility and liability, but ignore the 'fissured' workplace, meaning there are gaps in the protection of workers (especially if they are not classified as employees).

These developments are in sharp contrast to the features of the old model of employment that included long-tenure jobs with steadily rising pay, extensive workplace and retirement benefits, and a psychological contract based on a *quid pro quo* of employee loyalty for job security (Kochan 2015). Increasingly, this model is seen as being displaced by a more fluid market-mediated relationship featuring shorter-term jobs and multiple employers, shift of employment risk to employees, and a new psychological contract that indicates the job only lasts as long as it is a beneficial proposition for both parties (Cappelli 2008; Wilkinson and Pickett 2009). Global supply chains are now estimated to make up some 80 per cent of world trade and 60 per cent of global production (ITUC 2016), presenting challenges for traditional forms of labour market regulation (see Reinecke et al. 2018; Thomas in this volume).

Batt (2018) warns that the financial model of the firm points to why many employers don't want or need a relationship with employees in order to make money. She notes as follows:

> For a large swathe of activities, they simply need to contract for services rendered or buy technology, with labor already embedded as an input. This in turn suggests that a policy focus on the labor market alone – a strengthening or reform of labor and employment laws – is insufficient to achieve the kind of lasting reform needed to build a sustainable economy that provides decent jobs and income security for the majority of working people. (p. 466)

In conservative politics deregulation is seen as the answer to the new competitive context, and this has led to a questioning of old models of work regulation (Kaufman et al. 2020). Both the marginalisation of traditional labour market institutions, such as unions and collective bargaining, and the hegemony of neo-liberalism in many advanced societies have challenged the foundations of much of the traditional institutional regulation of work. The economic crisis has led both to pressures for a further paring back of governmental capabilities for regulation and enforcement, and a renewed interest in the possibilities for meaningful institutional redesign (Wilkinson and Wood 2012). In this sense the 'rules of the game' that impact the scope and authority of available work choice have been questioned (see Barry and Wilkinson 2019).

While much popular literature sees a context in which universal forces are unleashed upon the world of work (as if there were no human agency), analysis such as that presented in this volume (see for example Foden) suggests there is considerable unevenness in the workplace, not least as institutional arrangements at national level have a major impact on how broad trends play out in the workplace. What is needed, we argue, is a discussion of how existing institutions (albeit engineered for a different era) can be matched with the changing world of work. Is there scope to utilise Streeck's concept of beneficial constraints, to suggest that embedded institutions constrain free market behaviour in ways that in fact enhance economic performance (Streeck 1997)? Our hope is that the chapters in this volume contribute to a better understanding of what is actually happening in the world of work, which should then help inform policy and practice.

SETTING OUT A RESEARCH AGENDA FOR THE FUTURE OF WORK

This volume comprises a wide range of future of work topics, and it includes contributions from policy makers and practitioners as well as a number of academics. The book is set out as follows. Our contributions commence with a chapter by Chris Brewster and Peter Holland, who examine the transformation of employment in the 21st century and key aspects of work relationships. Globalisation, outsourcing, Artificial Intelligence (AI) and the changing nature of employment are all seen as reducing fairness, wellbeing and voice in the workplace. For some time, employment was not only the focus for people who needed work and the organisations they worked for; it was also the focus of governments that were judged by rates of employment and unemployment. It is in this context that the authors outline concerns relating to AI, noting that they are not new. For example, Karl Marx, in the famous 'Fragment on Machines' in *The Grundrisse* (1973), predicted that the rise of new machinery would create radical change in the role of workers, leading to the loss of jobs. However, while many have viewed technology as a means of job loss for workers, Brewster and Holland maintain that AI has potential to support positive employment relationships under leadership dedicated to fair and equitable workplaces. Without leaders who possess the skills and innovation to manage technology, the authors suggest that the threat of robotisation and AI will lead to searches for ever-cheaper ways of getting work done, pressuring people to move out of employment and to get them to provide work in other ways. Ultimately, Brewster and Holland argue that these changes are already occurring and are having a profound effect on employee voice

whether it is recognised or not. However, voice is likely to remain central to
the functioning of the work and/or employment relationship as a form of
communication and countervailing power.

Paula McDonald and Deanna Grant-Smith examine internships and
education-focused work experience, both on the rise and widely considered foundational in facilitating 'employability' and serving as a pathway
into the paid labour market. This form of labour may be organised by the
intern, the organisation or a broker, and may be voluntary or mandatory.
Although work experience may attract remuneration, it primarily consists
of unpaid work, distinguishing work experience from apprenticeships. The
authors address three streams of research that involve advanced knowledge of trends in relation to the future of (unpaid) work experience: (1)
modes and types of unpaid work; (2) the expansion and prevalence of
unpaid work; and (3) the impacts of unpaid work on participants and
other workers. The evidence presented on the expansion of unpaid work
and internships, the myriad of different forms that have evolved, and the
degree of support for their continuance, suggests the practice of unpaid
work and internships is likely to remain a permanent, though contested,
feature of youth employment, at least in industrialised economies. Yet the
potential for exploitation, inequity and negative impacts on the labour
market more broadly is significant. The research agenda canvassed here
provides an imperative for establishing sound evidence of how internships
and other forms of unpaid work experience can be structured fairly and in
a way that promotes, rather than diminishes, employment opportunities for
young people who currently face uncertain prospects in the transition from
education to work.

Gill Kirton focuses on workplace diversity and inclusion in modern
society across the dimensions of theory, context, practice and research.
Diversity and inclusion have arguably been the main drivers of change
in ER, which, according to Kirton, can be attributed to factors such as
growth in women's employment, an ageing workforce, the rising age of
retirement, and migration. Globalisation and technology have led to new
forms of employment – zero-hour contracts, temping, working remotely
– that deviate from the once-standard model of full-time employment in
a single organisation. Kirton reminds us that globalisation has increased
outsourcing for services, which has altered work conditions negatively, and
cost many jobs in countries with higher-paying wages. So, Kirton asks,
do these developments create a more flexible labour market and a better
work–life balance? Some research indicates that, despite improvements
in workplace diversity and inclusion, insecure forms of work, as seen in
the gig economy, can negatively impact mental health, as well as people's
economic wellbeing. Kirton calls the reader to acknowledge that social

and political contexts worldwide filter into organisations and workplaces. Thus, inequality is constant in the changing world of work, despite a plethora of laws and organisational level policies, in developed countries at least, meant to eliminate discrimination and promote a diversity agenda. Positive shifts in workplace diversity and inclusion must start with good practice models and bold actions to break down barriers to inclusion by building workforce diversity across occupations, hierarchies, functions, workgroups and teams.

Catherine Bailey and Adrian Madden explore the concept of meaningful work in the complex age of globalisation and technological advancements. The authors assert their position in the debate on whether meaningful work is a luxury rather than a necessity, by citing research indicating that meaningful work is highly significant for individual workers. They note that emerging forms of work such as crowdsourcing, gig work or digital microwork represent potentially exploitative work situations that may deprive individuals of a regular income, stability, supportive workplace relationships and connections with others, all of which may be important components of meaningfulness. Bailey and Madden draw on research from a wide range of discipline areas – philosophy, ethics and political theory, sociology, management studies and psychology – to map the terrain of meaningful work and evaluate the extensiveness of knowledge in the field. They then draw on this evidence base to pose a series of questions for future research and outline practical suggestions for individuals and the workplaces, such as employers demonstrating to workers the impact their work has on colleagues, the organisation and wider society, and promoting a positive and collaborative work environment.

David Foden examines the question of the quality of work and employment. He considers the extent to which the policy objective set by the European Union, of creating not only more jobs, but also better jobs, has been met. Taking as read that improving job quality is accepted as a valid endeavour, the chapter follows the International Commission on the Measurement of Economic Performance and Social Progress in placing wellbeing at the centre of economic and social policy debate. The idea here is that policies should be judged by more than their impact on income and wealth alone, and this applies to the policies and practices shaping our experience of work as much as to those shaping the quality of life more generally. Foden's analysis follows that of the European Foundation for the Improvement of Living and Working Conditions (Eurofound), which focuses on the level of the job (as opposed to the individual worker, the company, the wider labour market or economy) and identifies characteristics linked to seven distinct dimensions of job quality (including earnings), all of which are known to have causal links to health and wellbeing. A brief reflection on the role of institutions, policies and company practice precedes the conclusions.

Jean Cushen explores the role that financialisation is playing in changes to the world of work. She looks at how financial markets and investment decisions are leading firms to move away from the view that internal investment in labour is the best means to secure competitive advantage and profitability. In this way, Cushen sees the financial model of the firm as an existential threat to the traditional model of human resource management (HRM), built as it is on the notion of employee value creation rather than employee value extraction. The fear of financialisation is, then, that technology and analytics may render many employee skill sets redundant, and at the same time that the HR function will be tasked with distributing low-road strategies such as outsourcing work, managing redundancies, reducing or rejecting traditional employment benefits, and promoting peripheral employment and variable pay. Cushen's call is for HRM, both as a science and in practice, to be more assertive in arguing the case for firm investment in employee development and quality work to build sustainable productive value.

Sarah Kaine, Frances Flanagan and Katherine Ravenswood highlight the importance of understanding the consequences the current and pending changes to work and employment are having, and will continue to have, for gender. The chapter considers whether gig work provides new avenues to genuine flexibility, where women can balance work and family/caring commitments, or whether flexibility is more myth than reality, with gig work simply reproducing existing gender inequalities. In taking up this argument, the authors remind us that gig workers are not the only employees who are effectively working 'on demand', and that in non-gig work it is women in care industries who are disproportionately represented in such on-demand arrangements. Thus, despite claims that gig work may enhance female opportunity, there are signs that point towards its growth leading, as the authors state, to 'digitally "encase" much of the work performed by women within an ongoing paradigm of semi-informality.' The authors also argue for a research agenda for the future of work that considers whether the use of algorithmic data, such as provided by clients who rate and rank gig worker performance, is being used by platforms in ways that place additional burdens on women, or indeed gives rise to gender discrimination because such ratings contain underlying gender biases.

David Peetz and Georgina Murray open their chapter by acknowledging that most public debate about technology and robots focuses on how biotechnological change affects job loss. The authors state that, while forms of technology may change, their relationship to the production process and class are essentially the same. This chapter focuses on the implications of reaching towards the limits of technological capability and its insertion into or integration with the human body. The authors question what effect this technology will have on class and into which types of roles it will be inserted. When it comes to biotechnology, the topics of emotional labour, autonomy, stress, health and wellbeing are essential. The authors provide examples of the potential reduction in discretion that cyborg technology and its links with AI might bring and what workers' abilities will be to override a decision made by AI. No matter what forms of AI are mass produced, Peetz and Murray argue that, without conscious policy interventions, the rise of cyborg technology will impact the distribution of income and power. The rise of neural implant technology and other forms of cyborg technology raise major challenges, equal to that of the emergence of capitalism and climate change. The authors argue that society can choose what outcomes will arise from the development of neural technology: whether it will be a force for overcoming injury, illness and disability and improving living standards; or for pioneering a period of inequality; or both.

Joshua Healy and Andreas Pekarek return us to the theme of gig work. They argue that, while vitally important to the debate about gig work, the current academic preoccupation with the legal status of workers, as either employees or contractors, is too narrow. They call for a broader consideration of other mechanisms by which gig work can be assessed, and in doing so they invoke the notion of 'high road' and 'low road' employment. As the authors note, the high-road model proposes a broader standard: that employment is not just legal, but also that it is fair and reasonable. If, as the authors argue, workers need to consider different means of compelling platforms to offer fairness, one way to do this is by organising. Here, the authors show that gig workers are far from powerless, and indeed they cite examples of novel and emergent ways in which workers have used digital technology to resist employer control. A second avenue to promote improvement for workers is via shaping consumer preferences, and here there is evidence that some platforms are trialling high-road ER practices as a point of ethical differentiation in the market, even where this increases labour costs. The authors also see the prevailing labour market as a source of possible pressure on platforms, with tight labour market conditions acting as a pressure point to force platforms to enhance wages. As the authors conclude, however, predictions of how things will unfold are fraught because of the current lack of data on gig workers' earnings, how they vary and in what ways gig workers supplement those earnings with non-gig work.

Victor Gekara and Darryn Snell examine emerging workplace technologies and propose various questions for research in the next few years. Gekara and Snell argue that, while most of society agrees that new digital and automation technologies are expected to cause major industrial transformations and disruptions to people's lives, the nature and extent of impact has been the subject of policy and academic debate for many years. The authors examine this issue at the national economy and individual levels, and focus on who is most affected and/or most at risk in the unfolding workplace technological change, how those affected can be assisted, what systems of mitigation can be introduced to protect workers from the impacts experienced and, finally, who should be responsible for these tasks. Gekara and Snell suggest that research is required on these issues to inform effective policies and strategies on work and employment under emerging technologies. The authors argue that, due to the speed and complexity of these developments, governments require clear, empirically driven guidance on effective policies to manage technological change associated with economic transition. Similarly, industry requires informed strategies to effectively manage technological change while maintaining an appropriately skilled, engaged and motivated workforce.

Huw Thomas explores the role that Global Production Networks (GPNs) have in shaping the future of work. Thomas reminds us of how global capital can exploit what the literature refers to as 'spaces of exception' in ways that effectively allow them to operate outside the reach of regulation. Thomas notes that much of the early literature on production networks/ chains focused on understanding the networks themselves, how they operated and their degree of embeddedness, and largely saw workers as passive agents. However, in returning to the theme explored in Healy and Pekarek, Thomas argues that workers need not be seen simply as bystanders watching these processes of change unfold. Rather, as he argues, workers have agency, and here again the future of work provides exciting opportunities for researchers to explore new forms of worker resistance to the dominance of global capital. For Thomas, the future of work for workers in GPNs is not set, and indeed there are alternative possibilities: on the one hand there is a model of soft, private regulation that places few constraints on GPNs, and on the other hand there are models of governance that include a strong role for workers and public agencies. What is at stake here, according to Thomas, is whether GPNs incorporate equity, voice and efficiency, or just act according to economic efficiency.

Edwin Trevor-Roberts notes that, while our understanding of careers today has evolved over the past century, there remains an inherent assumption that careers are built in an environment of certainty or, at the very least, that an individual will purposefully move towards certainty in their career. The future of careers, however, is predicated on uncertainty. The pace of change, whether it be technological, societal or organisational, will continue to accelerate. Individuals face an increasing number of alternatives for their career structure, such as boundaryless, portfolio, gig or traditional. In addition, people can no longer expect clearly identifiable career paths mapped out by their organisation, as organisations themselves explore new methods for producing value, as discussed in earlier chapters. A successful career of the future will be characterised by a person's ability to manage the uncertainties they experience. The chapter explores what a career will look like in the future, starting with a re-conceptualisation of careers as subjective sense-making processes to be enacted within an environment of uncertainty.

The final contribution is an ambitious attempt to plot the future direction of employee engagement. In this chapter Bruce Kaufman and colleagues note that, despite its importance, there is little agreement between consultant and academic communities about what engagement actually is or how to measure it. While academic interest in employee engagement has grown rapidly only in the last decade, the authors note that efforts to engage workers are far from new; and if other words, such as energetic and industrious, are used then the study of engagement can be traced as far back as to the work of Adam Smith and John Commons. The second part of the chapter reports on the findings of the authors' large, four-country survey of workers and management, known by the acronym SWERS, which yields some engagement insights. While noting differences in measurement techniques, the SWERS results are not dissimilar to those of leading survey firms, such as Gallop, which show there is considerable room for improving employee engagement. An interesting finding of SWERS is that within-country differences are equal to, if not more significant, than cross-national differences, even though the latter are quite significant. Finally, the chapter seeks to assess the future of employee engagement, no small task given difficulties inherent in predicting the impact of influences such as rate of economic growth, employment/unemployment, the rise and decline of different industries, and so on. In this section the authors attempt to predict future patterns and possible growth in engagement by assessing the likelihood of greater dispersion of high-performance work systems (HPWS), which are predicated on engaged workers. The authors settle on a sober assessment, noting that, while some trends such as growth in knowledge-driven and high-technology industries favour an expansion in HPWS, other future-of-work trends, such as financialisation and employment insecurity, work against the adoption of HPWS.

NOTE

* The authors acknowledge financial support from the ARC (DP140100194), SSHRC (435-2015-0801) and the Innovation Resource Center for Human Resources (IRC4HR).

REFERENCES

Agrawal, Ajay, Joshua Gans and Avi Goldfarb (2018) *Prediction Machines: The Simple Economics of Artificial Intelligence*, Boston, MA: Harvard Business Review Press.

Alvesson, M. (2013) *The Triumph of Emptiness: Consumption, Higher Education, and Work Organization*, Oxford: Oxford University Press.

Bank of England KnowledgeBank (2019) 'KnowledgeBank: The economy made simple', accessed 4 October 2019 at https://www.bankofengland.co.uk/knowledgebank.

Barry, M. and A. Wilkinson (2019) 'Regulation, deregulation or re-regulation? The changing regulatory framework for HRM', in A. Wilkinson, N. Bacon, S. Snell and D. Lepak (eds), *The Sage Handbook of Human Resource Management* (2nd edition), London: Sage, pp. 65–81.

Batt, R. (2018) 'The financial model of the firm, the "future of work", and employment relations', in Adrian Wilkinson, Tony Dundon, Jimmy Donaghey and Alex Colvin (eds), *The Routledge Companion to Employment Relations*, London: Routledge, pp. 464–79.

Blanchflower, D. (2019) *Not Working: Where Have All the Good Jobs Gone?* Princeton, NJ: Princeton University Press.

Briken, K. and P. Taylor (2018) 'Fulfilling the "British way": beyond constrained choice – Amazon workers' lived experiences of workfare', *Industrial Relations Journal*, 49(5–6), pp. 438–58.

Cappelli, P. (2008) *Employment Relationships: New Models of White-Collar Work*, Ithaca, NY: Cornell University Press.

Dundon, T., N. Cullihane and A. Wilkinson (2017) *A Very Short, Fairly Interesting and Reasonably Cheap Book about Employment Relations*, London: Sage.

Fleming, P. (2019) 'Robots and organization studies: why robots might not want to steal your job', *Organisation Studies*, 40(1), pp. 23–38.

Goos, M. and A. Manning (2007) 'Lousy and lovely jobs: the rising polarization of working Britain', *Review of Economics and Statistics*, 89(1), pp. 118–33.

Gratton, L. (2011) *The Shift: The Future of Work is Already Here*, London: Collins.

Howcroft, D. and P. Taylor (2014) ' "Plus ça change, plus c'est la même chose": researching and theorising the new technologies', *New Technology, Work and Employment*, 29(1), pp. 1–8.

ITUC (2016) Supply Chain Resources Hub, accessed 5 October 2017 at https://www.ituc-csi.org/supplychains-resources-hub?lang=en.

Kaufman, B., M. Barry, R. Gomez and A. Wilkinson (2020) 'Measuring the quality of workplace relations and organizational performance with alternative balanced scorecards from strategic HRM and employment–industrial relations', *Human Resource Management Journal*.

Keynes, J.M. (2009) 'Economic possibilities for our grandchildren', in *Essays in Persuasion*, London: Classic House, pp. 321–32.

Kochan, T.A. (2015) *Shaping the Future of Work: What Future Worker, Business, Government, and Education Leaders Need to Do for All to Prosper*, New York: Business Expert Press.
Marx, K. (1973) *Grundrisse: Foundations of the Critique of Political Economy* [*Grundrisse der Kritik der Politischen Ökonomie*], London: Penguin Books.
McKinsey Global Institute (2017) 'A future that works: automation, employment, and productivity', [Report].
Milkman, R. (2018) Winners and Losers: The Future of Work Symposium on New Social Inequalities and the Future of Work, 19 June, The University of Queensland, Australia.
Piketty, T. (2014) *Capital in the Twenty First Century*, Cambridge, MA: Harvard University Press.
Quiggin, J. (2020) The Future of Work, The Keith Hancock Lecture, Academy of the Social Sciences in Australia, The University of Queensland, Australia.
Reinecke, J., J. Donaghey, A. Wilkinson and G. Wood (2018) 'Global supply chains and social relations at work: brokering across boundaries', *Human Relations*, 71(4), pp. 459–80.
Rifkin, J. (1995) *The End of Work*, London: Putnam.
Ross, A. (2016) *The Industries of the Future*, New York, NY: Simon & Schuster.
Scott, N. (2019) 'The 50 greatest Yogi Berra quotes', USA Today Sports, 28 March, accessed 4 October 2019 from https://ftw.usatoday.com/2019/03/the-50-greatest-yogi-berra-quotes.
Shriver, L. (2016) *The Mandibles: A Family, 2029–2047*. London: Borough Press.
Streeck, W. (1997) 'Beneficial constraints: on the economic limits of rational voluntarism', in J. Hollingsworth, J. Rogers and R. Boyer (eds), *Contemporary Capitalism: The Embeddedness of Institutions*, Cambridge: Cambridge University Press, pp. 197–219.
Taylor review (2017) *The Taylor Review of Modern Working Practices*, July, London: Department for Business, Energy and Industrial Strategy.
Toffler, A. (1970) *Future Shock*. New York, NY: Random House.
Weil, D. (2014) *The Fissured Workplace: How Work Became So Bad for So Many and What Can be Done to Improve It*, Cambridge, MA: Harvard University Press.
Wilkinson, A. and G. Wood (2012) 'Institutions and employment relations: the state of the art', *Industrial Relations: Journal of Economy and Society*, 51(2), pp. 373–88.
Wilkinson, A., M. Barry, R. Gomez and B. Kaufman (2018) 'Taking the pulse at work: an employment relations scorecard for Australia', *Journal of Industrial Relations*, 60(2), pp. 145–75.
Wilkinson, R. and K. Pickett (2009) *The Spirit Level: Why More Equal Societies Almost Always Do Better*, London: Allen Lane.

PART II

Changing practices

2. Work 'or' employment in the 21st century: its impact on the employment relationship

Chris Brewster and Peter Holland

INTRODUCTION

> [R]esearch and development has further advanced fast moving technologies, companies have adopted new approaches, and new empirical evidence has emerged of the disruptive impacts of emerging technologies and new business models on the labour markets, social relationships and political systems. (Schwab, 2018, p. 1)

This quote highlights the major changes we have experienced in the 21st century and continue to experience at an accelerating rate. An all-pervading theme of the times is disruption and whilst in itself this is a way to progress and enhance the economy, the speed and depth of change is something that has not been experienced in living memory. Offshoring is eroding high-skilled white-collar jobs and long-established models of business, work and employment in major sectors such as hotels, fast food, taxi and the publishing industries have been 'blown to bits' (Evans & Wurster, 2000) by major technological innovation increasingly supported by artificial intelligence (AI) and globalisation. What has often been side-lined in this transformation is the changing nature of employment, where working in the 21st century 'gig' economy is seen as cutting edge and/or inevitable. This 'new' world of work has major implications for the employment relationship and key aspects underpinning this relationship of fairness, well-being and voice. We therefore look to explore and map out some of these issues in this changing workplace terrain through the dislocation between work and employment as we know it in Advanced Market Economies (AMEs). From this we hope to provide a research framework or agenda to explore in the next decades of accelerating change and disruption.

BACK TO THE FUTURE?

All AMEs have been through a number of major technological and organisational revolutions. The first industrial revolution involved the introduction of mechanisation and new power sources and amongst other consequences it created '*employment*'. Prior to that, people had worked as cultivators, as subsistence labourers in agriculture, as hired help who worked for food and lodging as servants to rich people, who had run their own businesses, or had worked as craft workers who made products at home, selling them directly or being paid for each piece by an agent between them and the market (Thompson & McHugh, 2002). This process became known as 'putting out' and was the earliest form of the subcontracting system (Mathews, 1989). No one was in 'employment' and the primary market was local or regional. The second revolution involved mass assembly and production. The revolution was a shift to the organisation of work and production in (manu)factories, which meant taking advantage of the new technology embodied in machinery by bringing together often hundreds, or in some cases even thousands, of workers into the same workplace, mainly because of the need for a central power source (Watson, 1997). A new model of engagement had to be found and that was (full-time) employment: the owner of the facilities, the employer or the employing organisation, paid for (purchased) the time of the workers and in return the workers completed the tasks that were allocated to them. In a short time the model spread to other sectors of the economy (though never to all) and became a norm: work became conflated with employment, so that unpaid work, mostly by women, ceased to be counted as work. Another development during this period of radical change in the merger of work and employment was the appearance of trade unions in response to the appalling conditions under which this work was undertaken. The key role of these trade unions was to provide a countervailing power or voice for employees as a means of regulating the employment relationship: in particular, addressing conditions of work, levels of exploitation and precarious employment (Acker et al., 1996).

As market economies developed, they adopted the same model, and the attention of government policy and gradually economists and then management scholars became focused on employment. When the International Labour Organization (ILO) was established in the 20th century, this was so much the norm that it focused on employment (and initially at least, like industrial relations scholars, on organised and negotiated employment). Nowadays in much of the West, the question 'What do you do?' is typically answered with details of the individual's occupation; in the East, the question is typically answered with details of the individual's employer, followed by occupation. Unemployed people have 'looked for employment', but increasingly this appears to be changing to 'looking for work'.

Employment became the focus not just of people who needed work and the organisations they worked for; it also became the focus of governments, which were often judged by the rates of employment and unemployment in the state. It became the focus of many intermediaries (intergovernmental agencies like the ILO, trade unions, pressure groups, charities, employment agencies, 'head-hunters', consultancies). Increasingly, it became the focus of academic activity: labour economists, personnel administration specialists, human relations, and health and safety specialists mirrored the development of these roles in industry and tried to understand, explain and improve them. The development of the collective representation of workers led to the development of the academic study of industrial relations and in the late 20th century to the development of human resource management (and now, perhaps, to 'human capital' management or 'talent' management). All of these constituted scholarly attempts to understand employment (Piore & Sabel, 1984; Boxall & Purcell, 2016). There were limited attempts to study self-employment, co-operative labour systems and other alternatives, but these were outliers: employment was the issue.

The third industrial revolution involved automation and computerisation, and coincided with several economic shocks in the 1970s and the emergence of neo-liberalism ideology with a focus on economic efficiency and deregulation (Harvey, 2005). This gave impetus to the increased outsourcing and offshoring of initially unskilled but gradually semi-skilled and skilled work to emerging economies (Holland et al., 2015). This has been a far from comfortable process for those in employment or seeking employment. In addition, during the recent period of economic transformation there have been major structural changes both inside and outside the workplace. In particular the decline (and offshoring) of blue-collar work in AMEs, and the rise of human resource management with its focus on direct relationships with the individual employee combined with hostile legislation towards trade unions in many AMEs resulted in a decline in the countervailing power and voice of employees representatives, mainly trade unions (Fernie & Metcalf, 2005). Whilst these changes have been uneven across AMEs, there is a clear trend, and with the decline in trade unions, the question has to be asked. Are we heading back to the future? Who will voice concern and rally against exploitation in the work and employment space?

What each revolution has shown us is that various kinds of work have become redundant and other kinds of work have been created. All these changes come with displacements as employment in different areas either just disappeared or emerged – work evolved. As MIT economist David Autor has commented, if you told an American farmer in 1900 the coming century would bring a 95% reduction in farm employment, it's a safe bet the farmer would not have predicted we would be developing apps instead (cited in Engelbert, 2017).

However, with the current or fourth industrial revolution (Schwab, 2016), we are experiencing a revolution in work and employment not seen since the first industrial revolution. So what is the difference? In each previous revolution various kinds of work have become redundant and other kinds of work have been created. That is happening in the current revolution, but now many of the new kinds of work can also be performed by robots and AI. In other words, the new jobs that are being created as replacements for the jobs destroyed by robots will themselves be done by robots. In this fourth industrial revolution a combination of communication technologies and AI is providing machines with ever-more human-like capacity to sense, reason, understand and learn, so that they will increasingly be able to replace human workers. Klaus Schwab, the founder of the World Economic Forum, argues (2016) that the single most important challenge facing humanity in the 21st century is how to understand and shape the new technological revolution. Revolutions are not comfortable: in most cases enormous numbers of people have been put into extreme jeopardy, and starvation, misery and migrations have accompanied the process. Taking time to think about this can provide a profound understanding of the future of work and employment as we know it.

For those who can get employment in this emerging industrial revolution, old employment structures are being replaced, and what appears to be happening is a move to an increasing amount of people who seek (or can only achieve) work – but not employment. This new and increasingly unregulated 'gig' economy is progressively inhabited by individuals who work for themselves, who have no employer, and who see no relevance in collective representation (voice) by institutions, which are seen as part of the industrial era reflective of 20th-century employment models. There are as yet no answers to questions about how work in this new economy will be fashioned, and how it can be regulated for fairness, well-being and voice.

Other important changes in society can be examined separately but are off-shoots of the technological changes. The spread of globalisation would not have taken place without easy communication around the world, and in particular the ability to transfer work (and the financial outcomes of work) instantaneously, as the world becomes knowledge and service led (Friedman, 2016). What we suggest is that today's revolution is different in kind from that of previous technological revolutions, and in the following sections of this chapter we explore the nature of the current revolution, its impact on employment in the developed societies, and the implications for those of us who study work and employment.

FORECASTING WORK AND EMPLOYMENT

None of our concerns are new of course. Karl Marx, in the famous 'Fragment on Machines' in *Grundrisse* (1993), predicted that the rise of new machinery would create radical change in the role of workers, leading to the loss of jobs. Norbert Wiener, who established the science of cybernetics in the interwar years, predicted similar things (1950); and at around the same time, on the other side of the Atlantic in France, Georges Friedman also predicted job losses (2009). In the UK John Maynard Keynes (1937) and more recently Stephen Hawking (2016) were also concerned about the effect of technologies on jobs (employment) as we understood them.

In each case they were both right and wrong. Technological advances did create massive changes in jobs, but economies adjusted – though often after much pain – so that eventually most people managed to find employment. Now, however, we argue, with Hawking, that things have reached a tipping point. Hawking (2016) noted that automation in factories has decimated jobs in traditional manufacturing, and the rise of AI is likely to extend this job destruction deep into the middle classes, with only the caring, creative or supervisory roles remaining – a point reinforced by Susskind and Susskind (2015), who argue that even the supervisory roles may be replaced by AI. However, as Minku and Levesley (2018) note, AI systems are being used to recognise eye diseases and diagnose cancer, with similar AI progress in writing software and evaluating legal contracts. However, they argue that this is largely happening in a way that shows how AI will be more of a tool than a threat to skilled workers. From this perspective, they argue that it may become more common for professionals to learn how to benefit from the power of AI, than for entire jobs to simply disappear. A further issue raised by Hawking (2016) and made by others is that new technology will widen the inequalities in society and make it possible for small groups of individuals to make enormous profits while employing very few people, which he says is both inevitable and socially destructive.

There is clear evidence that robotisation and the development of AI is another in a long list of technological developments that have continued through the centuries, and that in all previous cases new employment has been developed to replace those that have become redundant. We have known since Meehl in the 1950s (Meehl, 1954) that statistical prediction invariably outperforms subjective judgement, and this approach has been applied to the world of work too. It is easy to find many other examples of people through the years claiming that technological developments would lead to the destruction of various kinds of employment. In fact, other kinds of work have arisen and unemployment has remained at historical lows. But there is a difference now, as we have noted: the new jobs that are being created as replacements by robots and AI, will themselves be replaced by robots and AI. This is an intellectual revolution, in which brain, rather than physical, power is being replaced.

We, of course, follow the more successful forecasters (Tetlock, 2005) and note that nothing is impossible and that things will not follow any simple trajectory, but it does seem that the new technological changes will have a greater effect on work and employment than previous ones. We do not suggest that these changes will be straightforward or that there will be any 'straight-line' trajectory of change. As Minku and Levesley (2018) indicate there is the potential for a high and low road in how we address these changes, a key point also made by Schwab (2018). As ever, things will be haphazard, unplanned and inconsistent. But we do believe that the end result, with the statistical smoothing that can be done in hindsight, will be that standard employment will progressively be destroyed and not replaced. We suggest that the threat of robotisation and AI will lead (is leading) to searches for ever-cheaper ways of getting work done. This will lead, at more or less the same time, to pressures to move people out of employment and to get them to provide the work in other ways. We foresee the development of broad trends as following in two broad stages.

Stage One

We can be relatively confident about the first stage because it is already well under way. Stage One has two streams, both focused on ensuring that work can be done even more cheaply and simply than robotisation and AI can offer: the outsourcing and offshoring of work, in a very similar form, to under-developed countries where it can be done more cheaply; and, in the developed countries, changes to the relationship between work and employment that constitute the degradation of salaries and working conditions.

Work that can be transferred, in more or less the same form, to poorer countries where living standards and social and work regulation and protection are low or non-existent will be transferred, so that production can continue 'efficiently', at prices lower than even robotisation can offer. Scholars in international business (IB) and comparative human resource management (HRM) have long noted the importance of subsidiary-specific advantages, with examples including human resource advantages such as well-educated workforces, but more common is the search for 'cost-effective' labour – so much outsourcing goes to poor countries with low, non-existent or unenforced labour standards. The Rana Plaza disaster in 2013, in which over 1100 Bangladeshi apparel workers, providing cheap products for famous Western 'brand name' clothing companies, were killed and over 3000 injured, is the most dramatic recent example of the consequences of such a model. This outsourcing and offshoring is continuing to develop from basic blue-collar work to advanced areas such as computer systems maintenance, health analysis and commerce (Holland et al., 2015).

For the roles that cannot be transferred, because the work is immediate and/or 'hands-on' (transport, services, caring), work will become increasingly divorced from employment and there will be a drive to reduce the terms and conditions of employment of those who remain in employment – the 'low road' approach. Despite the 'high road' argument of Minku and Levesley (2018) and Schwab (2018) creating 'collaborative fusion' of employees and AI, under the neo-liberalist policies exhibited in many AMEs we argue that the same thing will happen to the ever-increasing types of work that the robots and computers can do in all other fields. This will be exacerbated by the availability of labour freed up by robotisation and AI. As Fleming (2018) notes, despite the changes to automation and AI that have been occurring over the last decade or so, there has been no commensurate rise in unemployment in the developed societies (we would add, at least in the richer developed societies, as the situation is not so healthy in the Southern and Eastern European countries for example).

Within this discussion, it is important to note that these changes are a matter of managerial choice (high or low road). Managers are no more likely than anyone else to appreciate and want to implement new technologies (indeed, some of the younger 'geeks' at the lower levels of organisations may be much keener). Managers will only use robots and AI when they can see obvious and verifiable benefits for them in doing so, or when driven by the pressures of competition or economic opinion (shareholder expectations as expressed by the media) to do so. But they will not be offering employment of the same kind as we have been used to. They are increasingly seeking ways of getting work completed in ways that remain cheaper than the technological equivalents. Thus, there is an increasing drive in the developed countries amongst employers, economists and politicians who support the neo-liberal approach of deregulation, 'getting rid of' the 'red-tape', or what used to be called 'checks and balances'. Accepting this argument was at least part of the reason for the UK's decision to leave the European Union and for the election of Donald Trump in the USA.

If work with minimal regulation cannot be or is slow to be implemented then 'work without employment' is an alternative option. These changes are already upon us as the technology increasingly becomes part of the everyday language and discourse in developed societies where people no longer 'look something up'; they 'google' it or talk about *uberisation*, a word developed from the name of Uber, one of the major companies involved in technological disruption. So what does this new world of work (not employment) look like? Typical examples are set out below.

Zero-hour contracts and the gig economy

An emerging aspect of these changes in work and employment is the rise of work with no basic framework in terms of on-going employment (zero-hour contracts) with no secure or guaranteed income. This is best highlighted in the rise of this new or 'gig' economy and its effects on those working in it. Ironically, it has been badged by many as the 'happening' or dynamic part of the economy of many advanced nations.

Fake self-employment

'Employers' are asking their 'employees' to set themselves up as self-employed subcontractors, responsible for their own tax and insurance (the 'Uber' model). In the short term they may keep more of their earnings, but in the long term they lose their employment rights, any guarantee of work or income, and they have to pay the outstanding costs.

Internships

In some industries it is now common to offer unpaid internships as part of a supposed recruiting system. Employees work for free for some weeks or months in order to develop their skills and contacts in the industry and to be able to claim 'experience' when they apply for their next job. Some employers replace them at the end of their internship with other interns.

Exploitation – wage theft – working for nothing?

Despite the regulation of terms and conditions in AMEs, issues of wage exploitation including under and non-payment of wages, even by multinational organisations, is becoming a major concern. With the sophisticated HRM systems now available it is hard not to conclude that this is anything but deliberate wage theft. If there is no countervailing force (trade unions), how do you challenge this system?

   We tend to agree with Fleming (2018) in arguing that employment will continue, but it will continue in a much-debilitated state compared with what we are used to. What is also clear is that issues of fairness, equity and voice are increasingly challenged, under these conditions.

Stage Two

As some kinds of work are already transferred to poor countries and other work is deregulated or divorced from employment, there will come a time (it is already here in some industries such as auto-manufacture) when robotisation and AI become cheaper for the employer than using human beings. Development will be patchy – in some industries this is already the case and the process will just be one of continual improvement and cost reduction. In other industries the change will occur much more quickly than most people now assume. And in others there will be much longer delays before such changes take place. Finally, there will be some industries where such changes will never occur, or at least not in a time-scale that will impact any readers of this chapter. Further, developments are likely to be faster in some national contexts than in others; even regional differences within countries may occur.

However, at some point in the near future increasing numbers of humans will be replaced by robots and AI. There will be some work that human beings can still do. Face-to-face caring roles, for example, are unlikely to be replaced until considerably more time has elapsed; and there will be other work in the creative industries that people may choose to do even when the machines could do it more cost-effectively. However, even in these cases, technological support will be extensive, and the disconnect between work and employment is likely to be even more significant than now. So what alternative scenarios are there for work and specifically for employment? What then will be the value of our current understandings of, for example, human resource management or employee relations? Does much of our extant research examine yesterday's issues? Of equal importance is, how do we build fairness, equity and voice into these new systems of work?

HOW DO WE BUILD FAIRNESS AND EQUITY?

We emphasise that any developments will be disruptive, episodic, uneven and occasionally contradictory. But it seems impossible to conceive that technological development will cease to reconceptualise work and accelerate the dislocation with employment. We believe that any developments will be unlikely to change or even challenge significantly the existing power relationships in society. In our view, the more optimistic accounts of the way that the fourth industrial revolution might 'democratise' societies and enhance work and skills (see Minku & Levesley, 2018), will inevitably run into the determined resistance of current power holders. Indeed the evidence, post the Global Financial Crises of 2008, seems to be that the strength of the neo-liberal paradigm is being reinforced rather than weakened and that the rich and powerful owners of the new technologies, now often characterised as single, or a few individual owners of major technology companies, are becoming richer and more powerful than any previous elite.

Accepting that no trajectory is simple or straightforward, therefore, we pose in this exploratory chapter the following questions based on the assumption that there is an alternate road to a more fair and equitable workplace and further research for those of us who study work and employment.

IS THERE THE POTENTIAL FOR GLOBAL LABOUR MARKET ARCHITECTURE?

As noted, the power within the global economy is becoming increasingly concentrated, with information and communication technologies (ICTs) appearing to accelerate the process. This has seen a general decline in the regulatory power of states to control labour standards (Levi et al., 2012). Using the Rana Plaza disaster as a case in point, Hendrikx et al. (2016) argue for a more effective hybrid regulatory model combining public and private sector actors in parallel with state laws to enforce labour standards and regulations. They argue that improvements in AMEs were brought about with social regulation and such strategies could underpin this global labour market architecture, through legal frameworks and codes of conduct (Hendrikx et al., 2016). Ironically, the key catalyst for such change may be globalisation and ICTs as it was the coverage and the brands associated with the Rana Plaza disaster that brought the personal touch to many people in AMEs wearing the clothes that came out of these third world factories or more precisely sweatshops. The best practice model for such change may be the European Union (EU), which has concluded over fifty bilateral free trade agreements, and labour provisions. Whilst Campling et al. (2016) note these provisions are 'promotional' rather than 'conditional', it can be seen as a step in the right direction for bridging the gap.

An additional solution could be the development of a global auditing system (like the ISO system) to benchmark acceptable and unacceptable forms of work (Owens & Stewart, 2016). Again using the Rana Plaza disaster example, the focus on multi-stakeholder platforms could be more effective and developed to manage labour regulation within supply chains with independent third parties monitoring the supply chain (Marx & Wouters, 2016). Whilst there are examples of such systems at work, the reaction of many international brands associated with the Rana Plaza disaster that they were not aware or monitoring the supply chain indicates the need for real policies and practices, and not rhetoric when these principles are endorsed by transnational corporations (TNCs). What this point strikes at is the quality and power of enforcement of such auditing systems. This is likely to be the only way to help build a system of decent work (McCann & Fudge, 2017). Whilst we don't anticipate these changes will stop the tide of change, they may help create a better alternative.

HOW DO WE BUILD VOICE?

Employee voice has been a much-researched aspect of the workplace in recent decades. It could be argued this is aligned with the significant change we have seen in work and employment over the last three decades (see Holland et al., 2018; Wilkinson et al., 2014). Adopting this trajectory, we explore potential alternative scenarios as to how voice could emerge in this new landscape. The disruptive nature of the fourth industrial revolution is likely to unleash much broader and more dynamic communication patterns and practices. Through new communication channels such as social media the impact of these platforms has already been seen (Holland et al., 2018). So what do we see as potential scenarios and future research areas for voice?

The first scenario could be that, with the rise of AI and offshoring in many AMEs, voice will become less significant as employment and work become increasingly fragmented and separated. In the individualised or 'gig' economy where individuals (labour) effectively bid against each other for work, in this 'race to the bottom' scenario (in terms of pay rates), there is likely to be little enthusiasm for collective action. Even here, however, there are examples of IT-savvy individuals who have not been paid putting up web 'walls' warning other workers against particular organisations.

A second scenario emerging in this market combines traditional labour institutions and the strategic use of social media. For example in the UK a new union – the Independent Union of Great Britain (IUGB) – has emerged to address the unique circumstances of the 'gig' worker. Whilst only a new and relatively small union campaigns for couriers, Uber drivers and cleaners, using social media strategies, it has campaigned successfully and created an increasing multi-media profile (voice) and alternative scenarios for organised labour.

This use of social media as well as being central to this new economy can also be a powerful tool if used strategically by the individual. A third level of countervailing power is the practice of naming and shaming of bad experience with certain clients particularly in the 'gig' economy. As the HMV case showed (employees were live tweeting in the middle of a redundancy round), the broad and immediate impact of such media can be very damaging to a brand (Holland et al., 2018). Such 'corporate' campaigns have also been run by trade unions, and in coalition with like-minded institutions can create damage to a brand (Holland & Pyman, 2012). So what we may be seeing here is the emergence of an electronic hybrid voice of institutional and social mechanisms, where the combination of these strategies enables the individual contractor and labour institutions (unions) to campaign and place some regulation into the market specifically through their voice.

A third scenario is that, where workers are in 'stable' employment, we could see an internalised technology-enabled hybrid voice develop. Direct voice can be filtered through internal systems and algorithms identifying issues and trends that management can identify and react to in real time. Where unions remain relatively strong in this hybrid model, their voice may remain central to negotiating terms and conditions of employment and grievance procedures, which again can emerge in real time and allow unions to be increasingly proactive in addressing concerns. In addition, and as the HMV case highlighted, for employees who believe they are being silenced or management is turning a deaf ear to their concerns (Pinder & Harlos, 2001) or disagree with management practices, and feel the need to blow the whistle on inappropriate behaviours, the new technology highlighted by social media provides a voice on workplace issues on open ICT platforms. It may also be seen as providing a countervailing power to the employer, creating immediate and potentially global awareness of issues that generates pressure for management to respond.

A final scenario is that the further deregulation of the economy and employment sets in train a backlash (as noted above), and legislation for more formal employment regulation through similar platform voices as seen in Europe through work councils.

What is clear is that changes already moving through the employment relationship are having a profound effect on employee voice in one form or another. However, voice is likely to remain central to the functioning of the work and/or employment relationship as a form of communication and countervailing power. As such we have provided what we would argue is fertile ground for future research in this field.

CONCLUSION

As we have acknowledged, we believe we are on the cusp of major change in the nature of work and employment. Whether we shall see a high road or a low road to the management of technology, employment and work remains open for debates. Current evidence supports both a dystopian and utopian view. As one of the most influential writers on the subject has succinctly noted – we all sense it – something big is going on (Friedman, 2016).

REFERENCES

Acker, P., C. Smith & P. Smith (1996). *The New Workplace and Trade Unionism*. London: Routledge.

Boxall, P. & J. Purcell (2016). *Strategy and Human Resource Management* (4th edn). Houndmills: Palgrave.

Campling, L., J. Harrison, B. Richardson & A. Smith (2016). 'Can labour provisions work beyond the border? Evaluating the effects of EU free trade agreements', *Labour Review*, *155*(3), pp. 357–82.

Engelbert, C. (2017). 'Job stealing robots? Millennials see hope, fear in automation', *The Wall Street Journal*. Retrieved from https://deloitte.wsj.com/cio/2017/05/04/job-stealing-robots-millennials-see-hope-fear-in-automation (accessed on 4 October 2019).

Evans, P. & T. Wurster (2000). *Blown To Bits: How New Economics of Information Transforms Strategy*. Cambridge, MA: Harvard University Press.

Fernie, S. & D. Metcalf (2005). *Trade Unions: Resurgence or Decline?* London: Routledge.

Fleming, P. (2018). 'Robots and organization studies: Why robots might not want to steal your job', *Organization Studies*. doi:10.1177/0170840618765568

Friedman, G. (2009) *The Next 100 Years: A Forecast for the 21st Century*. New York, NY: Doubleday.

Friedman, T. L. (2016). *Thank You For Being Late: An Optimist's Guide to Thriving in the Age of Accelerations*. New York, NY: Allen Lane.

Harvey, D. (2005). *A Brief History of Neoliberalism*. Oxford: Oxford University Press.

Hawking, S. (2016). 'This is the most dangerous time for our planet', *The Guardian*. Retrieved from https://www.theguardian.com/commentisfree/2016/dec/01/stephen-hawking-dangerous-time-planet-inequality (accessed on 4 October 2019).

Hendrikx, F., A. Marx, G. Rayp & J. Wouters (2016). 'The architecture of global labour governance', *International Labour Review*, *155*(3), pp. 339–54.

Holland, P. & A. Pyman (2012). 'Trade unions and corporate campaigning in a global context: The case of James Hardie', *Economics and Industrial Democracy*, *33*(4), pp. 555–79.

Holland, P., B. Cooper & R. Hecker (2018). 'Social media: A new form of employee voice?', in P. Holland, J. Teicher & J. Donaghey (eds), *Employee Voice at Work*. Singapore: Springer, pp. 73–90.

Holland, P., C. Sheehan, R. Donohue, A. Pyman & B. Allen (2015). *Contemporary Issues and Challenges in HRM* (3rd edn). Melbourne, Australia: Tilde Press.

Keynes, J. M. (1937). 'The general theory of employment', *Quarterly Journal of Economics*, *51*(2), pp. 209–223.

Levi, M., C. Adolph, D. Berliner, A. Erlich, A. Greenleaf, M. Lake & J. Noveck (2012). *Aligning Rights and Interests: Why, When and How to Uphold Labour Standards. World Development Report*. Washington, DC: World Bank.

Marx, A. & J. Wouters (2016). 'Redesigning enforcement in private labour regulation: Will it work?', *International Labour Review*, *155*(3), pp. 435–57.

Marx, K. (1993) *Grundrisse: Foundations of the Critique of Political Economy* [*Grundrisse der Kritik der Politischen Ökonomie*]. London: Penguin Books.

Mathews, J. (1989). *Tools of Change: New Technology and the Democratisation of Work*. Sydney, Australia: Pluto Press.

McCann, D. & J. Fudge (2017). 'Unacceptable forms of work: A multidimensional model', *International Labour Review*, *156*(2), pp. 147–84.

Meehl, P. E. (1954). *Clinical versus Statistical Prediction: A Theoretical Analysis and a Review of the Evidence*. Minneapolis, MN: University of Minnesota Press. doi.org/10.1037/11281-000

Minku, L. & J. Levesley (2018). 'AI doctors and engineers are coming – but they won't be stealing high-skill jobs', *The Conversation*. Retrieved from https://theconversation.com/ai-doctors-and-engineers-are-coming-but-they-wont-be-stealing-high-skill-jobs-101701 (accessed on 4 October 2019).

Owens, R. & A. Stewart (2016). 'Regulating for decent work experience: Meeting the challenge of the rise of the intern', *International Labour Review*, *155*(4), pp. 679–707.

Pinder, C. & K. Harlos (2001). 'Employee silence: Quiescence and acquiescence as responses to perceived injustice', in K.M. Rowland & G.R. Ferris (eds), *Research in Personnel and Human Resource Management*. London: Emerald, pp. 331–69.

Piore, M. & C. Sabel (1984). *The Second Industrial Divide: Possibilites and Prosperity*. New York, NY: Basic Books.

Schwab, K. (2016). *The Fourth Industrial Revolution*. Harmondsworth: Penguin.

Schwab, K. (2018). *Shaping the Future of the Fourth Industrial Revolution*. Geneva, Switzerland: World Economic Forum.

Susskind, R. & D. Susskind (2015). *The Future of the Professions: How Technology will Transform the Work of Human Experts*. Oxford: Oxford University Press.

Tetlock, P.E. (2005). *Expert Political Judgment: How Good Is It? How Can We Know?* Princeton, NJ: Princeton University Press.

Thompson, P. & D. McHugh (2002). *Work Organisation: A Critical Introduction* (3rd edn). London: Macmillan Business.

Watson, T.J. (1997). *Sociology, Work and Industry* (3rd edn). London: Routledge.

Weiner, N. (1950). *The Human Use of Human Beings*. Illinois, US: The Riverside Press

Wilkinson. A., T. Dundon, J. Donaghey & R. Freeman (2014). *The Handbook of Research on Employee Voice*. Cheltenham, UK and Northampton, MA, USA: Edward Elgar Publishing.

3. Unpaid work experience and internships: a growing and contested feature of the future of work

Paula McDonald and Deanna Grant-Smith

A central feature of work and workplace transformations globally has been the rapid expansion of internships and educationally focused work experience. Such experiences are now widely considered foundational in facilitating 'employability' and as a pathway into a reconfigured paid labour market. Work experience refers to a period when an individual attends a workplace and participates in its everyday functions but is not considered an employee. Participation is typically unpaid. Placements can be characterised as a mandatory or optional component of an education course (also known as shadowing, supervised work experience, industry attachment, practicum, field placement, professional practice or clinical rotation), or of an active labour market programme established to assist job-seekers to secure paid work (Grant-Smith and McDonald 2018b). Increasingly, internships and other forms of unpaid work experience can be organised on the open market, initiated either by the participant themselves, the organisation hosting them, or a commercially oriented intermediary or broker. Now a frequent component of young people's transitions from education to work, the practice is therefore a crucial, yet under-recognised dimension of debates about the future of work and employment relations.

The literature addressing unpaid work and internships sits at the nexus of education and employment relations, spanning the fields of higher education, employment relations, labour economics and youth studies. Dominating extant research are higher education perspectives that focus on the role of work-integrated learning (WIL) in enhancing the employability of university students. Graduate employability has been defined as 'the perceived ability to attain sustainable employment appropriate to one's qualification level' (Rothwell et al. 2008, p. 2). First appearing in the employment literature around the mid-19th century, employability has successively shifted emphasis from initiative in the 1980s (Chertkovskaya et al. 2013), to job-related skills and knowledge in the 1990s (Smith 2010), and more recently, to frameworks of core competencies (Boden and Nedeva 2010). In contrast, a more modest literature has addressed internships undertaken outside a formal course of study.

Since the parameters of the field are imprecise and definitions contested, some qualifiers in terms of the scope of this chapter are necessary. First, although work experience can attract remuneration, our focus is on work experience that is unpaid because this is where the practice is most contested and participants are most likely to experience exploitation (Grant-Smith and McDonald 2016). Second, although there is a large body of educationally focused literature on the learning outcomes of, for example, clinical placements and WIL, we privilege here the connection between work experience and the labour market. That is, our primary emphasis is the perceived employability enhancing aspects of unpaid work experience rather than its educational outcomes (Grant-Smith and McDonald 2018a). Third, we distinguish work experience from apprenticeships, which in their contemporary form comprise a structured combination of periods of theoretical instruction and practical work experience as part of an indentured period of paid employment (Fuller and Unwin 2013).

Consistent with the overarching themes of this book, the chapter addresses three streams of research that have advanced knowledge of trends in relation to the future of (unpaid) work experience. These themes comprise: (1) modes and types of unpaid work; (2) the expansion and prevalence of unpaid work; and (3) the impacts of unpaid work on participants and other workers. Each section presents a critical summary of current knowledge and explores the associated debates. The final section of the chapter canvasses a forward agenda for future research and practice in the field.

CONCEPTUALISING UNPAID WORK EXPERIENCE

The different forms of contemporary unpaid work experience can be distinguished by their distinctive characteristics. These include whether the experience has explicit educational goals and outcomes (i.e., directly supervised by an educational institution or employer, or unsupervised); what motivated the participant (i.e., altruism, improving employability, acquiring knowledge and skills); and the primary beneficiary of the unpaid work (i.e., the participant themselves or the organisation). However, these purposes and motivations often overlap. For example, some university degree programmes have a mandatory unpaid work experience component, the length of which can vary between a single day to extended periods of full-time work (Baldwin and Rosier 2016).

Traditionally, longer periods have been the case for occupations for which this experience is a requirement of professional registration, such as teaching or nursing (Grant-Smith and Gillett-Swan 2017; Grant-Smith et al. 2018). However, a mandatory period of work experience has become an increasingly common graduation requirement in other disciplines such as the creative industries, where participation in unpaid work experience is ubiquitous both pre- and post-graduation (Ashton 2016; Figiel 2013; Frenette 2013; Hope and Figiel 2012; Percival and Hesmondhalgh 2014; Siebert and Wilson 2013).

To provide what is perceived to be a positional advantage in the increasingly competitive graduate jobs market (Tomlinson 2008), increasingly universities and colleges are offering a range of non-mandatory or elective opportunities for student placements in industry as supplemental to the core curriculum. Some unpaid work experience may therefore have an overt educational or learning focus while other experiences differ little from paid work, other than non-receipt of payment. Indeed, Malik (2015, p. 1186) suggests that there is a confluence of 'ambiguous statutory language, unclear legal precedent, and non-binding agency interpretation' around the notion of interns.

Grant-Smith and McDonald (2018b) distinguish between four distinct types of unpaid work, which are conceptualised along two key dimensions: the degree of participatory discretion and the purpose of the experience (see Figure 3.1). They suggest that participatory discretion can be either mandatory, where unpaid work is directed by a third party and where a benefit such as a qualification, employment contract or welfare payment is conditional on participation; or elective, where an outcome is not dependent on participation. They also differentiate unpaid work on the basis of type of experience, separating participation in unpaid work that is educationally focused and where the principal benefit is participant learning, from unpaid work experiences that involve the conduct of productive work undertaken primarily for the benefit of the employer rather than the participant.

This typology provides some broad definitional clarity based on distinctions between different forms of unpaid work. However, the simplicity of its two-dimensional structure can obfuscate the nuance of very different experiences that are captured within the same quadrant. For example, unpaid open market internships are co-located with altruistic volunteering as elective productive work. Both these forms of unpaid work are undertaken 'voluntarily' but can be distinguished by the motivation of the unpaid worker and the obligations placed on the 'employer'. Another example is open market internships that are typically undertaken with the intention of improving employment prospects through the development of professional

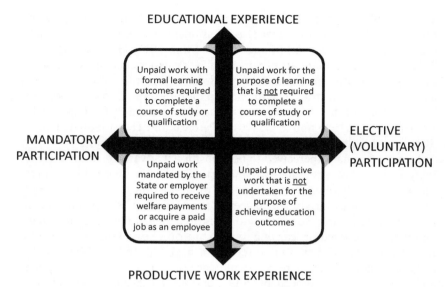

EDUCATIONAL EXPERIENCE

Unpaid work with formal learning outcomes required to complete a course of study or qualification

Unpaid work for the purpose of learning that is *not* required to complete a course of study or qualification

MANDATORY PARTICIPATION

ELECTIVE (VOLUNTARY) PARTICIPATION

Unpaid work mandated by the State or employer required to receive welfare payments or acquire a paid job as an employee

Unpaid productive work that is *not* undertaken for the purpose of achieving education outcomes

PRODUCTIVE WORK EXPERIENCE

Source: Adapted from Grant-Smith and McDonald 2018b.

Figure 3.1 Distinguishing types of unpaid work according to the level of participatory discretion and purpose of the experience

experience, skills and contacts; in this case the primary beneficiary is most often the employer, who can profit from free, if somewhat inexperienced, labour. In contrast, volunteering for a non-profit service organisation (such as a church, charity or club) generally provides direct benefits to the organisation and its clients (Oliver et al. 2016). Yet not all unpaid work described as volunteering is undertaken on a purely altruistic basis. Participants may volunteer because they anticipate employability benefits and it is not difficult to imagine the incentives for organisations to use the preferred term 'volunteering' over 'internship' in recruitment processes.

Providing clarity around the distinctions between different forms of unpaid work is more than mere pedantry. It is crucial for guiding the design of robust research studies and enabling a comparison of findings on risks and benefits both across settings and contexts and for different types of unpaid work experience, thus avoiding the 'apples and oranges' effect. Avoiding definitional ambiguity is also important for advocacy. The characterisation of unpaid work experiences as 'not working but learning' has been used to 'legitimately den[y] a whole range of rights, protections and claims to wages and working conditions that are granted to other workers' (Sukarieh and Tannock 2017, p.250). Unambiguous terminology around different forms of unpaid work can also be used to support the argument that payment should be made in instances where instead of 'learning to labour' (Chillas et al. 2015, p. 12), interns are expected to be productive workers.

MEASURING THE EXPANSION OF UNPAID WORK

Research, including representative prevalence studies, has clearly demonstrated that unpaid work has become a 'majority experience' for those transitioning from education to the labour market. In Australia, a survey of the working-age population revealed that more than half (58%) of respondents aged 18–29 had participated in at least one episode of unpaid work experience in the previous five years (Oliver et al. 2016). In the UK, Roberts (2017) reported that some 11,000 internships are advertised annually across a wide range of occupations and organisation types, with the actual number taking place estimated to be as high as 70,000.

A European study of 27 countries showed 46 per cent of 18–35-year-olds had participated in at least one traineeship and more than half of these were unpaid (European Commission 2012). Similarly in Canada and the US, around half of university students have reported that they have undertaken an institutionally organised unpaid work placement (Kramer and Usher 2011; Perlin 2011). There is also some early evidence of an increasing reliance on unpaid work in certain industries and types of businesses such as start-ups (Papageorgiou 2016). Similarly, there has been recent interest in expanding the numbers of virtual internships in small to medium enterprises (SMEs) to access global talent as such arrangements have few overheads and require limited organisational investment (Jeske and Axtell 2016).

The expansion of unpaid work experience, in particular WIL, has enjoyed strong levels of support from businesses, students, parents and higher education institutions, including those in the vocational training sector. In the Australian survey reported above (Oliver et al. 2016), around half of participants' most recent experiences of unpaid work were associated with formal education or training. This high level of participation is motivated in part by the goal of providing graduates with a labour market advantage through the acquisition of skills and knowledge they cannot acquire in the formal classroom and which are in excess of those required to perform a standard, entry-level graduate role (Burke and Carton 2013; Phillips 2014; Orrell 2011). However, providing such arrangements also provides an opportunity for universities to create and maintain relationships with industry partners (Cook et al. 2015) and for businesses to access highly educated and motivated unpaid workers at no cost.

A recent study of pathways into employment in the UK Midlands, based on interviews with young people and employers, found that pre-employment work experience is a strong prerequisite for all but the lowest-paid, lowest-skilled jobs (Purcell et al. 2017). Similarly, it has been reported that nearly half of British employers believe that job candidates who have not gained work experience through an internship will 'have little or no chance of receiving a job offer' for their organisations' graduate programmes, irrespective of their academic qualifications and performance (Roberts 2017, p. 1). Consequently, students and graduates often rationalise their decisions to participate in internships and other unpaid work experiences in complex, class-conscious, politicised ways that emphasise the acquisition of desirable social and cultural capital to be(come) competitive with their job-seeking peers (Leonard et al. 2015).

Supply-side factors are also relevant to the growth of unpaid work in the transition from education to work. These include contracting graduate labour markets and increased competition for scarce jobs, which have allowed employers to be more selective in their recruitment decisions and to reduce their investment in staff training and skill development (Hall 2011; Keep and James 2012). Increasing labour market competition has also contributed to credential inflation (Tomlinson 2008), where young people experiencing barriers to employment such as family, health or social problems and/or who exhibit low levels of literacy and numeracy, must compete with adults and better-qualified young people for lower-skilled jobs (Thompson 2010).

A key question arising from these research studies is whether unpaid work experience will continue to confer purported competitive labour market advantages when the practice has become so widespread. Put another way, as unpaid work becomes a normative practice, either to gain professional registration or to differentiate oneself from graduate peers in a tight labour market, it seems entirely possible that any competitive advantage may be progressively erased. This possibility poses significant threats to notions of workplace fairness and equity in the future because it means a progressive erosion of benefits that accrue from the investment by the unpaid worker and the opportunity costs of participation.

IMPACTS OF UNPAID WORK ON PARTICIPANTS AND OTHER WORKERS

The increasingly ubiquitous practice of unpaid work experience raises complex questions about exploitation, where unpaid interns may represent 'a uniquely vulnerable, growing sector of the workforce' (Fredericksen

2013, p. 253). Although unpaid work in the form of WIL is rationalised on the basis that it may result in experiential learning in an authentic workplace setting, there are increasing critiques of the effectiveness of this approach, especially in relation to graduate employment outcomes (Grant-Smith and McDonald 2018a; Rickhuss 2015). Globally, in response to concerns about exploitation, there has been an emergence of organisations that work to advocate for the interests of interns and other unpaid workers and to inform them of their rights. These include the Precarious Workers Brigade and Interns Aware in the UK, Génération précaire in France, Repubblica degli Stagisti in Italy and Students Against Unpaid Internship Scams in Canada.

Research into the employment outcomes of unpaid internships is typically based on self-report student feedback surveys (e.g., Matthew et al. 2012) or studies of employer perceptions (e.g., Gault et al. 2010). Results are generally positive, with students judging these experiences as essential to enhancing their competitiveness in the employment marketplace and important for improving their analytical thinking and skills (Cannon and Arnold 1998; Kramer and Usher 2011).

A review of 57 peer-reviewed studies of the impacts of internships pointed to several student-identified benefits including better career decision-making, improved job-related and social skills, and improved employment outcomes following graduation (Sanahuja Velez and Ribes Giner 2015). However, these benefits are often conditional on, for example, the disciplinary field of the participant, opportunities to reflect on experiences, the quality of mentoring and the degree to which exploitative practices occur such as unethical or risky physical tasks or unreasonable workloads (Jackson 2017; Lawton and Potter 2010; Moorman 2004; Perlin 2011; Sanahuja Velez and Ribes Giner 2015).

In contrast to student-identified benefits, empirical evidence to support claims that participation in unpaid work has a significant positive influence on securing employment, or that these benefits are shared equally across disciplines, has been scarce and the evidence more mixed (Oliver et al. 2016; Peters et al. 2014; Silva et al. 2018). Swan (2015) argues that the perceived value of internships, especially those undertaken in high-status organisations, may lead interns to accept very poor conditions while also conveying positive evaluations about their experiences. There are also challenges associated with directly comparing studies due to variations across target samples (tertiary/vocation students, graduates), type of work experience (WIL, open market, paid/unpaid), the duration and quality of the placement, and the time that has elapsed between the work experience and the measurement of employment outcomes.

Some studies have found positive relationships between educationally focused internships and labour market outcomes in Australia (Polidano and Tabasso 2013), Finland (Hakkinen 2006), Denmark (Joensen 2009), and Spain and Italy (Passaretta and Triventi 2015). The importance of work experience quality in determining positive employment outcomes was further highlighted in a European Commission (2012) study of traineeships. O'Higgins and Pinedo (2017) differentiated between paid and unpaid internships, finding that paid internships are associated with more advantageous employment outcomes than if they are unpaid. They suggest some possible explanations for this finding: that paid interns may already have good prospects in the labour market; that they are able to better focus on learning outcomes because they are not burdened by financial hardship; and because paid internships may offer better training opportunities because companies view them as trial recruitment periods.

Other studies have revealed no benefits (National Association of Colleges and Employers 2013) or even negative outcomes associated with participation in unpaid work experiences. In the UK, Holford (2017) found that university graduates who participated in an unpaid internship post graduation were earning less 3.5 years later than peers who had gone immediately into paid work or on to further study. Such results have been echoed in other countries including Germany (Cerulli-Harms 2017).

An Australian prevalence study (Oliver et al. 2016) highlighted another important indicator of quality that is important to job market outcomes. Respondents who had participated in open market internships that were described by the authors as 'potentially unlawful' (defined as involving the same work as that done by regular employees and which did not predominantly involve observing or performing mock or simulated tasks) were more likely than respondents who had completed apparently lawful unpaid work experience to be neither employed nor looking for work at the time the survey was completed (see Stewart et al. 2018). Finally, when considering unpaid work experience undertaken as part of a mandatory active labour market programme, research suggests a reduced likelihood of separating from unemployment payments or no positive effect on labour market success (Borland and Tseng 2011; Heckman et al. 1999).

Another impact of unpaid work experience that has been receiving increased attention is equity of access. Concerns include that students from low socio-economic backgrounds may be excluded from participation in unpaid experiential learning activities because they struggle to exercise the class- and place-based habitus that enables them to recognise competitive opportunities as an option and to navigate opaque recruitment practices (Allen and Hollingworth 2013; Roberts 2017). In particular, they may experience difficulties accessing international internships and field experiences that may provide access to professional labour markets. As Hunt and Scott

(2017) assert, social class can stamp an imprint on the role of internships, extending and intensifying the mechanisms of socio-economic reproduction already apparent in the education system.

Importantly, while concerns about equity of access are often levelled at open market internships, they can also be associated with higher education sponsored WIL programmes. This is because poorer students may not be able to afford the costs of travel and accommodation while participating in unpaid work (Oliver et al. 2016), especially if there is an opportunity cost associated with working fewer hours in paid work such as in a retail or hospitality job. Such limits to participation can constrain access to particular employment pathways and career opportunities for those with fewer economic, social and educational resources (Curiale 2010; Frenette 2013).

At a socio-political level, unpaid work has been referred to as a prop for neoliberal market economies where 'capital finds novel ways to offload its responsibilities for a workforce' (McRobbie 2002, p. 518), particularly in terms of training and development. The unchecked expansion of unpaid work has the potential to cheapen and make precarious all labour by applying downward pressure on the wages, training and employment opportunities for those seeking to enter the labour market, as well as those already within it (Siebert and Wilson 2013; Standing 2011). It also creates the expectation that unpaid work is an obligatory rite of passage (Discenna 2016), which may result in more numerous and longer periods of unpaid work. A broader employment relations concern is also that, in the future, unpaid interns may displace paid workers (Grant-Smith and McDonald 2016) and that precarious work conditions may become more entrenched because employers offer neither secure employment nor high-quality working conditions (Broughton et al. 2016).

FUTURE RESEARCH AND PRACTICE

Knowledge of how choices around elective or voluntary forms of unpaid work are practised and shaped is nascent. The notion of choice is often dismissed as self-evident and simply a response to worsening labour market conditions rather than being influenced by a neoliberal discourse that positions job-seekers as responsible for their own employment success (Johnson 2011). Some researchers have begun to question the persuasiveness of uncritical employability discourses and their normalisation, particularly in higher education (Osborne and Grant-Smith 2017). The financial and psychological wellbeing of those participating in unpaid work has become an increasing focus in critical scholarship in recent years (e.g., see Baglow and Gair 2018; Gair and Baglow 2018; Grant-Smith and Gillett-Swan

2017; Gillett-Swan and Grant-Smith 2018). Further research is required, however, to understand the extent to which participation in unpaid work is a constrained choice and has come to occupy a default occupational closure function in some industries.

Comparatively little attention has been afforded – either in education or employment relations scholarship – to the unpaid work practices and experiences of international higher education students, vocational education and training students, secondary school students, and job-seekers not engaged in education or training. Considering emerging evidence of the impacts of unpaid work on participants and workplaces, it is important that the experiences of these cohorts are given adequate attention in future research. For example, international students may find it more difficult to access quality unpaid work experiences and may face unique workplace challenges associated with cultural differences and language skills requiring higher levels of workplace support (Jackson 2017). While most measures of participation in unpaid work focus on students and young workers, there has also been a troubling rise in participation rates of experienced professionals undertaking unpaid internships following job loss or to facilitate career change (Magaldi and Kolisnyk 2014; Reid 2014; Steffen 2010). This trend requires further investigation.

Given the classed, raced, gendered and geographical inequalities in access to unpaid work opportunities and the potential for exploitative and unlawful practices, there is a pressing need to determine the effectiveness and outcomes of different types of unpaid work to inform educational and industrial relations policy responses that effectively balance 'worker autonomy and worker protection' (Magaldi and Kolisnyk 2014, p. 184). Despite numerous rhetorical claims to the contrary, we have at present only formative knowledge of the extent to which unpaid work is effective in facilitating employability and employment. Some emerging evidence suggests unpaid work experience is at best neutral or in some cases even detrimental to securing paid employment. However, there is an urgent need for more empirical evidence of the conditions under which unpaid work experience successfully develops the capacities and skills considered desirable by employers and facilitates the acquisition of paid and secure employment in a chosen field. A more concerted focus on supply-side issues is also warranted in future research. This includes exploring the motivations of different types of employers to create unpaid work opportunities and how unpaid work experience is judged alongside other capacities by employers in recruitment decisions.

The recent emergence of virtual internships, or e-internships, also appears to be a feature of the evolving contours of unpaid work. While such experiences offer the promise of international and capital city work experience without leaving home (Channell and Anderson 2010), the extent to which they provide appropriate learning opportunities remains unclear, especially if they are undertaken outside the education context. Further, many of these opportunities originate in countries that do not have a strong record of regulation of unpaid work. As a result, the unpaid worker may be engaging in an arrangement that violates the laws of their own country and they may find themselves without legal redress in cases of intellectual property or other disputes. Of particular concern are the high levels of participant motivation and self-management that are required to succeed in undertaking virtual work, skills that are likely to be significantly less developed in those lacking working experience (Leath 2015).

As a result, the benefits for the e-intern in terms of autonomy and flexibility in the timing and location of work may be offset by increased difficulties in building professional relationships, networks and trust with colleagues (Jeske and Axtell 2016). Compared with traditional internships, e-internships seem to provide few opportunities for workplace socialisation (Leath 2015) or exposure to corporate culture and professional etiquette through job shadowing (Jeske and Axtell 2016). It is therefore important that e-internships are supervised by staff with experience working in virtual environments and managing virtual teams and that, rather than simply focusing on the delivery of tasks, participant development is also factored into the e-internship programme.

Anecdotally, internship intermediaries, or brokers as they are sometimes termed, appear to have proliferated in the graduate employment field (Perlin 2011). Although some universities have promoted and supported such agencies, they have generated significant critique for undermining the graduate labour market, exploiting young people by extracting their labour and ideas for free, and entrenching class inequalities (Purtill 2017; Tweedie and Ting 2018). Although internship intermediaries are likely to become increasingly visible in the employment landscape of the future, no published research to date has systematically addressed how these organisations operate, nor the characteristics of the internships they offer. Finally, there is a need to research why, albeit that unpaid work appears to be increasing across most disciplines and jurisdictions, in select professions such as engineering it remains uncommon and students are routinely paid while undertaking mandatory work placements as part of their studies (Grant-Smith and McDonald 2016; Smith et al. 2015). This too may change over time as unpaid work becomes an even more normalised and entrenched practice.

The evidence presented here on the expansion of unpaid work and internships, the myriad of different forms that have evolved, and the degree of support for its continuance, suggests the practice of unpaid work and internships is likely to remain a permanent, though contested, feature of the youth employment landscape in the future, at least in industrialised economies. Yet the potential for exploitation, inequity and negative impacts on the labour market more broadly is significant. The research agenda canvassed here provides an imperative for establishing sound evidence of how internships and other forms of unpaid work experience can be structured fairly and in a way that promotes, rather than diminishes, employment opportunities for young people who currently face uncertain prospects in the transition from education to work.

REFERENCES

Allen, K. and S. Hollingworth (2013) ' "Sticky subjects" or "cosmopolitan creatives"? Social class, place and urban young people's aspirations for work in the knowledge economy'. *Urban Studies*, 50(3), pp. 499–517.

Ashton, D. (2016) 'Creative contexts: Work placement subjectivities for the creative industries'. *British Journal of Sociology of Education*, 37(2), pp. 268–287.

Baglow, L. and S. Gair (2018) 'Australian social work students: Balancing tertiary studies, paid work and poverty'. *Journal of Social Work*, pp. 1–20.

Baldwin, C. and J. Rosier (2016) 'Growing future planners: A framework for integrating experiential learning into tertiary planning programs'. *Journal of Planning Education and Research*, 37(1), pp. 43–55.

Boden, R. and M. Nedeva (2010) 'Employing discourse: Universities and graduate "employability"'. *Journal of Education Policy*, 25(1), pp. 37–54.

Borland, J. and Y. Tseng (2011) 'Does "work for the dole" work? An Australian perspective on work experience programs'. *Applied Economics*, 43, pp. 4353–4368.

Broughton, A., M. Green, C. Rickard, S. Swift, W. Eichhorst, V. Tobsch, I. Magda, P. Lewandowski, R. Keister, D. Jonaviciene and N.E. Ramos Martin (2016) *Precarious Employment in Europe*. Strasbourg: European Parliament.

Burke, D. and R. Carton (2013) 'The pedagogical, legal and ethical implications of unpaid internships'. *Journal of Legal Studies Education*, 30, pp. 99–130.

Cannon, J.A. and M.J. Arnold (1998) 'Student expectations of collegiate internship programs in business: A 10-year update'. *Journal of Education for Business*, 73, pp. 202–204.

Cerulli-Harms, A. (2017) *Generation internship: The impact of internships on early labour market performance*. IZA DP No. 11163. Bonn, Germany: IZA Institute of Labor Economics.

Channell, T.L. and D.M. Anderson (2010) 'Creating virtual internships in the music business'. *Journal of the Music and Entertainment Industry Educators Association*, 10(1), pp. 173–183.

Chertkovskaya, E., P. Watt, S. Tramer and S. Spoelstra (2013) 'Giving notice to employability'. *Ephemera*, 13(4), pp. 701–716.

Chillas, S., A. Marks and L. Galloway (2015) 'Learning to labour: An evaluation of internships and employability in the ICT sector'. *New Technology, Work and Employment*, 30, pp. 1–15.

Cook, S.J., A. Stokes and R.S. Parker (2015) 'A 20-year examination of the perceptions of business school interns: A longitudinal case study'. *Journal of Education for Business*, 90(2), pp. 103–110.

Curiale, J. (2010) 'America's new glass ceiling: Unpaid internships, the Fair Labor Standards Act, and the urgent need for change'. *Hastings Law Journal*, 61, pp. 1531–1560.

Discenna, T.A. (2016) 'The discourses of free labour: Career management, employability, and the unpaid intern'. *Western Journal of Communication*, 80, pp. 435–452.

European Commission (2012) 'Towards a quality framework on traineeships: Second-stage consultation of the social partners at European level under Article 154 TFEU', 5 December. Available at http://ec.europa.eu/transparency/regdoc/rep/1/2012/EN/1-2012-728-EN-F1-1.pdf (accessed on 4 October 2019).

Figiel, J. (2013) 'Work experience without qualities?' *Ephemera: Theory and Politics in Organizations*, 13, pp. 33–52.

Fredericksen, L. (2013) 'Falling through the cracks of Title VII: The plight of the unpaid intern'. *Georgia Mason Law Review*, 21, pp. 245–273.

Frenette, A. (2013) 'Making the intern economy'. *Work and Occupations*, 40, pp. 364–397.

Fuller, A. and L. Unwin (2013) *Contemporary Apprenticeship: International Perspectives on an Evolving Model of Learning*. London: Routledge.

Gair, S. and L. Baglow (2018) ' "We barely survived": Social work students' mental health vulnerabilities and implications for educators, universities and the workforce'. *Aotearoa New Zealand Social Work*, 30(1), pp. 32–44.

Gault J., E. Leach and M. Duey (2010) 'Effects of business internships on job marketability: The employers' perspective'. *Education+Training*, 52, pp. 76–88.

Gillett-Swan, J. and D. Grant-Smith (2018) 'A framework for managing the impacts of work-integrated learning on student quality of life'. *International Journal of Work-Integrated Learning*, 19(2), pp. 129–140.

Grant-Smith, D. and J. Gillett-Swan (2017) 'Managing the personal impacts of practicum: Examining the experiences of Graduate Diploma in Education students'. In J. Nuttall, A. Kostogriz, M. Jones and J. Martin (eds) *Teacher Education Policy and Practice: Evidence of Impact, Impact of Evidence*. Singapore: Springer, pp. 97–112.

Grant-Smith, D. and P. McDonald (2016) 'The trend toward unpaid pre-graduation professional work experience for Australian young planners: Essential experience or essentially exploitation?' *Australian Planner*, 53(2), pp. 65–72.

Grant-Smith, D. and P. McDonald (2018a) 'Planning to work for free: Building the graduate employability of planners through unpaid work'. *Journal of Youth Studies*, 21(2), pp. 161–177.

Grant-Smith, D. and P. McDonald (2018b) 'Ubiquitous yet uncertain: An integrative review of unpaid work'. *International Journal of Management Reviews*, 20(2), pp. 559–578.

Grant-Smith, D., L. de Zwaan, R. Chapman and J. Gillett-Swan (2018) ' "It's the worst, but real experience is invaluable": Pre-service teacher perspectives of the costs and benefits of professional experience'. In D. Heck and A. Ambrosetti (eds) *Teacher Education In and For Uncertain Times*. Singapore: Springer, pp. 15–34.

Hakkinen, I. (2006) 'Working while enrolled in a university: Does it pay?' *Labour Economics*, 13(2), pp. 167–189.

Hall, R. (2011). 'Skills and skill formation in Australian workplaces: Beyond the war for talent?' In M. Baird, K. Hancock and J. Isaac (eds) *Work and Employment Relations: An Era of Change.* Sydney: Federation Press, pp. 78–92.

Heckman, J., R. Lalone and J. Smith (1999) 'The economics and econometrics of active labour market programs'. In O. Ashenfelter and D. Card (eds) *Handbook of Labour Economics*, Vol 3A. Amsterdam: Elsevier, pp. 1865–2097.

Holford, A. (2017) *Access to and returns from unpaid graduate internships.* ISER Working Paper Series, No. 2017-07. Colchester: Institute for Social and Economic Research.

Hope, S. and J. Figiel (2012) *Intern Culture: A Literature Review of Internship Reports, Guidelines and Toolkits from 2009–2011.* London: Artquest.

Hunt, W. and P. Scott (2017) 'Participation in paid and unpaid internships among creative and communications graduates. Does class advantage lay a part?' In N. O'Higgins (ed.) *Rising to the Youth Employment Challenge: New Evidence on Key Policy Issues.* Geneva: International Labour Office, pp. 113–162.

Jackson, D. (2017) 'Exploring the challenges experienced by international students during work-integrated learning in Australia'. *Asia Pacific Journal of Education*, 37(3), pp. 344–359.

Jeske, D. and C.M. Axtell (2016) 'Going global in small steps: e-internships in SMEs'. *Organizational Dynamics*, 45(1), pp. 55–63.

Joensen, J. (2009) *Academic and labour market success: The impact of student employment, abilities and preferences.* Working Article No. 1352077, 27 April. Stockholm: Social Science Research Network.

Johnson, J. (2011) 'Interrogating the goals of work-integrated learning: Neoliberal agendas and critical pedagogy'. *Asia-Pacific Journal of Cooperative Education*, 12, pp. 175–182.

Keep, E. and S. James (2012) 'A Bermuda Triangle of policy? Bad jobs, skills policy and incentives to learn at the bottom end of the labour market'. *Journal of Education Policy*, 27, pp. 211–230.

Kramer, M. and A. Usher (2011) *Work-integrated Learning and Career-ready Students: Examining the Evidence.* Toronto, ON: Higher Education Strategy Associates.

Lawton, K. and D. Potter (2010) *Why Interns Need a Fair Wage.* London: The Institute for Public Policy.

Leath, B. (2015) 'Solving the challenges of the virtual workplace for interns'. *Young Scholars In Writing*, 6, pp. 3–11.

Leonard, P., S. Halford and K. Bruce (2015) ' "The new degree?" Constructing internships in the third sector'. *Sociology*, 50(2), pp. 383–399.

Magaldi, J.A. and O. Kolisnyk (2014) 'The unpaid internship: A stepping stone to a successful career or the stumbling block of an illegal enterprise? Finding the right balance between worker autonomy and worker protection'. *Nevada Law Journal*, 14, pp. 184–209.

Malik, M.M. (2015) 'The legal void of unpaid internships: Navigating the legality of internships in the face of conflicting tests interpreting the FLSA'. *Connecticut Law Review*, 47, pp. 1183–1214.

Matthew, S.M., R.M. Taylor and R.A. Ellis (2012) 'Relationships between students' experiences of learning in an undergraduate internship program and new graduates' experiences of professional practice'. *Higher Education*, 64(4), pp. 529–542.

McRobbie, A. (2002) 'Clubs to companies: Notes on the decline of political culture in speeded up creative worlds'. *Cultural Studies*, 16, pp. 516–531.

Moorman, A.M. (2004) 'Legal issues and the supervised internship relationship: Who is responsible for what?' *Journal of Physical Education, Recreation and Dance*, 75, pp. 19–24.

National Association of Colleges and Employers (2013) *Unpaid internships: A clarification of NACE research*. Spotlight for Career Services Professionals. Available at http://naceweb.org/s10162013/paid-internship-full-time-employment.aspx (accessed on 4 October 2019).

O'Higgins, N. and L. Pinedo (2017) *Interns and outcomes: Just how effective are internships as a bridge to stable employment?* International Labour Office Employment Working Paper No. 241. Geneva: ILO.

Oliver, D., P. McDonald, A. Stewart and A. Hewitt (2016) *Unpaid work experience in Australia: Prevalence, nature and impact*. Report prepared for the Commonwealth Department of Employment (January). Sydney: University of Technology Sydney.

Orrell, J. (2011) *Good Practice Report: Work-integrated Learning*. Sydney: Australian Learning and Teaching Council.

Osborne, N. and D. Grant-Smith (2017) 'Resisting the employability doctrine through anarchist pedagogies and prefiguration'. *Australian Universities Review*, 59(2), pp. 59–69.

Papageorgiou, A. (2016) *Living in 'Beta': Hubs, Collectives and the Emergency of Moral Economies in Athens*. Hertfordshire: COST Action IS 1202, University of Hertfordshire.

Passaretta, G. and M. Triventi (2015) 'Work experience during higher education and post-graduation occupational outcomes: A comparative study on four European countries'. *International Journal of Comparative Sociology*, 56(3–4), pp. 232–253.

Percival, N. and D. Hesmondhalgh (2014) 'Unpaid work in the UK television and film industries: Resistance and changing attitudes'. *European Journal of Communication*, 29(2), pp. 188–203.

Perlin, R. (2011) *Intern Nation: How to Earn Nothing and Learn Little in the Brave New Economy*. London: Verso.

Peters, J., P. Sattler and J. Kelland (2014) *Work-integrated Learning in Ontario's Postsecondary Sector: The Pathways of Recent College and University Graduates*. Toronto, ON: Higher Education Quality Council of Ontario.

Phillips, K.P.A. (2014) *Engaging Employers in Work Integrated Learning: Current State and Future Priorities*. Canberra: Department of Industry.

Polidano, C. and D. Tabasso (2013) *Making it real: The benefits of workplace learning in upper-secondary VET courses*. Melbourne, Australia: Melbourne Institute Working Paper no 31/13.

Purcell, K., P. Elias, A. Green, P. Mizen, M. Simms, N. Whiteside, D. Wilson and C. Tzanakou (2017) *Present Tense, Future Imperfect? Young People's Pathways into Work*. Coventry: Institute for Employment Research, University of Warwick.

Purtill, J. (2017) *Paying to work: Australian start-up offers 'learning platform of the future'*. ABC Triple J Hack, 20 February. Available at http://www.abc.net.au/triplej/programs/hack/would-you-pay-to-work-for-a-company/8281544 (accessed on 4 October 2019).

Reid, P.L. (2014) Fact Sheet #71: Shortchanging the unpaid academic intern. *Florida Law Review*, 66, pp. 1375–1402.

Rickhuss, T. (2015) 'Investigating the cost of unpaid internships for the UK Advertising Industry'. *Journal of Promotional Communications*, 3, pp. 363–380.

Roberts, C. (2017) *The Inbetweeners: The New Role of Internships in the Graduate Labour Market*. London: Institute for Public Policy Research.

Rothwell, A., L. Herbert and F. Rothwell (2008) 'Self-perceived employability: Construction and initial validation of a scale for university students'. *Journal of Vocational Behaviour*, 73(1), pp. 1–12.

Sanahuja Velez, G. and G. Ribes Giner (2015) 'Effects of business internships on students, employers and higher education institutions: A systematic review'. *Journal of Employment Counselling*, 52, pp. 121–130.

Siebert, S. and F. Wilson (2013) 'All work and no pay: Consequences of unpaid work in the creative industries'. *Work, Employment and Society*, 27, pp. 711–721.

Silva, P., B. Lopes, M. Costa, A.I. Melo, G. Paiva Dias, E. Brilo and D. Sebra (2018) 'The million-dollar question: Can internships boost employment?' *Studies in Higher Education*, 43(1), pp. 2–21.

Smith, S., C. Smith and M. Caddell (2015) 'Can pay, should pay? Exploring employer and student perceptions of paid and unpaid placements'. *Active Learning in Higher Education*, 16, pp. 149–164.

Smith, V. (2010) 'Review article: Enhancing employability: Human, cultural, and social capital in an era of turbulent unpredictability'. *Human Relations*, 63(2), pp. 279–300.

Standing, G. (2011) *The Precariat: The New Dangerous Class*. London: Bloomsbury Academic.

Steffen, H. (2010) 'Student internships and the privilege to work'. *Cultural Logic: Culture and Crisis*. Available at http://clogic.eserver.org/2010/Steffen.pdf (accessed on 4 October 2019).

Stewart, A., D. Oliver, P. McDonald and A. Hewitt (2018). 'The nature and prevalence of unlawful unpaid work experience in Australia'. *Australian Journal of Labour Law*, 31, pp. 157–179.

Sukarieh, M. and S. Tannock (2017) 'The education penalty: Schooling, learning and the diminishment of wages, working conditions and worker power'. *British Journal of Sociology of Education*, 38, pp. 245–264.

Swan, E. (2015) 'The internship class: Subjectivity and inequalities – gender, race and class'. In A.M. Broadbridge and S.L. Fielden (eds) *Handbook of Gendered Careers in Management: Getting In, Getting On, Getting Out*. Cheltenham, UK and Northampton, MA, USA: Edward Elgar Publishing, pp. 30–43.

Thompson, R. (2010) 'Reclaiming the disengaged? A bourdieuian analysis of work-based learning for young people in England'. *Critical Studies in Education*, 52(1), pp. 15–28.

Tomlinson, M. (2008) 'The degree is not enough: Students' perceptions of the role of higher education credentials for graduate work and employability'. *British Journal of the Sociology of Education*, 29(1), pp. 49–61.

Tweedie, B. and I. Ting (2018) *How working for free went mainstream*. ABC news online, 4 May. Available at http://www.abc.net.au/news/2018-05-03/what-job-ads-reveal-about-the-rising-internship-culture/9713918 (accessed on 4 October 2019).

4. Diversity and inclusion in a changing world of work

Gill Kirton

INTRODUCTION

Diversity in the labour market has been increasing in all advanced industrialized economies and it is one of the main drivers of change in the world of work. Many factors have generated increased workforce diversity, including exponential growth in women's employment, an ageing workforce associated with rising state pension ages, and international migration creating greater racial, ethnic and religious diversity (Kirton and Greene 2016). At the same time, aided and abetted by globalization and technology, developed countries are witnessing a far greater variety of modes of employment that deviate from the once-standard 'full time in a single organization' model, including part-time working, zero-hours contracts, temporary agency work, fixed-term contracts, remote working and various forms of self-employment including in the so-called 'gig economy'. Further, the reorganization of the state in the guise of privatization and outsourcing of public services seen in many countries has altered working conditions and the employment relationship for the worse for many workers previously in secure relatively well-paid jobs with 'standard' hours in unionized workplaces (Moore and Tailby 2015).

All of these developments have implications for diversity and inclusion in the workplace. One question is, does the more flexible labour market enable workers to balance more easily work and family life? This is likely to be particularly important for women, who, despite social changes around combining working and parenting, are still typically the primary family carers. There is much debate about the benefits of flexibility for employers, vis-à-vis employees. Certain forms of flexibility – flexible work arrangements – might be available to accommodate workers' need to reconcile paid work and family responsibilities, but it is clear that workers need some control over their working-time arrangements in order to achieve a satisfactory work–life balance. Those with caring responsibilities are likely to need predictable work schedules, which may not match employers' expectations of and desire for labour flexibility. Employers may offer flexible work arrangements only to the extent that it suits their operational needs (Fleetwood 2007). There is also plenty of evidence that precarious and insecure forms of work can have negative impacts on people's mental health and wellbeing as well as on their material conditions within and outside the workplace. Such forms of work are more likely to be experienced by women, black and minority ethnic individuals, and sometimes by older workers (Kirton and Greene 2016; see also Kaine et al. in this volume).

On a meso-organizational scale, the structure of workplaces reflects and at the same time tends to reproduce macro-level inequalities, including under-representation of women, black and ethnic minorities, and other minority groups (such as disabled and LGBT people) in positions of power and authority, from middle management through to boardrooms. Thus, one of the things that has remained constant, if not intensified, in this changing world of work is inequality, and this despite a plethora of laws and organization-level policies, in developed countries at least, all meant to eliminate discrimination and disadvantage and promote the valuing of workforce diversity (Moore and Tailby 2015). For individuals, inequalities at work can be manifest in myriad ways, for example in unequal and/or low pay, lack of career opportunities, unequal/unfair treatment at work, difficulties accessing decent work, job insecurity, de-valuing or undervaluing of skills and experience, among others. At occupational and organizational levels, horizontal and vertical forms of segregation by gender, race/ethnicity and possibly age continue to hamper progress on equalities at work (Kirton and Greene 2016).

Against this background, this chapter addresses diversity and inclusion across the dimensions of theory, context, practice and research.

THEORY: COMPETING OR OVERLAPPING DISCOURSES OF EQUALITY, DIVERSITY AND INCLUSION?

This section summarizes discourses of equality, diversity and inclusion, but for extended critical expositions of the shift from equality to diversity see Lorbiecki and Jack (2000), Noon (2007). Over time, the language of equality, diversity and inclusion has undergone shifts that symbolize changes in how societies, and organizations within them, are conceptualizing and responding to the challenges and demands of a diverse workforce. In the context of the USA, Dobbin (2009, p. 220) reminds us that it was Civil Rights activists who *fought* for equal opportunity in employment by literally taking to the streets and protesting against the acute and rife inequality, discrimination and disadvantage that black people and women faced. The same is true in other countries including Australia and the UK; that is, activists often coming from the women's and anti-racist movements were the ones who fought to have discrimination at work outlawed and, as a consequence, equality policies became commonplace in organizations. By the 1980s, a new concept – diversity management – began to permeate policy-making and public discourse, starting in the US but becoming widely adopted in developed economies across the globe including Australia, Canada, Continental Europe, New Zealand and the UK.

In the USA, the main allure of the diversity concept lay in its position as an alternative to the growing and virulent backlash against the social justice aims of the affirmative action approach to equality and its association with the demands of the Civil Rights movement. There was a widespread view in American business and politics that affirmative action either was of little help to or was even counter-productive for competitive organizations, especially for-profit companies supposedly burdened with over-regulation (Kelly and Dobbin 1998). Taylor Cox and Roosevelt Thomas, both African–American and both academics-cum-management consultants published some of the earliest pieces advocating for diversity policies and programs for the sake of business imperatives and goals, rather than in the name of social justice or purely to comply with government mandates (Cox and Blake 1991; Thomas 1990). Other management and practitioner-oriented authors in the US and beyond soon followed, positing that the business case rationale rendered diversity management a new paradigm and a new and positive way forward for organizational equality initiatives that had nothing to do with affirmative action (Dobbin 2009). Advocates argued that diversity management would hold more appeal for business and management, and hence be beneficial for employees too. As employers came to recognize workforce diversity as a vehicle for gaining competitive advantage, the theory stated that they would introduce policies to attract, retain and develop a diverse workforce (Cox and Blake 1991; Kandola and Fullerton 1994).

Globally critics of this new approach began to argue that a universalistic and decontextualized concept of diversity fails to acknowledge that countries have different histories of public equality concepts and legal/organizational equality policy-making, which inevitably create varying antecedents to the newer approaches. The UK, for example, never adopted the more controversial affirmative action approach to equality policy-making, and therefore did not witness the same level of backlash to the liberal 'equal opportunity' policies that organizations developed by way of implementation of the anti-discrimination legislation of the 1970s. Still, by the mid-1980s within a conservative climate the pejorative charge of 'political correctness' was being invoked in the UK to de-legitimize such policies and this climate paved the way by the 1990s for the supposedly new business-friendly diversity approach to capture the imagination of practitioners as a new way forward (Greene and Kirton 2009). Consultants Rachel Ross and Robin Schneider (1992) and Rajvinder Kandola and Johanna Fullerton (1994) led the diffusion of the diversity management approach in the UK via their practitioner/management-oriented books. They too claimed that organizations could leverage business benefits from diversity and therefore that diversity management would change the mind-sets inured against equality claims.

There has since been much debate about the business case for diversity and many attempts to capture exactly what it is; in other words, how do businesses and organizations gain from workforce diversity and proactive diversity management policies? The arguments put forward approximate to four main advantages: (i) ability to reap the benefits of diversity in the labour market, (ii) capability to maximize employee potential, (iii) capacity to manage across borders and cultures, and (iv) ability to create business opportunities and enhance creativity (Cornelius et al. 2001). Practitioner exponents of the business case for diversity see it as a superior rationale for securing organizational commitment to equality and diversity (Kandola and Fullerton 1994; Thomas 1990). However, critical authors agree with the words of Nkomo and Hoobler (2014, p. 252) that 'the battle to establish the business case or the "value-in-diversity" propositions has not been won'. Further, many contributions expose the many flaws and limitations of the business case for diversity, including its unproven and hollow claims, and the failure of diversity policies and programs to deliver the promised and necessary transformation of organizational culture to become more inclusive (e.g. Foster and Harris 2005; Greene and Kirton 2009; Litvin 2002; Lorbiecki and Jack 2000; Noon 2007; Sinclair 2006).

The linguistic evolution is still underway and a more recent shift is that from diversity to inclusion, again first coined by practitioners and now widely used in academic work (Nkomo and Hoobler 2014). While inclusion is usually tacked onto diversity, modifying the concept rather than replacing it (i.e. diversity and inclusion), Oswick and Noon (2014, p. 26) note that some academics and consultants try to make a distinction between the two concepts. Diversity is defined as concerned with recognizing the value of differences and managing them for commercial advantage, while inclusion is concerned with the processes that incorporate differences within business practices (Roberson 2006). Thus, scholars typically see inclusion as going *beyond* diversity management (Sabharwal 2014). Sabharwal (ibid.) defines diversity management as the 'first step' focused on policies and structural changes to remove barriers for specific groups and demographic categories, while inclusion takes the next step and creates an inclusive environment for all. In the inclusive organization, it is argued that the 'employees value diversity and all decisions are carried out based on these assumptions' (Scott et al. 2011, p. 739). For some, the linguistic shift to inclusion acknowledges the failure of the diversity concept alone to live up to its promise of dismantling the organizational architecture of privilege and disadvantage that stands in the way of gaining optimal value from workforce diversity, while offering a solution beyond diversity management. Others question whether inclusion is in fact merely 'old wine in new bottles' (Nkomo and Hoobler 2014) or more specifically, a new iteration of the identity-blind diversity approach (Roberson 2006).

Looked at in another way, the shift to inclusion may also reflect the growing concern that business case rhetoric might have run its course. It may symbolize recognition that diversity practitioners and organizations need to search for new rationales that acknowledge that diversity (in all its breadth) is both a labour market reality (whether or not it adds value) and a social expectation (Kochan et al. 2003). Thus, the addition of inclusion to the lexicon softens the potentially exploitative connotations of diversity and takes the debate back some way towards social justice as an aim and value. Reflecting this viewpoint, Bendick and Egan (2010) argue that employers need to be steered towards formulating a business case for *inclusion*, not diversity. This is in order to benefit from workforce diversity without (perhaps inadvertently) setting up more structures of inequality such as career cul-de-sacs or ethnic pay gaps for black and minority ethnic workers channelled into ethnic niches in the name of realizing the putative competitive benefits of workforce diversity. To this extent, they argue, the business case for *inclusion* recognizes the needs and rights of workers and not just those of businesses/organizations. However, Nkomo and Hoobler (2014) are far more critical, contending that the ideology of inclusion in its efforts to include 'everyone' represents a turn to colour blindness that denies the existence of racism that emphatically does not affect everyone. Similarly, Roberson (2006) argues that, as a more palatable approach, inclusion is proving ineffective for promoting the interests of historically marginalized groups; and for that reason, the turn to inclusion does not bode well from a social justice perspective.

Concepts of equality, diversity and inclusion have evolved over time but have their roots in the social justice claims of activist movements in the 1960s–70s. The contestation and controversy surrounding such claims led to a reformulation of equality principles into the diversity approach that marshalled a more business-friendly language (Kelly and Dobbin 1998). Thus for some, equality, diversity and inclusion are overlapping concepts with similar aims, albeit grounded in different rationales intended to appeal to different constituencies and audiences. For others, they are competing concepts that have differential consequences for socially marginalized groups and for organizational policy-making (discussed later) (Noon 2007).

CONTEXT: HOW AND WHY DOES IT MATTER FOR DIVERSITY AND INCLUSION?

As stated earlier, having originated in the USA, there was formerly a universalistic flavour within diversity discourse and writing, which assumed that a standard set of *diversity management practices* implemented within organizations in different countries, would have similar effects everywhere. Put another way, the implicit assumption was that national context did not matter. For many years now, diversity scholars have emphasized and continue to stress, the importance of country context for understandings of equality, diversity and inclusion as well as for the policies that flow from them (Jones et al. 2000). Strachan et al. (2004), for example, make the point that diversity management in Australian organizations will inevitably operate in concert with the 'equal employment opportunity' policies already in place since the 1980s, which, like those adopted in Britain, differed from the American affirmative action policies (Kirton and Greene 2016).

Of particular importance is the macro-national level context, which comprises societal and structural conditions in the economy and labour market, the law, the education system, the welfare regime and the family as an institution. These conditions may either inhibit or enhance equality at work for individuals (Syed and Ozbilgin 2009). The national institutional context has a substantive bearing on organizational diversity management, not least because it is where laws, rules, norms and expectations are set in regard to how the employment relationship is formed and managed. The role of government, employers, industry/professional bodies and trade unions in the processes of determining laws and rules and shaping outcomes varies enormously. Not least, legal regulation of employment terms and conditions and of equality at work varies among different countries although developed countries all have some equality legislation particularly on gender. Thus, a common assertion in critical literature is that diversity management practices are not the purely voluntary ones that orthodox theory of diversity would have us believe; that is, organizations do not adopt such practices purely for their own strategic reasons. Rather, national legislation certainly plays a critical role in shaping organizational equality, diversity and inclusion practices (Syed and Ozbilgin 2009; Strachan et al. 2004). In addition, in some countries, trade unions have played and continue to play a key role in representing employee interests in the national and organizational equality and diversity arena (Kirton and Greene 2016; Moore and Tailby 2015).

Further, some scholars observe that, beyond legislation and the regulation of employment, the wider social policy context also has a huge influence on the formulation of organizational diversity management policies as well as on how different groups experience the labour market and workplace including the opportunities and barriers encountered (Kirton and Greene 2016; Syed and Ozbilgin 2009). Jones et al. (2000) reveal how discussions about ethnic difference and policy-making in New Zealand mainly concern the indigenous Maori people. Indigenous status is a major basis of difference in New Zealand that has enormous consequences for employment opportunities and prospects. Activists and practitioners feared that the advent of diversity management imported from the very different context of the USA threatened to disrupt the attempts at partnership treaties between white New Zealanders and Maori people. In the European context, Kirton and Greene (2016) discuss how public policies impact on gender, race/ethnic, age, disability, LGBT and religious equality in the labour markets of different European Union countries. On race/ethnicity, Kirton and Greene (2016) observe how countries' approaches to immigration and citizenship of foreign-born people have implications for rights at and to work, welfare benefits, training opportunities, etc., and therefore how organizations treat foreign-born people may vary within and between countries. On women's employment, Kirton and Greene (ibid.) note that countries' welfare regimes provide different levels of support for the family responsibilities that women typically combine with paid work. Some welfare regimes offer little state support in the form of childcare and eldercare provisions or statutory parental leave and therefore reinforce a traditional gender division of domestic responsibilities (i.e. family caring as women's responsibility), and others, most notably the Scandinavian countries, enable women's participation in paid work through strong state supports for families.

Kirton and Greene (ibid.) also discuss how wider social attitudes towards equality and diversity impact upon the personal and working lives of marginalized groups. Thus, in addition to variation in the legal environment among countries, the equality, diversity and inclusion *climate* varies in different countries affecting subjective phenomena such as what it feels like or means to be black/ethnic minority, gay/lesbian/trans, or a member of a religious minority as well as objective regimes of inequality (Kirton and Greene, ibid.). For example, in many European countries, discrimination based on sexual orientation and gender identity is widespread even though most have legal measures in place covering the workplace in terms of equal treatment in promotion, dismissal, pay and other working conditions. To

give another example, far right nationalist movements that peddle xeno-
phobic and racist ideas and blame migrants and multiculturalism for social
and economic woes seem to be gaining popular support in a number of
European countries and beyond. Such attitudes will inevitably spill over
into the workplace. Bringing this wider context into the discussion about
equality and diversity at work highlights that in different countries different social groups enter the workplace with varying subjective experiences
and from different starting places in regard to achieving full inclusion in
organizations.

In terms of what the varying national context of diversity and inclusion means for organizational diversity management, many scholars have
criticized the notion that the voluntary nature of diversity management
meant that it represented the new and positive way forward for organizational equality policy promulgated by some practitioners (Kandola and
Fullerton 1994). Critical authors argue that leaving diversity to the voluntary action of employers/organizations risks only partial consideration
(at best) of employee needs and rights, and only when such needs coincide
with business interests (Jones et al. 2000; Noon 2007; Greene and Kirton
2009; Litvin 2002). Nevertheless, Klarsfeld et al. (2012) caution against the
simplistic assumption that legal rules are binding and therefore preferable,
and that voluntary organizational practices play no role in socially regulating diversity management.

PRACTICE: WHAT ARE DIVERSITY AND INCLUSION *DOING* IN ORGANIZATIONS?

The discussion in the previous section implies that, as well as understanding the outer context, we also need greater knowledge of how concepts
of equality, diversity and inclusion play out in policy terms in different
organizational contexts. This will aid understanding of the implications
for HR and diversity management *practice* (Farndale et al. 2015; Greene
and Kirton 2009; Jones et al. 2000; Kirton and Greene 2016; Nkomo and
Hoobler 2014; Syed and Ozbilgin 2009). However, whether the discursive
shifts described above have led to organizational policy shifts is a question
much debated in the literature. Organizations have certainly adopted the
rhetoric of diversity: as long ago as 2003, analysis of corporate websites
revealed that over 80 per cent of UK companies were using the term
'diversity' to describe their policies in the people management area (Point
and Singh 2003). However, in the UK case, the majority of organizational
diversity policies still appear to focus programs and practices mainly on
characteristics protected by British legislation (gender, ethnicity, disability,

religion and belief, age, and sexual orientation) (van Wanrooy et al. 2013). This suggests that organizations are still writing their policies in accordance with equality legislation rather than addressing a broader range of differences or strategic imperatives as promised by the diversity concept. Thus, despite business case rhetoric, today's diversity management policies appear to have only tenuous links to business goals (Tatli 2011) and stronger links to previous equal opportunity policies than proponents would like to admit. Sabharwal (2014), for example, includes fair and equitable treatment of employees by management as an organizational inclusion behaviour, which clearly highlights the overlapping nature of expected organizational inclusion practices and those expected by the more established equality and diversity approaches. Thus, 'inclusion' offers a new language, but not necessarily new practices.

In fact, many have commented that diversity management seems to be full of assertions and promises, but rather devoid of new policy measures to evidence those assertions and to fulfil those promises. Many diversity practices resemble those formerly falling under equal opportunities policies but with a new name and rationale (Kelly and Dobbin 1998; Kirton and Greene 2000; Oswick and Noon 2014) (e.g. diversity awareness training, diversity proofing HR procedures, targeted recruitment and talent/development programs, employee network groups, workforce/workplace culture audits). It is worth noting that originally such initiatives were designed to support the aims of compliance with anti-discrimination law and/or the social justice goals of equal opportunity approaches. They are now claimed to support the business goals of diversity management (Kelly and Dobbin 1998; Kirton and Greene 2000), even though there is little hard evidence that they actually do so (Kochan et al. 2003). In fact, failure to show return on investment (i.e. to prove the business case) beleaguers diversity policies and programs, which is obviously problematic in terms of attracting organizational value and resources.

Writing from a US perspective, Dobbin et al. (2013) claim that the prevalence of most diversity practices remains low and even things that can be done cheaply are not that popular among firms. Beyond the US, evidence from a survey of 300 senior company executives in three global regions identified that 61 per cent of firms had diversity-focused mentoring programs; 61 per cent had diversity-focused employee resource/networking groups; 58 per cent tied managers' performance to development and retention of diverse employees; 39 per cent conducted exit interview diversity tracking; and 35 per cent tracked promotion rates of diverse groups (Forbes 2011). As Dobbin et al. (ibid.) suggest, most of the diversity and inclusion initiatives mentioned appear inexpensive; and what is more, it is difficult to see how they contribute to leveraging the business benefits of workforce diversity or even to advancing inclusion. Looked at cynically, it is possible that such initiatives may enhance employee *perceptions* of inclusion simply by seemingly paying attention to the existence of workforce diversity. However, there is little evidence that notions of diversity and inclusion have led to a radical shake-up of organizational policies and practices. Thus, to the extent that new and distinctive policy programs and practices are largely absent, it seems most accurate to describe diversity and inclusion as a policy *paradigm*, which according to Kulik (2014, p. 132) 'represents an organisation's normative beliefs and expectations about employee diversity and its role in the organisation', rather than as a policy *approach* per se.

With regard to *who* is doing diversity and inclusion in organizations, many practitioners and researchers state that the business case for diversity requires embedding diversity in the core business functions of organizations (Shapiro and Allison 2007). Yet typically, diversity management is an HR policy area and one for which HR practitioners take responsibility in terms of not only design, but also implementation. According to a global survey, in 59 per cent of firms, responsibility for diversity lies with the HR director (SHRM 2009). Consequently, middle and senior managers often know very little about their organizations' diversity policies and some see little value in them (Foster and Harris 2005; Greene and Kirton 2009). Studies that have explored the work of specialist organizational diversity managers have identified lack of senior and middle management engagement and lack of buy-in to the objectives of diversity policy beyond HR as a structural barrier in the way of policies having the desired strategic impact (Greene and Kirton 2009; Shapiro and Allison 2007). Further, diversity managers often seem to end up supporting an overworked and undervalued HR manager such that they become primarily occupied with advising line managers on diversity-related problems with individual employees (i.e. firefighting), rather than contributing fully to organizational strategy about how to leverage the purported benefits of workforce diversity (Greene and Kirton 2009; Shapiro and Allison 2007; Sinclair 2006).

From the perspective of organizational diversity managers themselves, research finds that they are often somewhat critical of the business case when it prioritizes organizational interests and neglects those of employees (Kirton et al. 2007; Sinclair 2006; Tatli 2011). Hence, Kirton et al. (2007, p. 1981) argue that diversity managers 'exist in a position of uneasy tension in their organisations and within the diversity discourse', which may explain why some have incorporated 'inclusion' into their work, policies and job titles. Yet while diversity managers often seek to champion the rights and needs of employees, they also need to use the business case discourse to increase the support and resources for diversity initiatives (Kirton et al. 2007; Tatli 2011). An early pioneer of diversity management in the

USA, Thomas (2008) reflects upon his experiences as a *business-oriented* African–American diversity consultant and reveals just how difficult the role is. He pinpoints the main challenges as a struggle for legitimacy and his presumed lack of objectivity. Thomas (ibid.) is candid about how some (minority) people felt let down by his proposal of an alternative approach to the affirmative action policies for which the previous generation of African–Americans had fought so hard. Hence, the very people he hoped would benefit from positioning diversity as a mainstream business concern challenged the legitimacy and credibility of his arguments. Equally, Thomas believed that (white) senior business leaders failed to see how an African–American with supposedly a personal interest in programs to promote diversity, could offer impartial business advice. Thomas's story also reminds us that diversity practitioners are typically women or minority ethnic men who may themselves have faced workplace discrimination (Kirton et al. 2007). Even if they advocate for the business case, their personal life experiences surely lie in the hinterland informing their diversity work, which is poignantly demonstrated by Thomas's (2008) piece.

RESEARCH: WHAT AND WHO DO DIVERSITY SCHOLARS STUDY?

Since the discursive turn to diversity occurred, one large stream of literature mostly from scholars based in North America, investigates performance effects of workforce diversity (usually gender and race) at organizational and workgroup/team levels in order to provide an evidence base for the claims of business benefits from workforce diversity and effective diversity management (Nkomo and Hoobler 2014). Some studies have concluded that heterogeneous teams outperform homogenous ones and generate organization-level financial performance benefits. However, other studies indicate that diversity may not have any beneficial or meaningful effects at all for performance (Horwitz and Horwitz 2007; Kochan et al. 2003; Milliken and Martins 1998). Overall, existing research on the performance effects of workforce diversity is inconclusive although generally race diversity is seen as more problematic, and gender diversity as less relevant for performance. Arguably, this strand of research has reached a dead end in terms of providing an evidence base for the legitimation of organizational diversity efforts.

Although the above research focus dominated the US debate for some time, the totality of the diversity research base is now quite large and scholars come from different disciplines (psychology, sociology, employment relations, management, and organization studies) as well as from many countries. Some critical researchers argue that studies have hitherto focused too much on managerial perspectives such that little is known about employee perspectives on diversity and inclusion in the workplace (D'Netto et al. 2013). Greene and Kirton (2009) agree and make the case for research to take a 'stakeholder perspective' on diversity management in order to shift the focus away from the diversity–organizational-performance relationship back to how policies and practices impact upon employees and how such might be designed and implemented to allow individuals dignity, fairness and equality at the workplace. Within such an approach, a stronger focus on a range of 'actors' involved in development or implementation of organizational diversity management (middle/senior managers, HR/ diversity practitioners, trade unions) and their needs, perspectives, actions, behaviours, is also necessary.

Another significant strand of diversity literature that responds to the call for non-managerial voices to be heard, explores workplace experiences and career outcomes of diverse groups. As others have noted, despite the fact that the diversity discourse encompasses myriad group and individual differences, race/ethnicity and gender are the most popular foci of such research (Ozturk and Tatli 2016). That said, more recently we see other bases of difference gaining attention in scholarly work including LGBT issues, religion, disability and age, and such studies are enriching the knowledge base. Farndale et al. (2015), for example, note that patterns of age diversity are changing in many developed economies and that age is a salient factor for job involvement, job satisfaction and organizational commitment, all of which self-evidently have implications for HR policy and practice. Ozturk and Tatli's (2016) work contributes to expanding the diversity research agenda by focusing on gender identity and specifically on the workplace experiences of transgender individuals. They argue that presently diversity research and practice are not equipped to respond to the unique challenges transgender workers encounter. Similarly, Bell et al. (2011) argue that LGBT employees are unable to contribute fully and effectively to organizations – in the way that the inclusion concept suggests is desired – because new mechanisms are required to allow their voices (and those of other visible minorities) to be heard. Further, although Nkomo and Hoobler (2014, p. 255) rightly lament that diversity literature 'has been almost deaf' to the realities of intersectionality, the concept of intersectionality has started to filter through to diversity and inclusion research. Many researchers are at pains to highlight how different bases of difference and inequality combine to produce specific experiences that are presently not addressed effectively by diversity policy and practice (Moore and Tailby 2015; Tatli 2011). We can anticipate that this strand of research will grow and enrich the literature and evidence base.

CONCLUSION

As a fundamental principle within diversity and inclusion research and practice, there is a need to acknowledge that what is going on in the external context inevitably impacts upon organizations and workplaces in myriad ways. Smith Rachele (2017, p. 6), a consultant who has worked in the UK and USA, remarks in her critique of current diversity management practice, 'while the world outside is raging, the harshness of its external realities seem to be kept at bay inside the corporate boardrooms and training rooms'. The critique of the diversity concept notwithstanding, in particular the business case rationale, the framing and positioning of the concept as of strategic importance, suggests that it should be a high priority for organizations, that it should be a highly valued management discipline/function, and that it should be well resourced. Its evolution as an organizational policy paradigm and as a field of practice indicates otherwise (Greene and Kirton 2009; Shapiro and Allison 2007). The discursive shift to inclusion does not seem to have shifted organizational policy and practice sufficiently to allow an optimistic vision of future prospects for better workplace experiences for those historically marginalized and excluded.

It is clear from everything we know about diversity and inclusion that things will improve with action and not with good intentions or with mission statements alone. Organizations need to start with a check on the basics, for instance ensuring fair and equitable treatment of all staff; implementing or improving employee engagement; diversity-proofing HR policies to eliminate unintended adverse impact on any groups of staff; and benchmarking diversity policies against those of other organizations. Organizations then need to take bold action where necessary – such as adopting legally allowable positive action measures or introducing sanctions against recalcitrant managers – in order to break down barriers to inclusion by building workforce diversity across occupations, hierarchies, functions, workgroups and teams. To help move the agenda forward in ways that will benefit those historically marginalized and excluded, those leading the charge – diversity scholars, diversity managers and equality activists – need to achieve a better understanding of how to 'sell' ethically grounded diversity management to organizations and managers. Such a project involves deep engagement with and among multiple stakeholders in order to improve awareness of differing viewpoints and experiences, as well as exchanges of information and experiences among diversity experts in order to enhance our understanding of what works where. While this all may sound like a big ask, it is achievable by those organizations willing to step up to the challenge and invest in workforce diversity.

REFERENCES

Bell, M., M. Özbilgin, T. Beauregard and O. Sürgevil (2011). 'Voice, silence and diversity in 21st century organizations: strategies for inclusion of gay, lesbian, bisexual, and transgender employees.' *Human Resource Management* **50**(1), pp. 131–146.

Bendick, M. and M. Egan (2010). 'The business case for diversity and the perverse practice of matching employees to customers.' *Personnel Review* **39**(4), pp. 468–486.

Cornelius, N., L. Gooch and S. Todd (2001). 'Managing difference fairly: an integrated "partnership" approach.' In *Equality, Diversity and Disadvantage in Employment*, (eds) M. Noon and E. Ogbonna. Basingstoke: Palgrave, pp. 32–50.

Cox, T. and S. Blake (1991). 'Managing cultural diversity: implications for organizational competitiveness.' *Academy of Management Executive* **5**, pp. 545–556.

D'Netto, B. (2013). 'Human resource diversity management practices in the Australian manufacturing sector.' *International Journal of Human Resource Management* **25**(9), pp. 1243–1266.

Dobbin, F. (2009). *Inventing Equal Opportunity*. Princeton, NJ, and Oxford: Princeton University Press.

Dobbin, F., S. Kim and A. Kalev (2013). 'You can't always get what you need: organizational determinants of diversity programs.' *American Sociological Review* **76**(3), pp. 386–411.

Farndale, E., B. Biron, D. Briscoe and S. Raghuram (2015). 'A global perspective on diversity and inclusion in work organisations.' *International Journal of Human Resource Management* **26**(6), pp. 677–687.

Fleetwood, S. (2007). 'Why work–life balance now?' *International Journal of Human Resource Management* **18**, pp. 387–400.

Forbes (2011). *Global Diversity and Inclusion: Fostering Innovation Through a Diverse Workforce*. New York, NY: Forbes Insights.

Foster, C. and L. Harris (2005). 'Easy to say, difficult to do: diversity management in retail.' *Human Resource Management Journal* **15**(3), pp. 4–17.

Greene, A.M. and G. Kirton (2009). *Diversity Management in the UK: Organizational and Stakeholder Experiences*. London: Routledge.

Horwitz, S. and I. Horwitz (2007). 'The effects of team diversity on team outcomes: a meta-analytic review of team demography.' *Journal of Management* **33**(6), pp. 987–1015.

Jones, D., J.K. Pringle and D. Shepherd (2000). '"Managing Diversity" meets Aotearoa/New Zealand.' *Personnel Review* **29**(3), pp. 364–380.

Kandola, R. and J. Fullerton (1994). *Managing the Mosaic: Diversity in Action*. London: Institute of Personnel and Development.

Kelly, E. and F. Dobbin (1998). 'How affirmative action became diversity management: employer response to antidiscrimination law, 1961–1996.' *American Behavioral Scientist* **41**, pp. 960–984.

Kirton, G. and A.M. Greene (2000). *The Dynamics of Managing Diversity* (1st edition). Oxford: Butterworth Heinemann.

Kirton, G. and A.M. Greene (2016). *The Dynamics of Managing Diversity* (4th edition). London: Routledge.

Kirton, G., A.M. Greene and D. Dean (2007). 'British diversity professionals as change agents – radicals, tempered radicals or liberal reformers?' *International Journal of Human Resource Management* **18**(11), pp. 1979–1994.

Klarsfeld, A., E. Ng and A. Tatli (2012). 'Social regulation and diversity management: a comparative study of France, Canada and the UK.' *European Journal of Industrial Relations* **18**(4), pp. 309–327.

Kochan, T., K. Bezrukova, R. Ely, S. Jackson, A. Joshi, K. Jehn, J. Leonard, D. Levine and D. Thomas (2003). 'The effects of diversity of business performance: report of the diversity research network.' *Human Resource Management* **42**(1), pp. 3–21.

Kulik, C. (2014). 'Working below and above the line: the research–practice gap in diversity management.' *Human Resource Management Journal* **24**(2), pp. 129–144.

Litvin, D. (2002). 'The business case for diversity and the "Iron Cage".' In *Casting the Other*, (eds) B. Czarniawska and H.H. Höpfl. London: Routledge, pp. 160–184.

Lorbiecki, A. and G. Jack (2000). 'Critical turns in the evolution of diversity management.' *British Journal of Management* **11**(Special Issue), pp. S17–S31.

Milliken, F. and L. Martins (1998). 'Searching for common threads: understanding the multiple effects of diversity in organizational groups.' *Academy of Management Review* **21**(2), pp. 402–433.

Moore, S. and S. Tailby (2015). 'The changing face of employment relations: equality and diversity.' *Employee Relations* **37**(6), pp. 705–719.

Nkomo, S. and J. Hoobler (2014). 'A historical perspective on diversity ideologies in the United States: Reflections on human resource management research and practice.' *Human Resource Management* **24**, pp. 245–257.

Noon, M. (2007). 'The fatal flaws of diversity and the business case for ethnic minorities.' *Work, Employment and Society* **21**(4), pp. 773–785.

Oswick, C. and M. Noon (2014). 'Discourses of diversity, equality and inclusion: trenchant formulations or transient fashions?' *British Journal of Management* **25**, pp. 23–39.

Ozturk, M. and A. Tatli (2016). 'Gender identity inclusion in the workplace: broadening diversity management research and practice through the case of transgender employees in the UK.' *International Journal of Human Resource Management* **27**(8), pp. 781–802.

Point, S. and V. Singh (2003). 'Defining and dimensionalising diversity: evidence from corporate websites across Europe.' *European Management Journal* **21**(6), pp. 750–761.

Roberson, Q. (2006). 'Disentangling the meanings of diversity and inclusion in organizations.' *Group and Organization Management* **31**(2), pp. 212–236.

Ross, R. and R. Schneider (1992). *From Equality to Diversity*. London: Pitman.

Sabharwal, M. (2014). 'Is diversity management sufficient? Organizational inclusion to further performance.' *Public Personnel Management* **43**(2), pp. 197–217.

Scott, K.A., J.M. Heathcote and J.A. Gruman (2011). 'The diverse organization: finding gold at the end of the rainbow.' *Human Resource Management* **50**(6), pp. 735–755.

Shapiro, G. and M. Allison (2007). *Reframing Diversity*. London: Diversity Professionals' Forum.

SHRM (Society for Human Resource Management) (2009). *Global Diversity and Inclusion: Perceptions, Practices and Attitudes*. Alexandria, VA: SHRM.

Sinclair, D. (2006). 'Critical diversity management in Australia: romanced or co-opted?' In *Handbook of Workplace Diversity*, (eds) P. Prasad, J. Pringle and A. Konrad. London: Sage, pp. 511–530.

Smith Rachele, J. (2017). *Dismantling Diversity Management*. London: Routledge.

Strachan, G., J. Burgess and A. Sullivan (2004). 'Affirmative action or managing diversity: what is the future of equal opportunity policies in organisations?' *Women in Management Review* **19**(4), pp. 196–204.

Syed, J. and M. Ozbilgin (2009). 'A relational framework for international transfer of diversity management practices.' *International Journal of Human Resource Management* **20**(12), pp. 2435–2453.

Tatli, A. (2011). 'A multi-layered exploration of the diversity management field: diversity discourses, practices and practitioners in the UK.' *British Journal of Management* **22**, pp. 238–253.

Thomas, R. (1990). 'From affirmative action to affirming diversity.' *Harvard Business Review* **68**(2), pp. 107–117.

Thomas, R. (2008). 'Consulting in the midst of differences and similarities: related tensions and complexities.' *Consulting Psychology Journal* **60**(2), pp. 203–214.

van Wanrooy, B., H. Bewley, A. Bryson, J. Forth, S. Freeth, L. Stokes and S. Wood (2013). *The 2011 Workplace Employment Relations Study*. London: Department for Business, Innovation and Skills.

5. Contemporary challenges in meaningful work

Catherine Bailey and Adrian Madden

Writing forty years ago, the psychiatrist Viktor Frankl (1978) argued that life in modern, affluent western societies poses significant challenges for individuals' innate will for meaning. If many of us are in fact superfluous to society's requirements, he asked, how can we find a source of meaning or purpose in our work and in our daily lives? Since then, the world of work has for many changed radically. Some have proposed that increased globalization, technological advancements and new business models have led to ways of organizing work that have upturned the employment relationship leading to growing precarity, and the increased concentration of wealth and power into the hands of an elite minority (Yeoman et al., 2019). Work and society have fragmented, leading some to question whether circumstances have moved beyond even Frankl's assessment, rendering employment in today's economy ultimately meaningless (Michaelson, 2019). Emerging forms of work such as crowdsourcing, gig working or digital microwork represent potentially exploitative work situations that may deprive workers of a regular income, stability, supportive workplace relationships and connections with others, all of which may be important components of meaningfulness (Kost et al., 2018; Petriglieri et al., 2018; Schwartz, 2018).

Although some have argued that meaningful work is a luxury rather than a necessity, research has repeatedly shown that meaningful work is highly significant for individual workers (Lepisto and Pratt, 2017; Michaelson et al., 2014). For example, one study of job design and motivation in the US showed that workers 'report important, meaningful work is the job feature they value most – above promotions, income, job security, and hours' (Grant, 2007, p. 394). The quest for meaningful work has moreover been found to be significant across many cultures (Harpaz and Fu, 2002). If meaningfulness is so important for workers, the fact that contemporary employment situations may not foster the kinds of environments where we can find meaning poses a significant challenge for individuals, employers and wider society.

It is within this context that we are witnessing heightened interest in the notion of meaningful work among both academics and practitioners. The purpose of this chapter is threefold. First, we critically review the literature on meaningful work to ascertain what we know so far about the topic. In doing this, we draw on treatments from across a wide range of discipline areas. This enables us to map the terrain of meaningful work and evaluate the breadth and depth of knowledge in the field. We then draw on this evidence base to pose a series of questions for future research in the field and, finally, we outline the practical implications for individuals and the workplace.

MEANINGFUL WORK: WHAT DO WE KNOW SO FAR?

The only thing that there is agreement about in the literature is that no one can agree what 'meaningful work' means. It remains a contested and controversial term (Michaelson et al., 2014; Yeoman et al., 2019). One of the main reasons behind this is that interest in the topic extends far beyond the management and human resource management (HRM) disciplines to include sociology, psychology, philosophy, ethics, political theory and theology. Within each of these discipline areas, meaningfulness is inevitably subject to its own epistemological and ontological debates and disagreements, rendering generalizations problematic.

Philosophy, Ethics and Political Theory

Within philosophy, ethics, political theory and theology, writings on meaningful work have largely been theoretical and conceptual rather than empirical. Within political theory, meaningful work is often defined as a fundamental human need rather than simply a preference for some, and signifies work that fulfils the 'constitutive values of autonomy, freedom and dignity' (Yeoman, 2014, p. 236). Meaningless work, in contrast, arises when the moral capacity of the individual is diminished, for instance through excessive workplace control or the encouragement of immoral behaviour (Bowie, 1998; Lips-Wiersma and Morris, 2009). The focus in this body of literature is generally on the normative value or worthiness of work as a political project (Moriarty, 2009), with a concern to address the unfair distribution of meaningful work within society and to assert the role of employers in ensuring the work they provide is meaningful.

A major concern within the ethics field is 'exploring what all work and workplaces should have in common to make it possible for workers to perform and provide meaningful work' (Michaelson et al., 2014, p. 81).

Bowie (1998) for example identifies six Kantian characteristics of meaningful work: it is freely entered into, it allows the worker to exercise autonomy, it enables the worker to develop rational capacities, it provides a sufficient wage, it supports moral development and it is not paternalistic. This perspective is grounded in the logic of deontology, notably the proposition that one should always treat the individual as an end and not merely a means. This goes to the heart of debates raised about unstable employment opportunities in the 'gig economy' (Taylor, 2017).

However, there is by no means widespread agreement within the field that these characteristics necessarily encompass meaningful work. There is some debate over whether meaningfulness resides in the objective conditions of work, or in the individual's subjective assessment of that work. Scholars such as Wolf (2010) argue for a 'bipartite value of meaningfulness' whereby meaningfulness comprises both objective and subjective dimensions; in other words, work has to meet certain objective standards of worth in order to be considered meaningful but must, at the same time, be subjectively experienced as meaningful by the individual. However, Ciulla (2019) argues in contrast that what Wolf might regard as the objective dimensions of meaningfulness, such as autonomy, fair pay and reasonable working conditions, in fact constitute the moral conditions that can form a pathway for experiencing work as subjectively meaningful.

One major factor relating to meaningfulness that has been identified within the political theory and ethics literatures is that of human freedom and autonomy. For example, Breen (2019) argues that meaningful work is associated with human freedom along three dimensions: freedom as self-determination, as self-realization and as non-domination. He argues that capitalist employers that permit managers to exercise 'authoritarian rule' over employees can lead to constant feelings of fear and anxiety on the part of employees, which stunt the experience of meaningfulness.

A further concern within the ethics field is the association between meaningful work and a meaningful life. Michaelson et al. (2014) note that there is no agreement over what a 'meaningful life' constitutes, and hence little consensus over how the two may be linked. For example, given that we spend so much time at work, is it necessary to have a meaningful job for our lives to be considered meaningful at a broader level? Is meaningfulness perhaps not equally significant to all, and therefore do individuals willingly trade off other factors such as pay against meaningfulness? Are individuals morally obligated to seek out meaningful work? What happens when an individual finds their work subjectively meaningful, yet it fails to fulfil the criteria for objective meaningfulness? As Michaelson et al. (2014, p. 87) argue, there is some concern that the necessity of work can distract us or detract from the possibility of leading a meaningful life, potentially requiring us to set aside other meaningful priorities such as family, hobbies and home. Thus, from the ethical perspective, work and life meaningfulness may be in a relationship that is either complementary or conflictual.

The ethics literature also considers the status of jobs that require the individual to visit harm in some way on others. Molinsky and Margolis (2005) use the term 'necessary evils' to encompass tasks that involve harming others in pursuit of a greater purpose. The notion of prosocial impact can provide employees with a utilitarian justification to rationalize harming others and to deviate from established norms (Michaelson et al., 2014). This raises further questions about how the individual may seek to balance their ethical responsibility to themselves, to live a meaningful life and to contribute towards the flourishing of others.

Sociology

The sociological tradition is grounded in an approach that seeks to understand human behaviour within the context of wider social structures (Bauman, 1990). Work is thus viewed as a 'system of production' (Giddens, 1993, p. 481), a pattern of collective human behaviour with institutionalizing effects of both positive and negative valence that, for some, represents a 'social duty' constituent of social solidarity (Troncoso, 1943, p. 288). Sociological theories about the meaning of work have been concerned with the social relations and organizational structures associated with labour. In these theories and approaches to work, sociological concerns overlap with those within philosophical and political theory. For example, Engels (1950, p. 7) argued that 'work was the prime basic condition for all human existence and this to such an extent that, in a sense, we have to say that labor created man himself'. In functionalist as well as in conflict-based approaches, work is seen to serve as the basis of society as social life is premised on the structures (forces) and institutions (relations) of production (Marx, 1995). Emphasis in the sociology of work has thus often centred on those structures, systems and institutions underpinning what work means in relation to worker autonomy and group or class identity; the labour process and quality of work (Braverman, 1974); work relations; and how these have been transformed since the twentieth century through the emergence of market economies and neo-liberalism (Polanyi, 1944; Harvey, 2005).

Although work is seen on the one hand to be integral to social existence, these sociological approaches to understanding the meaning of work have often emphasized the struggle and alienating effects of work at the individual level. For example, Braverman's (1974, p. 24) analysis of the changing nature of modern labour focused on increased job dissatisfaction with the degradation of work arising as a result of automation and the emergence of 'dumb jobs' for 'dumb people'. Terkel (1972, p. xxiii) on the other hand argued that it was not that 'the average working guy is dumb'; it was that work was 'by its very nature, about violence – to the spirit as well as the body' (ibid., p. xi). In sociology, a great deal of attention has thus been paid to the alienating or *meaningless* experience of work at the individual level (Seeman, 1959; Fromm, 1955), whereby the social arrangements of production have led to the estrangement of the worker not only from the work process, but also from his or her own 'essence'. Work alienates or becomes meaningless when it becomes depersonalized, such that individuals experience 'the loss of intrinsically meaningful satisfactions' such as pride in work, and the emergence instead of instrumentalized return or reward that is not linked to the nature or value of the work or to the work activity itself (Seeman, 1959, p. 790). Rather than contributing to the quality of social existence, the degradation of labour processes and the increasingly precarious nature of work relations means that work that has intrinsic usefulness, such as care work, is disregarded as labour, while work with exchange value is valorized (Standing, 2011).

Most research in the sociological tradition therefore has tended to focus on what work *means*, either at the individual level in terms of work–person fit, work centrality and 'interesting work' (England, 1986; England and Whitely, 1990), or at the structural level in terms of recent shifts from a work society to a knowledge society and the expansion of work casualization (Beck, 2000). In both instances, the focus on the *meaning* of work meaning has excluded the distinctive idea of *meaningful* work (Simpson et al., 2014). However, as Rosso et al. (2010) note, just because work has a particular meaning for someone does not mean that it is experienced as meaning*ful*.

Management Studies and Psychology

Within the field of management studies more broadly and organizational psychology more specifically, we have witnessed a significant upturn in interest in meaningfulness in the past two decades. Bailey et al. (2018b) report the results of an evidence synthesis on meaningful work from 1950 onwards. They uncovered four especially influential approaches to understanding meaningfulness (pp. 6–10), all of which conceptualize meaningfulness as a subjective experience.

The first approach derives from Hackman and Oldham's (1976, p. 256) job characteristics model in which meaningfulness is positioned as one of three psychological states experienced by individuals in relation to their work, along with experienced responsibility for the outcomes of work and knowledge of the actual results of the work activities. Experienced mean-ingfulness is associated in this model with high levels of skill variety, task significance and task identity. In turn, it is argued that the three psychologi-cal states lead to high levels of motivation, performance and satisfaction and low levels of absenteeism and turnover. Meaningfulness is described as 'the degree to which the individual experiences the job as one which is generally meaningful, valuable and worthwhile', thereby positioning mean-ingfulness as a subjective perception. This strand of the literature has been influential in more recent treatments such as Kahn's (1990) research on personal role engagement, in which he argues that meaningfulness, along with psychological safety and availability, is the precursor to high levels of engagement. It has also influenced the research on psychological empow-erment, in which meaningful work is positioned as one of four cognitions relating to the individual's orientation towards their work role, alongside competence, self-determination and impact (Spreitzer, 1996).

The second approach lies within the workplace spirituality literature, drawing in particular on the work of Ashmos and Duchon (2000). Within this body of literature, meaningfulness is defined as a fundamental human spiritual need with multiple dimensions, relating both to individually oriented work features such as self-fulfilment and joy, and to work that 'connects workers to a larger good' (Duchon and Plowman, 2005, p. 814). Within the humanities tradition, the third approach, scholars argue that the pursuit of meaning is inherent in the human condition rather than something that can 'be supplied' by the employer (Lips-Wiersma and Morris, 2009, pp. 503–4). According to this perspective, the most profound experience of meaningfulness arises from coherence across four domains: unity with others, expressing oneself, serving others, and developing and becoming oneself (Lips-Wiersma and Morris, 2009).

Positive psychological approaches constitute the fourth treatment, and here two main strands of thought can be discerned. According to the first, meaningfulness is regarded as a eudaimonic psychological state that includes the subjective sense of meaning derived from work, the link between meaningful work and life more broadly, and the desire to contrib-ute to the greater good (Steger et al., 2012). Work is considered meaningful when the individual judges their work to be significant and worthwhile and to have positive meaning (Tims et al., 2016). According to the second strand, work is considered meaningful when perceived by the individual as a calling (Bunderson and Thompson, 2009).

Beyond these, Bailey et al. (2018b) also found that meaningfulness has been defined in ways that fall outside the main theoretical and conceptual strands of the literature in two ways. First, as an occupation-specific phe-nomenon, such as in the work of Britt et al. (2001, 2007), who examined meaningfulness within the context of the military, or in McCarthy and Friedman (2006), whose focus was on meaningful work in nursing homes. Finally, some treatments of meaningfulness adopt idiosyncratic definitions, such as Scroggins' (2008) notion of meaningfulness as comprising consistency between one's self-perception and work role.

In summary, beyond broad agreement that meaningfulness is a subjective evaluation, there is no clear consensus over definition or the theoretical positioning of the meaningfulness construct within the management and psychology literatures, leaving the field open for further conceptual developments.

The Evidence Base for Meaningful Work

What do we actually know about meaningful work? In their review of empirical studies, Bailey et al. (2018b) found that 71 high-quality articles containing empirical data had been published between 1950 and 2017, the majority of which adopted a positive psychology perspective and a positivist epistemology. This body of work broadly suggests that meaningfulness is associated with a range of positive outcomes, such as engagement (Kahn, 1990), patient satisfaction in a medical setting (Duchon and Plowman, 2005), creativity (Cohen-Meitar et al., 2009), work-to-family enrichment (Tummers and Knies, 2013) or wellbeing (Littman-Ovadia and Steger, 2010). In their recent meta-analysis based on 44 articles, Allan et al. (2019) found meaningfulness to predict engagement, satisfaction and commitment, and that these in turn positively predict performance and organizational citizenship behaviours and negatively predict withdrawal intentions. They also found meaningfulness to be linked with life satisfaction, life meaning and general health. This represents the strongest case thus far for the positive effects of meaningfulness.

However, the positive findings reported in many studies should be weighed against those minority of studies that have either failed to find a link or that have found a negative association. For example, Steger et al. (2012) did not find that meaningfulness was associated with lower levels of anxiety; Albuquerque et al. (2014) failed to uncover a link between meaningfulness and organizational performance, and Lips-Wiersma and Wright (2012) found no association between meaningful work and extrinsic motivation.

Thus, we cannot assume, based on the extant evidence base, that meaningfulness is inevitably associated with positive outcomes. Alongside this, we also need to take into consideration limitations in study designs such as a preponderance of cross-sectional research and questions over the reliability and validity of extant measures of meaningfulness.

More recently, studies have additionally sought to uncover the potential negative effects of meaningful work, building on literature in the field of callings that has highlighted how perceptions of being 'called' to a particular line of work can lead individuals to accept mundane work or poor working conditions or pay, and to run the risk of exploitation (Bunderson and Thompson, 2009). For example, Oelberger's (2019) study of international aid workers shows how those engaged in deeply meaningful work may experience high levels of work–relationship conflict through their long, erratic working hours. Toraldo et al.'s (2019) research among music festival volunteers demonstrates that, when meaningful work is viewed through the lens of community, managers are able to exert neo-normative control over volunteers that obscures the economic realities of festival work. Thus, although the dominant view within the literature is that meaningfulness is positive and beneficial, there is some evidence that 'too much' meaningfulness may draw individuals into working practices that are harmful to their wider wellbeing, reflecting the themes of exploitation raised in the theoretical literature in sociology and ethics.

In terms of the factors that may influence meaningfulness, most research has focused on the role played by job design. Here, the weight of evidence suggests that job design features such as skill variety, job enrichment and autonomy are important for a sense of meaningfulness (e.g. de Boeck et al., 2019; Kahn, 1990; May et al., 2004; Schnell et al., 2013). It has also been suggested that meaningful work is negatively associated with perceived underemployment and a mismatch between the job and the worker (Allan et al., 2017). Equally, though, research has shown that relational factors may play a role in meaningful work; for instance, transformational and spiritual approaches to leadership have been found to be associated with meaningfulness (Pradhan and Pradhan, 2016; Duchon and Plowman, 2005), as well as positive work climates (Bailey and Madden, 2016) and recognition (Montani et al., 2017). Carton's (2017) research is especially interesting, as he demonstrates how it is possible for leaders to serve as meaning architects through processes of sense-giving in a case study of Kennedy's role at NASA. In particular, focusing on one 'ultimate aspiration', connecting this to a concrete purpose and communicating milestones emerged as important processes through which Kennedy helped workers at NASA find their work meaningful. Nonetheless, Bailey and Madden's (2016) research conversely suggests that the role of the leader in promoting meaningfulness may be marginal, and that a sense of meaningfulness is highly personal to the individual.

At the organizational level, some studies have suggested that certain types of work climates are more conducive to meaningfulness than others, such as spiritual climates or learning-focused climates, as well as work settings characterized by positive co-worker relationships (Duchon and Plowman, 2005; May et al., 2004; Pavlish and Hunt, 2012). It has also been proposed that there is a link between corporate social responsibility (CSR) and meaningful work (Akdogan et al., 2016), perhaps because CSR activities enable the individual to see a connection between their work and the greater good. In some cases, individuals may engage in corporate volunteering to compensate for an absence of meaning in their daily work (Rodell, 2013), which raises further questions about the link between meaningful work and a meaningful life.

Although there has been some research exploring occupational differences in meaningfulness, the findings have been equivocal. For instance, Albuquerque et al. (2014) found that doctors and nurses experience their work to be more meaningful than do administrators, and Lips-Wiersma et al. (2016) found that white-collar workers experience meaningful work more frequently than pink- or blue-collar workers. The fact that the researchers additionally found significant differences between the experience of the different facets of meaningfulness across the occupational groups, however, points to the complexity of the meaningfulness experience. Building on this point, Isaksen's (2000) study found that the individual's ability to construct meaning was more important than their occupation per se. Relatively little research has looked at demographic factors and meaningfulness, although one study by Weeks and Schaffert (2017) found that there are similarities across the generations in the experience of meaningfulness, but more research is certainly needed before any definitive conclusions can be drawn.

At the individual level, some research has explored whether certain personality types are more prone to experience their work as meaningful than others. One review concluded: 'weak to moderately positive correlations have been found with conscientiousness, openness and extraversion and a weak negative correlation with neuroticism' (Lysova et al., 2018, p. 377). Some associations have also been found between values such as benevolence and self-actualization with meaningfulness (Rosso et al., 2010). However, Lysova et al. (2018, p. 378) conclude that there is stronger evidence that goal directedness, prosocial motivation and a deep understanding of one's career narrative are more strongly associated with meaningful work than are personality traits.

Given that debates within the ethics and political theory literatures have emphasized the associations between individual-level experienced meaningfulness and wider organizational and societal imperatives, there is a notable gap in the research evidence around this theme. However, a small number of studies have addressed how 'good work', which might equate to the concept of 'objectively meaningful' work, is linked with individual perceptions of meaningful work, or 'subjective meaningfulness'. For example, Duffy et al. (2017) found that, although good work and meaningful work are correlated, they represent distinct constructs, opening up a promising avenue for future research.

There has also been some discussion of how meaningfulness varies at the societal level. Some research has suggested that meaningfulness may be more salient in some cultural settings than others (Magun and Rudnev, 2012; Schwartz et al., 2012). One recent article by Florian et al. (2019) highlights the point that shifting societal level discourses impact on individual experiences of meaningful work. In a study of volunteers in refugee centres in Germany, they found that societal level discourses initially framed voluntary work in refugee centres as highly meaningful, but when these discourses shifted towards a more negative perception of refugees, this posed significant challenges to the volunteers' sense of meaningfulness, leading to stress, burnout and growing hostility towards the refugees.

Research with a specific focus on meaningfulness among those working in precarious or atomized working situations is extremely sparse. There is one study that has focused specifically on meaningfulness among digital microworkers in the context of Amazon Mechanical Turk (MTurk; Kost et al., 2018). These workers undertake the remote completion of small digital tasks, and, as Kost et al. (2018, p. 101) argue, 'microwork lacks the relational and organizational architecture normally assumed to provide meaningful work', making this a particularly interesting setting to explore meaningfulness. Despite the ostensibly poor prospects for meaningfulness offered by this type of work, Kost et al. (2018) identify four pathways to meaningfulness: remuneration and autonomy of working, the opportunity for self-improvement, impact on specific beneficiaries and contribution to the greater good. The authors emphasize the role of the individual's choice to perceive meaningfulness in work, whatever the structural scaffolding that surrounds it. It is interesting to see the parallels in the pathways to meaningfulness between the microworkers and those of workers in more regular and traditional employment patterns (Lips-Wiersma and Morris, 2009; Rosso et al., 2010).

CONCLUSIONS AND IMPLICATIONS FOR FUTURE RESEARCH AND PRACTICE

Overall, there have been some significant advancements in our knowledge and understanding of meaningful work in recent years, in the wake of both theoretical and empirical research. Psychologists in particular have provided reasonably robust evidence of an association between meaningfulness and other positive attitudes such as engagement, commitment and satisfaction, and with outcomes such as performance and organizational citizenship behaviour (Allan et al., 2019). However, there are some important ongoing gaps in knowledge around meaningfulness that leave the field open for further development by researchers.

The diversity of research on meaningful work across discipline boundaries is of course a positive thing. These divergent perspectives have the potential to invigorate and enrich discussions of meaningfulness. However, there is a disappointing disconnect between the empirical literature on the one hand, which has taken place primarily within management and, more specifically, organizational psychology, and the theoretical/conceptual literature on the other, which has coalesced largely around debates within the ethics/political theory arenas. There have, nonetheless, been recent attempts to bring these two bodies of work together. For instance, Lepisto and Pratt (2017) draw attention to two broadly divergent perspectives on meaningfulness: the realization perspective and the justification perspective. They argue that most research to date has taken place within the realization paradigm, whereby meaningfulness is associated with the fulfilment of individual needs, motivations and desires. This aligns with the perspective taken by many organizational psychologists. The justification perspective, however, is associated with the individual's concern over whether their work is worthy or valuable, which connects with societal- and cultural-level discourses over what constitutes worthwhile work, and the processes through which this arises. According to this viewpoint, individuals struggle to find meaningfulness in their work if they believe their work lacks wider worth. The relative dearth of research from a justification perspective (for an exception see Florian et al., 2019) raises opportunities for further research by scholars wishing to connect conceptual and empirical debates. A future research agenda could incorporate consideration of the provenance of accounts of meaningfulness and worth, and the processes and conditions of account-making (Lepisto and Pratt, 2017).

The importance of such an agenda in the context of the future of work is lent additional weight in view of the proliferation of what Graeber (2019, pp. 9–10) refers to as 'bullshit jobs', or 'paid employment that is so completely pointless, unnecessary, or pernicious that even the employee cannot justify its existence even though, as part of the conditions of employment, the employee feels obliged to pretend that this is not the case'. According to Graeber (2019, p. 26) 37–40% of all jobs can be characterized in this way, including 'flunkies', 'goons', 'box-tickers', 'taskmasters' and 'duct tapers' (pp. 28–58). In his analysis, Graeber finds such work to be associated with stress, depression, misery and lack of meaning. He argues that the prevailing political, social and economic climate is especially conducive to the evolution of these forms of work. Little of the current evidence base on meaningful work has examined whether or how workers involved in these types of jobs derive a sense of meaning, and more research is needed that focuses on employees in such occupations.

In terms of evaluating whether and how meaningfulness is linked with some of the other more profound changes that are taking place in working life, such as growing precarity, increasing automation and digitization, as well as the growing potential for surveillance and control, there is a need for further research. So far, one study has addressed the issue of precarity (Kost et al., 2018), and this yielded some positive findings in terms of individuals' ability to find meaning even in 'a hopeless place'. More research among other types of precarious workers would be welcome, as would studies that address how current employment conditions interact with the subjective experience of meaningfulness. Recent research has begun to explore some of these issues. For example, Stein et al. (2019) found that increasing surveillance in the professional context of academia can undermine a sense of meaningfulness through reducing perceived autonomy. Symon and Whiting (2019)'s study of entrepreneurs showed that the use of digital technologies can cause individuals to lose control over their work and lead to a sense of diminished meaning. These studies suggest there is a risk that growing levels of automation and digitization can remove those elements of the work experience that are most conducive to a sense of meaningfulness, and studies that expand our understanding of the impacts of such trends would be welcome.

Bailey et al. (2018a) identify the paradoxical nature of meaningful work as a frame for understanding where the core tensions lie that are amenable to future research endeavours. One of the unresolved paradoxes centres on research that has identified both positive and negative features of meaningfulness. While on the one hand meaningfulness is part of a 'virtuous circle' of positive attitudes and behaviours within the psychology literature, there is also evidence of a darker side to meaningfulness that is associated with exploitation, self-sacrifice and denial (Oelberger, 2019). This raises unanswered questions concerning how meaningfulness may be effectively managed by both individuals and employers, and how meaningful work links with a meaningful life.

A further issue that requires more research is the extent to which meaningful work actually matters in practice to individual workers. Researchers within the humanities tradition generally adhere to the view that all humans have an innate will to meaning that impels them to seek out meaningfulness in their daily activities (cf. Frankl, 1978). However, studies have also shown that work can be associated with a wide range of potential meanings; for some it may be a curse, a disutility or a commodity (Budd, 2011). Thus, for some, work may not be the primary source of meaning in their lives but may instead be traded off against more valued leisure pursuits. Research that examines how and under what conditions these trade-offs are made would deepen our understanding of the nature of meaningful work.

Although the volume of research on meaningful work has increased, in terms of the quality of the extant evidence base, several commentators have referred to the preponderance of cross-sectional studies, which raises the common problem of how to demonstrate causality (Lysova et al., 2018). Another issue, which is more particular to research on meaningfulness, is the proliferation of different measurement scales used within the literature to assess meaningfulness. Bailey et al. (2018b) found 28 different measurement scales to be in use, plus variants thereof. Many of these are single-item measures with sometimes doubtful validity in terms of capturing a construct as complex as meaningfulness. Alternatively, one measure contained as many as 53 items across several different dimensions. This disparity in terms of measuring meaningfulness reflects the general uncertainty around precisely what meaningfulness means, how many dimensions it has and how these dimensions are interrelated. There is clearly scope for researchers to continue their efforts to develop new and more accurate measures of meaningfulness.

Implications for Practice

There is sufficient evidence that meaningfulness is associated with beneficial outcomes to encourage organizations to invest in interventions aimed at raising levels of experienced meaningfulness among their employees. One area that is of particular importance here is job design, since the weight of evidence supports the notion that meaningfulness is associated with job design features such as skill variety, task significance and task identity, alongside opportunities for autonomy and growth. Employers can consider how to ensure employees can gain feedback on their work that demonstrates the impact their work has on colleagues, the organization and wider society.

Equally important is the workplace climate; environments that are hostile, unfriendly or negative are unlikely to foster meaningfulness among their workers. Instead, employers should consider leadership development initiatives that emphasize collaborative working, devolution of responsibilities and positive relations among co-workers. The overarching organizational purpose and the role played by the organization in wider society should also be considered. Can employees see that the employer has a positive, affirming role to play (Bailey and Madden, 2016)? This links back to debates around the link between organizational purpose and meaningful work through mechanisms such as corporate social responsibility initiatives. Employers can consider how to build awareness of the organization's position and its impact on society, the community and the wider environment.

CONCLUSIONS

Meaningful work remains, for many, an unattainable ideal. Some have even suggested it is a greedy ideal that sets us up to fail (Muirhead, 2004). Yet, from Frankl onwards, research has repeatedly shown that individuals can experience profound meaning in their work even in adverse or challenging conditions. Despite the increased focus on meaningfulness in recent years, research has still not enabled us to answer some of today's pressing questions about how and why people find their work meaningful or meaningless. Almost all the existing evidence is based on studies that have taken place in the context of a traditional employment relationship; the challenge now is to explore how new forms of employment enable or constrain the imperative for meaning.

REFERENCES

Akdogan, A.A., A. Arslan and O. Demirtas (2016). 'A strategic influence of corporate social responsibility on meaningful work and organizational identification, via perceptions of ethical leadership'. *Procedia – Social and Behavioral Sciences*, 235, pp. 259–268.

Albuquerque, I.F., R.C. Cunha, L.D. Martins and A.B. Sa (2014). 'Primary health care services: Workplace spirituality and organizational performance'. *Journal of Organizational Change Management*, 27, pp. 59–82.

Allan, B.A., R.D. Duffy and B. Collisson (2017). 'Helping others increases meaningful work: Evidence from three experiments'. *Journal of Counseling Psychology*, doi: 10.1037/cou0000228.

Allan, B.A., C. Batz-Barbarich, H.M. Sterling and L. Tay (2019). 'Outcomes of meaningful work: A meta-analysis'. *Journal of Management Studies*, 56(3), pp. 500–528.

Ashmos, D. and D. Duchon (2000). 'Spirituality at work: A conceptualization and measure'. *Journal of Management Inquiry*, 9, pp. 34–145.

Bailey, C., and A. Madden (2016). 'What makes work meaningful – or meaningless'. *MIT Sloan Management Review*, Summer, pp. 52–63.

Bailey, C., M. Lips-Wiersma, A. Madden, R. Yeoman, M. Thompson and N. Chalofsky (2018a). 'The five paradoxes of meaningful work: Introduction to the special issue "Meaningful work: Prospects for the 21st Century"'. *Journal of Management Studies*, 56(3), pp. 481–499.

Bailey, C., R. Yeoman, A. Madden, M. Thompson and G. Kerridge (2018b). 'Meaningful work: An evidence synthesis'. *Human Resource Development Review*, doi.org/10.1177/1534484318804653.

Bauman, Z. (1990). *Thinking Sociologically*. Oxford: Blackwell.

Beck, U. (2000). *The Brave New World of Work*. Cambridge: Polity Press.

Bowie, N.E. (1998). 'A Kantian theory of meaningful work'. *Journal of Business Ethics*, 17, pp. 1083–1092.

Braverman, H. (1974). *Labor Monopoly and Capital: The Degradation of Work in the Twentieth Century*. New York, NY: Monthly Review Press.

Breen, K. (2019). 'Meaningful work and freedom: Self-realization, autonomy and non-domination in work', in Ruth Yeoman, Catherine Bailey, Adrian Madden and Marc Thompson (eds), *The Oxford Handbook of Meaningful Work*. Oxford: Oxford University Press, pp. 51–72.

Britt, T.W., A.B. Adler and P.T. Bartone (2001). 'Deriving benefits from stressful events: The role of engagement in meaningful work and hardiness'. *Journal of Occupational Health Psychology*, 6, pp. 53–63.

Britt, T.W., J.M. Dickinson, C.A. Castro and A.B. Adler (2007). 'Correlates and consequences of morale versus depression under stressful conditions'. *Journal of Occupational Health Psychology*, 12, pp. 34–47.

Budd, J. (2011). *The Thought of Work*. Ithaca, NY: Cornell University Press.

Bunderson, S.J. and J.A. Thompson (2009). 'The call of the wild: Zookeepers, callings, and the double-edged sword of deeply meaningful work'. *Administrative Science Quarterly*, 54, pp. 32–57.

Carton, A.M. (2017). '"I'm not mopping the floors, I'm putting a man on the moon!" How NASA leaders enhanced the meaningfulness of work by changing the meaning of work'. *Administrative Science Quarterly*, doi: 10.1177/0001839217713748.

Ciulla, J.B. (2019). 'The moral conditions of work', in Ruth Yeoman, Catherine Bailey, Adrian Madden and Marc Thompson (eds), *The Oxford Handbook of Meaningful Work*. Oxford: Oxford University Press, pp. 23–35.

Cohen-Meitar, R., A. Carmeli and D.A. Waldman (2009). 'Linking meaningfulness in the workplace to employee creativity: The intervening role of organizational identification and positive psychological experiences'. *Creativity Research Journal*, 21, pp. 361–375.

De Boeck, G., N. Dries and H. Tierens (2019). 'The experience of untapped potential: Towards a subjective temporal understanding of work meaningfulness'. *Journal of Management Studies*, 56(3) pp. 529–557.

Duchon, D. and D.A. Plowman (2005). 'Nurturing the spirit at work: Impact on work unit performance'. *The Leadership Quarterly*, 16, pp. 807–833.

Duffy, R.D., B.A. Allan, J.W. England, D.L. Blustein, K.L. Autin, R.P. Douglas ... E.J. Santos (2017). 'The development and initial validation of the decent work scale'. *Journal of Counseling Psychology*, 64, pp. 206–221.

Engels, F. (1950). *The Part Played by Labor in the Transition from Ape to Man*. New York, NY: International Publishers.

England, G. (1986). 'National work meanings and patterns – Constraints on management action'. *European Management Journal*, 4(3) pp. 176–184.

England, G. and W. Whitely (1990). 'Cross-national meanings of working', in A. Brief and W. Nord (eds), *Meanings of Occupational Work*. Lexington, KY: Lexington Books, pp. 65–106.

Florian, M., J. Costas and D. Karreman (2019). 'Struggling with meaningfulness when context shifts: Volunteer work in a German refugee shelter'. *Journal of Management Studies*, 56(3) pp. 589–616.

Frankl, V. (1978) *The Unheard Cry for Meaning*. New York, NY: Touchstone Books.

Fromm, E. (1955). *The Sane Society*. New York, NY: Holt, Winston & Rinehart.
Giddens, A. (1993). *Sociology*. Cambridge: Polity.
Graeber, D. (2019). *Bullshit Jobs*. London: Penguin.
Grant, A.M. (2007). 'Relational job design and the motivation to make a prosocial difference'. *Academy of Management Review*, 32, pp. 393–417.
Hackman, R. and G.R. Oldham (1976). 'Motivation through the design of work: Test of a theory'. *Organizational Behavior and Human Experience*, 16, pp. 250–279.
Harpaz, I. and X. Fu (2002). 'The structure of the meaning of work: A relative stability amidst change'. *Human Relations*, 55, pp. 639–667.
Harvey, D. (2005). *A Brief History of Neoliberalism*. Oxford: Oxford University Press.
Isaksen, J. (2000). 'Constructing meaning despite the drudgery of repetitive work'. *Journal of Humanistic Psychology*, 40, pp. 84–107.
Kahn, W.A. (1990). 'Psychological conditions of personal engagement and disengagement at work'. *Academy of Management Journal*, 33, pp. 692–724.
Kost, D., C. Fieseler and S.I. Wong (2018). 'Finding meaning in a hopeless place? The construction of meaningfulness in digital microwork'. *Computers in Human Behavior*, 82, pp. 101–110.
Lepisto, D.A. and M.G. Pratt (2017). 'Meaningful work as realization and justification: Toward a dual conceptualization'. *Organizational Psychology Review*, 7, pp. 99–121.
Lips-Wiersma, M. and L. Morris (2009). 'Discriminating between "meaningful work" and the "management of meaning"'. *Journal of Business Ethics*, 88, pp. 491–511.
Lips-Wiersma, M. and S. Wright (2012). 'Measuring the meaning of meaningful work: Development and validation of the Comprehensive Meaningful Work Scale (CMWS)'. *Group and Organization Management*, 37, pp. 665–685.
Lips-Wiersma, M., S. Wright and B. Dik (2016). 'Meaningful work: Differences among blue-, pink- and white-collar occupations'. *Career Development International*, 21, pp. 534–551.
Littman-Ovadia, H. and M. Steger (2010). 'Character strengths and well-being among volunteers and employees: Towards an integrative model'. *The Journal of Positive Psychology*, 5, pp. 419–430.
Lysova, E., B.A. Allan, B.J. Dik, R.D. Duffy and M.F. Steger (2018). 'Fostering meaningful work in organizations: A multi-level review and integration'. *Journal of Vocational Behavior*, 110, pp. 374–389.
Magun, V. and N. Rudnev (2012). 'Basic values of Russians and other Europeans'. *Problems of Economic Transition*, 54(10) pp. 31–64.
Marx, K. (1995). *Capital: A New Abridgement*. Oxford: Oxford University Press.
May, D.R., R.L. Gilson and L.M. Harter (2004). 'The psychological conditions of meaningfulness, safety and availability and the engagement of the human spirit at work'. *Journal of Occupational and Organizational Psychology*, 77, pp. 11–37.
McCarthy, J. and L.H. Friedman (2006). 'The significance of autonomy in the nursing home administrator profession: A qualitative study'. *Health Care Management Review*, 31, pp. 55–63.
Michaelson, C. (2019). 'Do we have to do meaningful work?' in Ruth Yeoman, Catherine Bailey, Adrian Madden and Marc Thompson (eds) *The Oxford Handbook of Meaningful Work*. Oxford: Oxford University Press, pp. 117–132.
Michaelson, C., M.G. Pratt, A.M. Grant and C.P. Dunn (2014). 'Meaningful work:

Connecting business ethics and organization studies'. *Journal of Business Ethics*, 121, pp. 77–90.

Molinsky, A. and J. Margolis (2005). 'Necessary evils and interpersonal sensitivity in organizations'. *Academy of Management Review*, 30, pp. 245–268.

Montani, F., J.-S. Boudrias and M. Pigeon (2017). 'Employee recognition, meaningfulness and behavioural involvement: Test of a moderated mediation model'. *The International Journal of Human Resource Management*, pp. 1–29. doi: 10.1080/09585192.2017.1288153.

Moriarty, J. (2009). 'Rawls, self-respect and the opportunity for meaningful work'. *Social Theory and Practice*, *35*(3) pp. 441–459.

Muirhead, C. (2004). *Just Work*. Cambridge, MA: Harvard University Press.

Oelberger, C. (2019). 'The dark side of deeply meaningful work: Work–relationship turmoil and the moderating role of occupational value homophily'. *Journal of Management Studies*, *56*(3) pp. 558–588.

Pavlish, C. and R. Hunt (2012). 'An exploratory study about meaningful work in acute care nursing'. *Nursing Forum*, 47, pp. 113–122.

Petriglieri, G., S.J. Ashford and A. Wrzesniewski (2018). 'Agony and ecstasy in the gig economy: Cultivating holding environments for precarious and personalized work identities'. *Administrative Science Quarterly*, doi: 10.1177/0001839218759646

Polanyi, K. (1944). *The Great Transformation: The Political and Economic Origins of Our Time*. New York, NY: Farrar & Rinehart.

Pradhan, S. and R.K. Pradhan (2016). 'Transformational leadership and job outcomes: The mediating role of meaningful work'. *Global Business Review*, 17, supplement, pp. 173–185.

Rodell, J.B. (2013). 'Finding meaning through volunteering: Why do employees volunteer and what does it mean for their jobs?' *Academy of Management Journal*, *56*(5) pp. 1274–1294.

Rosso, B.D., K.H. Dekas and A. Wrzesniewski (2010). 'On the meaning of work: A theoretical integration and review'. *Research in Organizational Behavior*, 30, pp. 91–127.

Schnell, T., T. Höge and E. Pollet (2013). 'Predicting meaning in work: Theory, data, implications'. *The Journal of Positive Psychology*, 8, pp. 543–554.

Schwartz, D. (2018). 'Embedded in the crowd: Creative freelancers, crowdsourced work, and occupational community'. *Work and Occupations*, *45*(3) pp. 247–282.

Schwartz, S.H., J. Cieiuch, M. Vecchione, E. Davidov, R. Fischer, C. Beierlein . . . M. Konty (2012). 'Refining the theory of basic individual values'. *Journal of Personality and Social Psychology*, 103, pp. 663–688.

Scroggins, W.A. (2008). 'Antecedents and outcomes of experienced meaningful work: A person–job fit perspective'. *Journal of Business Inquiry: Research, Education and Application*, 7, pp. 68–78.

Seeman, M. (1959). 'On the meaning of alienation'. *American Sociological Review*, *24*(6) pp. 783–791.

Simpson, R., J. Hughes, N. Slutskaya and M. Balta (2014). 'Sacrifice and distinction in dirty work: Men's construction of meaning in the butcher trade'. *Work, Employment and Society*, 28, pp. 754–770.

Spreitzer, G. M. (1996). 'Social structural characteristics of psychological empowerment'. *Academy of Management Journal*, *39*(2) pp. 483–504.

Standing, G. (2011). *The Precariat: The New Dangerous Class*. London: Bloomsbury.

Steger, M.F., B.J. Dik and R.D. Duffy (2012). 'Measuring meaningful work: The

Work and Meaning Inventory (WAMI)'. *Journal of Career Assessment*, 20, pp. 322–337.

Stein, M.-K., E.L. Wagner, P. Tierney, S. Newell and R.D. Galliers (2019). 'Datification and the pursuit of meaningfulness in work'. *Journal of Management Studies*, 56(3) pp. 685–716.

Symon, G. and R. Whiting (2019). 'The sociomaterial negotiation of social entrepreneurs' meaningful work'. *Journal of Management Studies*, 56(3) pp. 655–684.

Taylor, M. (2017). *Good work: The Taylor review of modern working practices*. Independent Report, 11 July. London: Department for Business, Energy and Industrial Strategy.

Terkel, S. (1972). *Working: People Talk about What They Do All Day and How They Feel about What They Do*. New York, NY: New Press.

Tims, M., D. Derks and A.B. Bakker (2016). 'Job crafting and its relationship with person–job fit and meaningfulness: A three-wave study'. *Journal of Vocational Behavior*, 92, pp. 44–53.

Toraldo, M.L., G. Islam and G. Mangia (2019). 'Serving time: Volunteer work, liminality and the uses of meaningfulness at music festivals'. *Journal of Management Studies*, 56(3) pp. 617–654.

Troncoso, M. (1943). 'Work as an institution'. *Social Forces*, 22(1) pp. 287–290.

Tummers, L.G. and E. Knies (2013). 'Leadership and meaningful work in the public sector'. *Public Administration Review*, 73, pp. 859–868.

Weeks, K. and C. Schaffert (2017). 'Generational differences in definitions of meaningful work: A mixed methods study'. *Journal of Business Ethics*, doi: 10.1007/s10551-017-3621-4.

Wolf, S. (2010). *Meaning in Life and Why It Matters*. Princeton, NJ: Princeton University Press.

Yeoman, R. (2014). 'Conceptualising meaningful work as a fundamental human need'. *Journal of Business Ethics*, 125, pp. 235–251.

Yeoman, R., C. Bailey, A. Madden and M. Thompson (2019). 'Introduction and overview', in Ruth Yeoman, Catherine Bailey, Adrian Madden and Marc Thompson (eds), *The Oxford Handbook of Meaningful Work*. Oxford: Oxford University Press, pp. 1–22.

6. Employment and work in Europe: improvement or just change?

David Foden

INTRODUCTION

This chapter approaches the overall theme of "the future of work" by discussing the important issue of the quality of work and employment. Specifically, it examines the extent to which the policy objective set by the European Union (EU) of creating not only more jobs, but also better jobs, has been met. The first section looks at structural change in the labour market and is based on the European Jobs Monitor (EJM). The EJM – a data-set established by Eurofound covering the EU as a whole, and each EU Member State – is designed to analyse changes in employment structure, taking a jobs-based approach whereby jobs (defined as a given occupation in a given sector) are listed, ranked in terms of hourly wage and assigned to quintiles of employment. It is then possible to track job creation and destruction in each quintile, to look at net change in employment over a period and to describe employment shifts.

Looking at the labour market in this way allows a qualitative assessment of structural change. Does the ongoing process of job creation and job destruction, which is inherent to economic change, lead to upgrading? To the more and better jobs sought by policymakers?

In the subsequent section, the chapter looks beyond the wage as a criterion of the quality of work and employment. Taking as read that improving job quality is accepted as a valid endeavour, it follows the International Commission on the Measurement of Economic Performance and Social Progress (Stiglitz et al., 2009) in placing well-being at the centre of economic and social policy debate. The idea here is that policies should be judged by more than their impact on income and wealth alone, and this applies to the policies and practices shaping our experience of work as much as to those shaping the quality of life more generally.

However, if it is accepted both that the quality of work and employment is important, and that it encompasses more than earnings, how should it be measured? The approach taken in this chapter follows that of Eurofound, which focuses on the level of the job (as opposed to the individual worker, the company, the wider labour market or economy) and identifies characteristics linked to seven distinct dimensions of job quality (including earnings), all of which are known to have causal links to the health and well-being of the worker (Eurofound, 2012; Marmot et al., 1991; Karasek, 1979; Karasek and Theorell, 1992; Siegrist, 1996; Bakker and Demerouti, 2007). Data from the recent editions of the European Working Conditions Survey (EWCS) (available at https://www.eurofound.europa.eu/surveys/european-working-conditions-surveys) have been used to assess job quality on this basis, and some key findings over time of this work are summarised. A brief reflection on the role of institutions, policies and company practice precedes the conclusions.

METHOD: THE EUROPEAN JOBS MONITOR (EJM) AND STRUCTURAL CHANGE

This section looks at how the structure of employment in Europe has changed from 1998 onwards, focusing mainly on the more recent years from 2011 to 2015. As mentioned in the introduction, the EJM does this taking the "job" as the unit of analysis. A job is defined as an occupation in a sector, and the approach is operationalised using ISCO, the International Standard Classification of Occupations, and NACE, Nomenclature of Economic Activities, the established classification of economic activity. The EU Labour Force Survey (EU-LFS) uses these classifications, so data are widely available on a comparable basis.

Using these classifications, a matrix of jobs is created in each country. In practice, many of the theoretical job cells do not contain employment. The country total of job cells with employment varies between around 400 and just over 2,000 and is largely determined by country size and labour force survey sample size.

The jobs in each country are ranked, based on the mean hourly wage. The job–wage rankings are based on combining data from the EU-LFS and the Structure of Earnings Survey (SES). Jobs are allocated to quintiles in each country based on the job–wage ranking for that country. The best-paid jobs are assigned to quintile 5, the lowest-paid to quintile 1. Each quintile in each country should represent as close as possible to 20% of employment in the starting period. Thereafter, the job-to-quintile assignments remain fixed for each country. The EU-LFS employment data are used to track the change in the stock of employment at quintile level in each country, and net employment change between starting and concluding periods (in persons employed) for each quintile in each country is summed to establish whether net job growth has been concentrated in the top, middle or bottom of the employment structure.

The resulting quintile charts give a simple, graphical representation of the extent of employment change in a given period, as well as an indication of how that change has been distributed across jobs of different pay. (A similar classification of jobs can be done using job-holders' skills or job quality more broadly defined as a ranking criterion, as shown in the series of EJM annual reports, available at https://www.eurofound.europa. eu/observatories/emcc/european-jobs-monitor.) The EJM can thus show us the different patterns of employment change in the EU over recent periods.

Key Findings

First (Figure 6.1) we look at data for the EU as a whole in the period 1998 to 2015 and at the sub-periods 1998–2007, 2008–2010, 2011–2013 and 2013–2015. In the relatively long expansion of the European economy from 1998 to 2007, there was growth in employment across all parts of the earnings distribution, though the growth was stronger at the top and bottom of the distribution, and weaker in the middle. In 2008–10, with the onset of the financial crisis, there was a decline in employment in all categories except the highest paid quintile. The decline was most marked, however, in the middle sections of the distribution, reflecting, inter alia, the loss of jobs in construction and manufacturing.

This pattern, which can be described as the "polarising" or "hollowing-out" of the labour market, continued in the second phase of the recession, 2011–13, though with a slower rate of job loss in general. This pattern of structural change can be seen as a consequence, at least in part, of long-run shifts in economic activity from industry to services and a decline in the availability of traditional blue-collar jobs. The onset of recession exacerbated the effect, and the process is seen as being interlinked to such drivers as globalisation (increased competition from low wage–cost economies) and (some forms of) technical change. However, as we will see below, the picture varies from one country to another.

Technical change influences the structure of employment by its impact on the demand for different categories of labour. One important effect is the routine bias in technical change – meaning that routine tasks can typically be performed to an increasing extent by technology, in particular through increased use of computer and digital technologies. As routine tasks are frequently embedded in jobs in the middle part of the wage–jobs distribution, such jobs are open to displacement by routine-biased technical change, thus contributing to the polarising effect noted above.

In contrast, skill-biased technical change occurs when computerisation

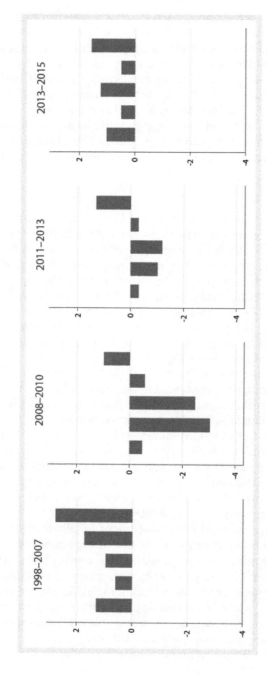

Notes: Different EU country aggregates due to data availability as follows: EU23 (no data for Cyprus, Malta, Poland or Romania), 1998–2007, based on annual LFS data. EU28 for remaining periods, based on second-quarter data in each year.

Source: Eurofound (2016(b)).

Figure 6.1   Employment shifts by job–wage quintile, EU, 1998–2015

increases the demand for highly skilled labour. This process can be seen in the generation of "new" occupational categories, such as data analytics, which rely on a combination of technology and relatively high skills. In this case, the effect of technology is to support the creation of jobs at the higher end of the distribution – an upgrading.

A second oft-cited cause of the polarisation observed in the labour market is trade and globalisation. The jobs most affected by increasing openness to trade are, it is argued, more likely to be in the middle of the distribution. This is due to the fact that jobs with more social interaction, and therefore inherently less amenable to the pressures of international competition, are located at the top and bottom of the distribution.

So technology and globalisation might be expected to contribute to the polarisation, albeit the impact of technology is more nuanced. But what, then, is behind the more mixed picture of the period from 2013 to 2015, when job growth appeared to take place more generally across the wage distribution? And further, what lies behind the different experiences at national level?

Figure 6.2 shows the findings for the EU Member States for the whole of the 2011–2015 period. To illustrate some of the diversity of experience, we take three examples – the UK, Austria and Italy. We can see that the UK – where the shift away from industry into service activities (both highly paid and otherwise) has been very marked – displays a classic polarising pattern. But different patterns are found in other countries. To take the example of Austria, the pattern is clearly one of "upgrading" of employment, with employment growth in the higher-paid jobs, and job loss in the lower-paid jobs. This is suggestive of the shift to "better jobs", which formed part of the EU's policy goal. In the third example, Italy, we see "downgrading" with no significant employment growth outside the lowest-paying quintile, and with higher job loss in the higher-paying quintiles (except for a very marginal increase in the top quintile). In this case there is a clear failure to deliver the "better jobs" part of the equation (at least as measured by hourly wages).

If we look at the information for other countries summarised in Figure 6.2, we can see examples of these three types of outcome – polarisation, upgrading and downgrading – combined with different patterns of overall expansion or decline in growth. For such diversity, and whatever the relevance of general trends such as the shift away from industrial activity, or the introduction of new technologies, or of the largely common economic cycle, no general explanation can be sufficient.

But what further (presumably national) factors can be adduced to explain such differences? There are several candidates. First, on the side of labour supply, there are differences between countries that may be significant.

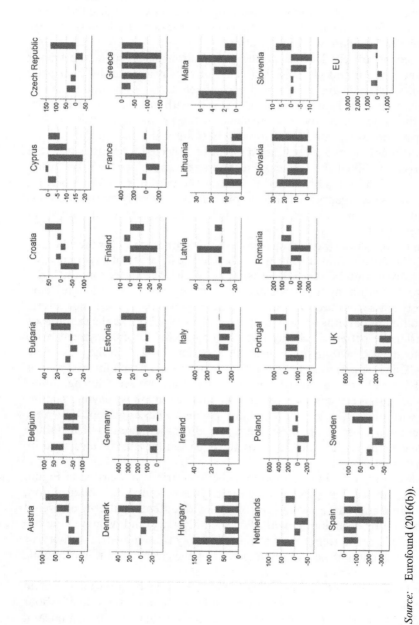

Source: Eurofound (2016(b)).

Figure 6.2 Employment shifts by job-wage quintile, 2011–15

They may influence the composition as well as the volume of employment. Growing female participation in the labour market is a general phenomenon, but to different degrees in different countries, and the same remark applies to the increase in educational attainment of labour market entrants. And the extent to which the different countries have been open to inward migration in the period in question also varies considerably.

Second, there are factors influencing the structure of demand for labour. Despite the suggestion above that the economic cycle is common to all Member States of the EU, the reality is more nuanced and the business cycle is not perfectly synchronised across the EU. Furthermore, other differences between the macroeconomic situation of the Member States, such as the growth rate or stage of development, might have an influence. Another factor might be differences in patterns of inequality across countries. In those Member States with more pronounced inequalities of income and wealth there may be a larger group of consumers with extensive financial resources but who are "time poor". Such individuals may be expected to spend heavily on basic services, creating demand for jobs in the lower-paying quintiles.

Finally, and perhaps most interestingly, there is the role of the different institutional settings for regulating the labour market. The institutions and policies in question shape the interaction of demand and supply to influence patterns of structural change. They include collective bargaining arrangements, and particularly the degree of centralisation and/or coordination mechanisms for wage-setting; the nature and functioning of employee representation in companies (and whether it can be part of a "productivity coalition" with management); employment protection rules, and their implementation; the organisation of welfare regimes, and especially how they are financed; and the institutions for developing skills formation. The interplay of institutions and policies can have an important impact on the pattern of structural change in employment in many ways: the setting of wage floors, contributing to the fostering or deterring of productivity growth, in subsidising low-wage employment, etc. Perhaps the principal conclusion to be drawn from the information in Figure 6.2 is that national-specific factors really matter in shaping labour market outcomes. However important the general framework and macroeconomic conditions, institutional settings are crucial too.

THE EUROPEAN WORKING CONDITIONS SURVEY AND THE DIMENSIONS OF JOB QUALITY

The EWCS was conducted for the sixth time in 2015 (Eurofound, 2017). The first survey was run in 1990, covering the then 12 EU Member States. In 2015, workers were interviewed in the EU28, Norway, Switzerland, Albania, the Republic of North Macedonia, Montenegro, Serbia and Turkey – in total almost 44,000, of whom nearly 36,000 were in the EU. In each wave, a random sample of workers (both employees and self-employed) has been interviewed face to face in their home. The scope of the survey questionnaire has widened substantially since the first edition, and themes covered in 2015 include employment status, working-time duration and organisation, work organisation, learning and training, physical and psychosocial risk factors, health and safety, work–life balance, worker participation, and earnings. The core objectives of the survey are to measure working conditions across Europe on a harmonised basis, analyse the relationships between different aspects of working conditions, monitor trends and contribute to the development of European policy on issues relating to work and employment. The broad scope of the questionnaire (available at https://www.eurofound.europa.eu/surveys/european-working-conditions-surveys/sixth-european-working-conditions-survey-2015/ewcs-2015-questionnaire) makes it an unrivalled source of comparative information on the various dimensions of job quality.

Both academic research and policy-making bodies have shown interest in conceptualising and measuring the quality of work in recent years. It is two decades since the International Labour Organization (ILO) launched the "decent work" agenda, which recognises that all workers, whether employees or self-employed, should have access to work that is productive, delivers a fair income, provides security and social protection, safeguards basic rights, ensures equality in relation to opportunities and treatment, offers prospects for personal development, and offers the chance for recognition and to have one's voice heard.

In the EU, quality of work is part of the European employment strategy. The set of indicators of job quality endorsed by the 2001 European Council meeting in Laeken were updated in 2010 by the European Union Employment Committee (EMCO), which defined four dimensions of work quality and proposed a set of indicators for monitoring purposes: socioeconomic insecurity; education and training; working conditions; and work–life balance and gender balance. The United Nations Economic Commission for Europe (UNECE), the ILO and Eurostat have developed a multi-dimensional framework to measure and analyse the quality of employment (UNECE, 2015). The OECD has focused on those aspects of employment that are most important for the well-being of workers and builds on three complementary factors that determine it: earnings quality, labour market security and quality of the working environment (OECD, 2014).

All of these approaches, and academic work (Gallie et al., 1998; Green, 2006; De Bustillo et al., 2011) reflect the multi-dimensional nature of the quality of work. This is central to Eurofound's approach, based on the seven dimensions of the physical environment, work intensity, working-time quality, the social environment, skills and development, prospects, and earnings. Each dimension reflects attributes at the level of the job, where the contractual relationship between employers and workers is set, and where the policies and regulations governing work are implemented. They are measured with data from the EWCS, using indicators of job character-istics that are related to meeting people's needs from work and reflect the job resources (physical, psychological, social or organisational aspects) and job demands. Through epidemiological studies, these characteristics have been demonstrated to have a causal effect – positive or negative – on the health and well-being of workers. The following subsections provide a brief description of key features captured in each dimension.

Physical Environment

The absence of physical hazards that pose a risk to health and well-being is an acknowledged feature of job quality. Eliminating or minimising these risks is at the core of occupational safety and health policy in EU Member States and is a longstanding plank in European social policy. Numerous preventive actions across traditional manufacturing industries have been implemented with the objective of minimising physical risks. Yet, despite these efforts and the shift to service industries in the economy, the level of exposure to physical risks is not declining significantly. Some risks are even increasing – for example, use of chemicals or exposure to electromagnetic fields – while the industrial application of new technologies such as nano-materials can generate new hazards.

Work Intensity

Demanding work, especially when combined with limited latitude for deci-sion-making and limited support, is associated with an increased risk of serious ill-health, as well as negative implications for organisations. Work intensity takes different forms, including "quantitative demands" such as working at very high speed, working to tight deadlines, frequent disrup-tive interruptions and not having sufficient time to do the job. These are reported most frequently in industry, construction and transport, followed by health and commerce and hospitality.

The number of pace-determinants and their interdependency are considered an objective indicator of work intensity. Determinants include performance targets, demands from clients, supervisor instructions and machine speeds. Interdependency refers to a multiplication of such determinants – the greater their number, the higher the interdependency. In terms of occupations, craft workers and plant and machine operators report the highest levels of interdependency (three or more pace-of-work determinants) and are most likely to report working to tight deadlines and working at speed.

Emotional demands refer to situations where emotions must be hidden, dealing with angry clients and working in emotionally disturbing situations. They have been found to be a predictor of mental health issues, fatigue and burnout. Service and sales workers and professionals report the highest incidence of emotional demands, with the health, commerce and hospitality sectors also reporting high levels.

Working-time Quality

In addition to the duration of working time, the notion of working-time quality also includes atypical working hours (working at night or weekends, shift work), control of working-time arrangements, advance notice of changes to working time (predictability) and flexibility of working time.

Some 16% of workers in the EU28 overall habitually work long weekly hours (48 hours or more per week) in 2015, compared with 19% in 2005 and 17% in 2010. (The proportion reporting long working days, at least once in the month prior to the survey, has also fallen – from 36% in 2005 to 32% in 2010 and the same figure in 2015.) Self-employed workers are much more likely to work long weeks: 55% of those self-employed with employees and 34% of those self-employed without employees. In contrast, only around 10% of employees work long weekly hours. Working Time Directive 2003/88/EC entitles workers to a daily rest period of 11 consecutive hours in every 24-hour period. Some 23% of workers reported that, at least once in the month prior to the survey, they had taken a break of less than 11 hours between the end of one working day and the start of the next. This is substantially more prevalent among self-employed workers (34% of self-employed workers without employees and 43% of self-employed with employees) than employees (about 20%). Men are more likely to have longer (paid) working hours and they work to "atypical" schedules more frequently than women. Flexibility – both available to and required from workers – is higher for men than for women. Similar proportions of men and women work shifts, and an equal proportion of men and women (each 19%) are able to adapt their working hours within certain limitations. Women, however, tend to have more regular working hours and are more likely to have their working hours set by their employer. And it is well established that, when unpaid work (including domestic work, care, etc.) is taken into account, on average women have longer overall working time than men.

The degree of working-time autonomy enjoyed by workers is closely linked to their employment status. Most workers in the EU (56%) have their working-time arrangements set by their employer and are not granted any flexibility to change them. For the majority of workers (69%), changes to their working-time arrangements do not happen regularly. However, almost 40% of those surveyed were asked to come into work at short notice in the 12 months prior to the survey. In terms of flexibility to suit a worker's needs, 65% of workers surveyed in the EU28 said it is easy for them to take an hour or two off work during working hours in order to take care of personal matters. However, this is not the case for all occupations: around 45% of plant and machine operators and service and sales workers said they find it difficult to take time off work during working hours to take care of personal matters.

Social Environment

Work is not only the main source of income for most people, but also an important opportunity for social interaction and integration. The quality of the social environment in the workplace is thus critical for integration and cohesion. On the plus side, the social support provided by colleagues and managers contributes to a positive environment, as does high-quality management. On the negative side, exposure to adverse social behaviour such as bullying or harassment is known to have a serious impact on worker well-being and is also strongly associated with outcomes that are negative for the enterprise, such as increased absenteeism and higher staff turnover.

In the EWCS 2015, respondents were asked if they had been exposed to different forms of adverse social behaviour in the month prior to the study, such as verbal abuse (reported by 12%), unwanted sexual attention (2%), humiliating behaviour (6%) and threats (4%). They were also asked whether they had been exposed to certain forms of behaviour in the 12 months prior to the study, with 2% reporting having experienced physical violence, 1% sexual harassment and 5% bullying/harassment. All forms of adverse social behaviour are experienced by women to a much greater extent than by men, except for threats (about 60% of the people who reported having been threatened were men). There are considerable differences in the reporting of adverse social behaviour between countries, which may in part be a result of cultural differences. The tolerance of undesired behaviours may differ from country to country, while underreporting may be more of a problem in some countries than in others.

In terms of occupation, almost all forms of adverse social behaviour are most commonly reported by service and sales workers. Workers in this occupational group are considerably more likely to report having been subjected to unwanted sexual attention (4%) and sexual harassment (2%). They are also considerably more likely to have experienced verbal abuse (16%), humiliating behaviour (8%) and threats (7%). As many as 5% of workers in this group report having been subjected to physical violence at work in the past 12 months and around 6% to bullying/harassment.

Adverse social behaviours are particularly prevalent in some sectors. The health sector reported the highest percentage of workers for all of the adverse social behaviour indicators, with the exception of workplace threats, which was found to be highest in public administration (11%).

In the EU28, some 7% of workers felt they had been discriminated against in the 12 months prior to the survey on grounds of sex, race, religion, age, nationality, disability or sexual orientation. As mentioned, European legislation protects workers against all these types of discrimination and provides for equal treatment in employment and occupation. The consequences of discrimination can be very serious for the individuals concerned, and include negative effects for their health and well-being, as well as on their career.

Ensuring a positive social climate, organisational justice, mutual trust between management and employees, recognition, and good cooperation are all important aspects of organisational management. Conversely, failure to provide these may be harmful both for the enterprise and the well-being of the workers, resulting in adverse outcomes such as poorer worker performance, lower organisational commitment and absenteeism. In the EWCS 2015, employees were asked about different aspects of the social environment in their workplaces. Almost three-quarters (73%) agree or strongly agree that employees are appreciated when they have done a good job. Some 73% agree or strongly agree that work is distributed fairly in their enterprise and 71% agree or strongly agree that conflicts are resolved in a fair manner. Around 82% agree or strongly agree that the management trusts the employees to do their work well. Some 69% agree or strongly agree that, in general, employees trust management in their workplace. The vast majority of employees in the EU28 (89%) agrees or strongly agrees that there is good cooperation between them and their colleagues.

Skills and Discretion

"Skills use and discretion" is a dimension of work allowing workers to develop and grow through their experience of work. The EWCS gathers data to measure the following four elements: the skill content of the job (the cognitive dimension of work), decision latitude, worker participation in the organisation, and training.

There is, in general, a high level of creativity and task variety associated with work in the EU28, as indicated by the large proportion of workers who report that their job involves solving unforeseen problems on their own (83%) or applying their own ideas in their work (78%). Moreover, a considerable proportion of workers say that their job involves learning new things (72%) and that they carry out complex tasks (63%). These proportions have also grown over time (see Table 6.1).

However, the data also show that almost half of all workers report that their job involves monotonous (46%) and/or repetitive tasks (40% perform repetitive tasks with a duration of less than 10 minutes); in other words, their jobs have little task variety. The lowest levels of creativity at work and task variety are reported by workers in elementary occupations, plant and machine operators, workers with part-time or fixed-term contracts, and younger workers.

Discretion is of high importance for workers, as it allows them to deal with the demands of their job and to work safely and in the way that best suits them. Between 2005 and 2015, there was an increase in the proportion of workers who reported having discretion to change aspects of their work (Table 6.2).

About half of all workers in the EU are involved in decisions that directly affect their work: 46% of all workers are consulted (always or most of the time) before objectives are set for their work, while 49% are involved in improving the organisation of work or processes in their department or

Table 6.1   Cognitive dimensions of work

| | Proportions of workers in the EU (%) | | |
	2005	2010	2015
Solving unforeseen problems	81	82	83
Ability to apply own ideas in work ("sometimes", "most of the time", "always")	77	75	78
Learning new things	69	68	72
Carrying out complex tasks	60	58	63

Table 6.2　　Decision latitude

	Proportions of workers in the EU (%)		
	2005	2010	2015
Ability to choose or change order of tasks	63	66	68
Ability to choose or change speed or rate of work	69	70	71
Ability to choose or change methods of work	67	67	69
Having a say in choice of work colleagues ("always" or "most of the time")	24	27	29

enterprise. In addition, some 47% report that they are able to influence decisions that are important for their work. However, there are substantial differences between occupations: only a third of plant and machine operators and workers in elementary occupations are involved in decisions that affect their work, but this figure rises to 8 out of 10 for managers.

Lifelong learning has been an objective of EU policy since the 1990s. EWCS data show that access to training has increased over time: for example, the proportion of workers who report having received training paid for by their employer (or by themselves if self-employed) rose from 26% in 2005 to 38% in 2015. Workers appreciate training for its direct benefit in improving their job, and for its potential benefits for job security and employability. When it comes to workers who have received training paid for or provided by their employer, 42% strongly agree that the training has helped improve the way they work and a further 41% agree with this statement, 60% agree or strongly agree that their job is more secure because of their training and 29% strongly agree that their prospects for future employment have improved because of the training. There are substantial inequalities in terms of access to training. Of particular concern is the fact that workers who might need training the most have the least access to it – workers in lower-level occupations and with lower levels of education, and those on fixed-term or part-time contracts or with no contract.

Prospects

The prospects dimension of job quality includes job security and the prospect of career advancement. The inverse of job security – job insecurity – is recognised as a significant cause of stress; when prolonged, it can have damaging effects on people's career paths and health and well-being. In 2015, 22% of workers reported downsizing of their workplace in the previous three years. Similarly, 16% of workers report that they are insecure about their jobs. Nevertheless, there has been some improvement. Almost 4 out of 10 workers (39%) agree with the statement that their job offers good prospects for career advancement – seven percentage points more than in 2010 (32%) and eight more than in 2005 (31%). In contrast, 38% of workers disagreed with this statement in 2015.

Men rate their prospects better than women. A high proportion of older workers (women in particular) feel that their prospects are poor – 50% of those aged 50 or over. There are also clear differences by occupation: a majority of managers agree that their job offers good prospects for career development; most elementary workers and plant and machine operators disagree in relation to their job.

Earnings

Monetary rewards are a crucial element of working life, even if non-material features of work have rightly gained greater attention in recent years. Earnings are the means to secure a livelihood as well as a factor in motivation to work. In this context, the level of earnings is of obvious importance. A further factor is the perception of the worker whether they are, or are not, paid appropriately. About half of all workers agree or strongly agree that they are paid appropriately based on their efforts and achievements, though there are differences across the earnings distribution.

Change Over Time

For four of the dimensions of job quality discussed above, there is at least partial information over time. This is the case for the physical environment, work intensity, working-time quality, and skills and discretion. Although indices have been created to measure the other dimensions, not all indicators used are available for the three time points when the EWCS was most recently administered.

For the four dimensions where we can compare over time, we can see in general that changes in job quality are relatively slow. In the case of the physical environment, the index comprising 13 indicators showed an increase of two index points between 2002 and 2015 – denoting a modest improvement. This improvement has been experienced more by men than by women, though this is a dimension of job quality in which women fare better overall. Figure 6.3 shows change over time by country.

Working-time quality also improved slightly overall (two index points) between 2005 and 2015, but all the improvement was in the first period, from 2005 to 2010. Similarly, there was an improvement in relation to

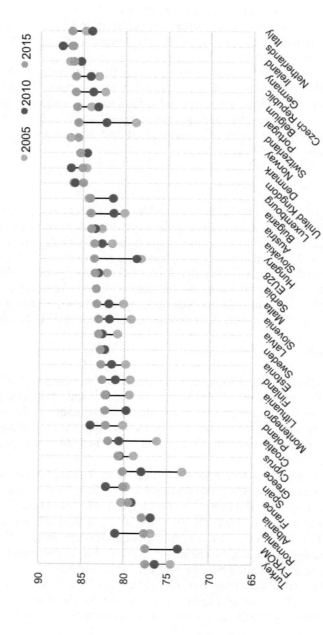

Source: Eurofound (2017).

Figure 6.3 Physical environment index (0–100), by country, 2005–2015

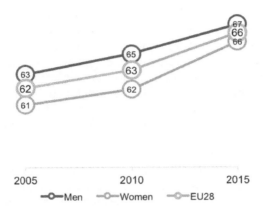

2005   2010   2015
●—Men   ○—Women   ○—EU28

Source: Eurofound (2017).

Figure 6.4   Skills and discretion index, men and women, EU28, 2005–2015

work intensity in the first phase. The work intensity index (which captures the level of demands in the job) shows a small (one point) decrease overall between 2005 and 2015, but with a slight re-intensification since 2010.

The dimension where there has been an unambiguous improvement over time, is skills and discretion. The index increased from 62 to 63 between 2005 and 2010, and then to 66 in 2015. Figure 6.4 shows the trend, also broken down by sex.

WHAT IS THE SOURCE OF IMPROVEMENT?

Accepting that job quality tends to change rather slowly, what are its origins? And how can it be encouraged? Clues can be found in the material already considered above. First in relation to structural change, the role of labour market institutions and industrial relations systems seems important in influencing which parts of the job–wage spectrum see growth, and which see decline. Countries in which minimum wages set by government and/ or social partners provide an effective floor to the labour market, in which wage-setting in general is predominantly shaped by collective bargaining, in which social partners have the organisational strength to coordinate pay outcomes at macro level, and perhaps especially where they are institutionally engaged in efforts to upgrade skills and support mobility may be best placed to see "upgrading" in structural change.

Second, there is a crucial role for policy and practice in shaping job quality. Policy interventions set the boundaries for the employment relationship, and all that is implied for employment security, for occupational safety and health, for social protection, for access to training opportunities, etc. But it is at a more local level that many key characteristics of the job – and job quality – are set, with company and workplace practice shaping such elements as job design and work organisation, and efforts to improve management quality and leadership. For this reason, Eurofound (2016(a)) includes workplace practices among the range of policies and strategies relevant to promoting sustainable work. In particular, social dialogue in companies (including collective bargaining and agreements at company level) can play a crucial role.

The importance of initiatives at local level inevitably raises the question of consistency across different workplaces, companies, sectors and regions, and how to ensure effective coordination and learning. Again in this context, the institutional framework matters, with countries where social partners are engaged in shaping public policy – through bipartite or tripartite negotiations or consultations – well placed to ensure coherence across different domains.

CONCLUDING REMARKS

This chapter has drawn on two European data sources – the European Jobs Monitor and the European Working Conditions Survey, to discuss structural change in the labour market and whether the processes of job creation and destruction were leading to more and better jobs in terms of pay; and then to provide a multi-dimensional description of job quality and a brief description of change over time.

For the EU as a whole, the EJM suggests that job growth was, for a long period from the 1990s until the middle of the present decade (2015), predominantly at the top and bottom of the job–wage distribution and, similar to evidence from the US, there was a hollowing out of the middle. More recently this pattern is less clear. Perhaps more interestingly, it does not hold across all Member States of the EU. We find patterns of upgrading and downgrading as well as polarisation. This suggests that mega-trends of deindustrialisation, globalisation and technological shifts – even in a framework where macroeconomic variables have much in common – play out differently according to national factors. In particular, the institutional arrangements for setting pay, developing skills, etc. would seem to retain a crucial importance despite the intensification of economic integration across borders.

From the data on job quality derived from the EWCS, once again the diversity of experience in Europe emerges. Different dimensions of job quality are reported to different degrees across sectors and occupations, and with different experiences for men and women, for older and younger workers. Yet given the importance of job quality for the health and well-being of workers, perhaps the simple and overriding message is that improvement in some dimension is possible for any job and for all. And linked to this, there is scope for positive intervention at many levels – from policy-making and regulation (at European, national and other levels), to the company and workplace. In this regard, the Future of Work is something we can all contribute to shaping.

REFERENCES

Bakker, A.B. and E. Demerouti (2007), "The job demands–resources model: State of the art", *Journal of Managerial Psychology*, Vol. 22, No. 3, pp. 309–328.

De Bustillo, R.M., E. Fernández-Macías, J.I. Antón and F. Esteve (2011), *Measuring More Than Money: The Social Economics of Job Quality*, Edward Elgar Publishing, Cheltenham, UK and Northampton, MA, USA.

Eurofound (2012), *Trends in Job Quality in Europe*, Publications Office of the European Union, Luxembourg.

Eurofound (2016(a)), *Sustainable Work throughout the Life Course: National Policies and Strategies*, Publications Office of the European Union, Luxembourg.

Eurofound (2016(b)), *What Do Europeans Do At Work? A Task-based Analysis: European Jobs Monitor 2016*, Publications Office of the European Union, Luxembourg.

Eurofound (2017), *Sixth European Working Conditions Survey – Overview Report (2017 update)*, Publications Office of the European Union, Luxembourg.

Gallie, D., M. White, Y. Cheng and M. Tomlinson (1998), *Restructuring the Employment Relationship*, Clarendon Press, Oxford.

Green, F. (2006), *Demanding Work: The Paradox of Job Quality in the Affluent Economy*, Princeton University Press, Princeton, NJ.

Karasek, R.A. (1979), "Job demands, job decision latitude, and mental strain: Implications for job redesign", *Administrative Science Quarterly*, Vol. 24, No. 2, pp. 285–308.

Karasek, R.A. and T. Theorell (1992), *Healthy Work: Stress, Productivity, and the Reconstruction of Working Life*, Basic Books, New York, NY.

Marmot, M.G., S. Stansfield, C. Patel, F. North, J. Head, I. White et al. (1991), "Health inequalities among British civil servants: The Whitehall II study", *The Lancet*, Vol. 337, No. 8754, pp. 1387–1393.

OECD (2014), *OECD Employment Outlook 2014*, OECD Publishing, Paris.

Siegrist, J. (1996), "Adverse health effects of high-effort/low-reward conditions", *Journal of Occupational Health Psychology*, Vol. 1, No. 1, pp. 27–41.

Stiglitz, J., A. Sen and J.P. Fitoussi (2009), *Report by the Commission on the measurement of economic performance and social progress*, available online at https://ec.europa.eu/eurostat/documents/118025/118123/Fitoussi+Commission+report (accessed on 4 October 2019).

UNECE (2015), *Handbook on Measuring Quality of Employment: A Statistical Framework*, United Nations, New York, NY, and Geneva.

PART III

The future of the future of work

7. Financing the future of work: who pays?

Jean Cushen

INTRODUCTION

Literature on financialisation and labour links macroeconomic movements of capital with firm-level employment outcomes. Scholars of financialisation conclude that, far from seeking a competitive advantage by investing in people to create *productive value*, financial markets pressure business leaders to destabilise and *extract value* from the employment relationship (Cushen and Thompson, 2016; Batt, 2018). This chapter explores how financial market pressures shape expenditure decisions within firms and the implications this has for human resource management (HRM) in the context of the 'Future of Work' (FoW). The chapter looks beyond HRM theory to consider how financial markets are shaping firm-level innovation, growth and productivity and the likely consequences this has for the HRM FoW agenda. Recent trends indicate that an expanding number of firms are less inclined to invest in the developmental secure employment arrangements required for innovation and creation of sustainable productive value. This, I argue, will push HRM into a period of epistemic uncertainty due to employees being increasingly marginalised as a source of productive, competitive advantage. Consequently, employment developments associated with FoW require an earnest reflection amongst scholars and practitioners regarding the strategic role HRM plays in delivering value within firms.

FROM MANAGERIAL TO FINANCIAL CAPITALISM AND FOW SCENARIOS

In earlier models of 'managerial capitalism' business managers cultivated industry knowledge to invest in their firms' productive capacities, drive innovation and secure competitiveness in the consumer market (Chandler, 1984). Financial investors provided capital to productive firms and, as an early commentator remarked, 'where enterprise leads finance follows' (Robinson, 1952, p. 86). Within managerial models of capitalism a firm's value is derived from how managers organise resources to deliver to consumers. Strategic HRM (SHRM) theory continues to develop primarily within this understanding through evaluating the HRM processes, line management capabilities and optimal resource base that best 'fits' with the firm's consumer market objectives (Paauwe and Boon, 2018). This managerial, consumer market frame of reference also dominates discussions of HRM's role in delivering the FoW. Such discussions explore how HRM is facing novel resource skills and allocation decisions as technology expands the boundaries of what is possible in how work is organised to meet consumer needs. On the one hand, HRM is tasked with creating adaptable organisation structures that avail of novel and more disposable sources of labour via, for example, crowd platform and gig channels, which erode traditional employment obligations (Bamber et al., 2017). On the other hand, individuals or roles worthy of traditional, longer-term employment should possess important technical and cognitive skills as well as the novel competencies deemed essential for the changing workplace, such as 'agility' and 'resilience' (Braun et al., 2017). The practice of 'talent management' has emerged as the FoW frontrunner, the practice deemed most capable of providing the decision-making architecture to identify, attract, select, develop and retain the best employees in the most strategic roles for the FoW (Collings et al., 2018). Ultimately, a managerial understanding of capitalism assumes HRM FoW priorities and outcomes are evaluated largely in the context of optimal resource allocation to enhance the firm's performance within the consumer market.

Conversely, the literature on financialisation explores how managerial capitalism has been supplanted by financial capitalism as financial market priorities dominate and override consumer market concerns (Fine, 2011). Internal firm investments and divestments are guided by financial evaluation metrics favoured by investment analysts. Managerial judgements on the resources required to compete in the consumer market remain important but secondary to how resources can be restructured to optimise returns to investors (Froud et al., 2006). Investors strive to have their fund outperform the market index, or benchmark, by deriving value from investments within a continuous, largely short-term time horizon. This focus on short-term fund performance is deemed to be a fundamental shift whereby financiers do not see themselves as guardians of the economy's longer-term stability nor a firm's success within consumer markets and this makes institutional investors fundamentally different from the earlier leaders of finance (Sawyer, 2013). Consequently, strategists have described contemporary investors as 'bad for business' (Caulkin, 2014) and responsible for creating a prolonged and increasing divergence between financial and real economies; with finance undermining industry (Boyer, 2000). Indeed, across most Organisation for Economic Co-operation and Development (OECD) economies a refrain of 'too much finance' is emerging as evidence mounts that financialisation is inhibiting 'real' economic growth and functional income distribution that sustains consumer markets and societies (Arcand et al., 2015; Gimet et al., 2018; Moosa, 2018). The burgeoning evidence pointing to how a financialised model of capitalism dominates developed economies means it is important to explore what this means for HRM. New technology associated with the FoW creates opportunities for ongoing short-term value extraction that enhance an organisation's performance against financial metrics, but not necessarily firm performance within the consumer market. New technologies have also caused the terms and conditions under which labour is provided to become ever negotiable and adjustable; a source from which value can be routinely extracted to absorb risk and heighten gains for investors (Lazonick and Mazzucato, 2013). Value extraction initiatives are executed within firms by the HR department via adjustment of core and periphery headcount, reorganisations, redundancies, centralisation, outsourcing, variable and flexible reward, erosion of benefits, reduced training, and rejection of collective negotiations (see Thompson and Cushen, 2019 for a review). Value extraction is prompting the collapse of traditional employment models replaced by overworked employees or underemployed individuals performing multiple jobs (Batt, 2018). Ultimately, a financialised understanding of capitalism assumes HRM FoW priorities and outcomes are evaluated in the context of optimal resource allocation to enhance firm performance against financial metrics.

These contrasting views on how a firm accumulates and distributes value are mirrored within the FoW scenario-based discussions offering diverging 'low road' and 'high road' outcomes for employees (McKinsey and Company, 2017; Brown et al., 2017; World Economic Forum [WEF], 2018). High road outcomes depict workplaces in which concerns about talent gaps and the disruptive potential of technological change lead companies to secure headcount and invest in developmental HRM. Retention of skilled, adaptable employees to create value is propelled to the forefront of business strategy. Employees are supported to navigate disruptive change and to carve out new roles that deliver competitive advantage. There is a strong demand for employees to innovate novel, once unknown ways of working, to complement new technology and machinery. A new ethos prevails that embraces investments in lifelong learning, enhanced innovation, and dynamism, and this leads to productivity developments across a range of industries and sectors. Low road scenarios are those where firm investment in developmental HRM is slow and low-skilled workers face a rapidly shrinking range of opportunities as analytics and technology renders their skill sets redundant. Devoid of a compelling vision regarding the role of intangible assets in creating value, employee displacement and de-skilling is propelled to the forefront of business strategy. Subsequent low employee productivity and a lack of appropriate talent development for emerging roles leads business to lose faith in people and the competitive advantage that HRM investments can deliver. Consequently robotics, algorithms and machine learning, managed by a few, deliver most of industry production and distribution.

The varying HRM FoW scenarios must be paid for via firm investment and expenditure decisions, making some more or less likely (WEF, 2018). Understanding contemporary firm expenditure patterns, namely and what firms are paying for and why, yields insights into the FoW that HRM is likely to be tasked with delivering.

CAPITAL EXPENDITURE TRENDS: INVESTING FOR GROWTH OR HOARDING INVESTOR RETURNS?

The central assumption underpinning FoW commentaries and scenarios is disruptive technological innovation (OECD, 2017). Capital expenditures are the investments made within firms to acquire, upgrade and maintain assets such as property, technology, software, equipment and machinery. Capital expenditure is therefore considered a diffuser of innovation as consistent levels of capital expenditure are required to spread an innovation throughout sectors and the wider economy (Stewart and Atkinson, 2013, p. 2). Higher capital expenditure is a sign of firms seeking to expand capacity and productivity. Looking at recent capital expenditure trends within firms, it seems that, far from being on the precipice of a radical overhaul of workplace physical and technological infrastructure, capital expenditure is stagnant relative to earlier phases of innovation; this is particularly pronounced when oil and energy capital expenditures are removed from analyses (Stewart and Atkinson, 2013). Declining capital expenditures in firms' innovative capacities is attributed to financialisation, and is pronounced even when contractions associated with the global financial crisis are controlled for. For example, panel data from non-financial publicly listed companies for the period of 1995–2015 across Western Europe reveal robust evidence of an increasing orientation of companies towards financial activities leading to lower capital expenditure (Tori and Onaran, 2018). Non-financial firms across Europe have been increasingly engaging in non-productive activities, and the ratio of financial assets to fixed assets increased most significantly in the UK and Germany (Tori and Onaran,

2018). While the pressures of financial markets are diffused by national institutions creating different 'shades' of financialisation, the pressures exist across developed economies (Faust and Kädtler, 2017). For example, declining capital expenditures amongst German firms, traditionally considered to favour longer-term, productive capital accumulation, have been noted by financial commentators who describe how 'the real profits being generated by the German corporate sector are not being reinvested in terms of [capital expenditure] or other forms of physical investment' (Chazan, 2018). Cash on the balance sheets of US S&P 500 companies (excluding financials and real estate) is now more than 40% higher than the average holdings over the last decade. In the US only once in the past six years have the Russell 1000 companies grown their new internal investments more than their returns to shareholders (Goldman Sachs, 2017).

Across OECD economies, innovative firm growth has taken a back seat to the return of capital to shareholders as companies are increasingly holding cash on balance sheets rather than putting it towards internal investment (Mazzucato, 2018). Within firms, financial evaluation metrics are deemed to be impeding on internal investment as cutting capital expenditure and operating costs to enhance financial returns is less risky in the short term than investing for value creation where returns are less predictable and distant (Christensen and Van Bever, 2014). As a recent example, IBM pursued a multi-year strategy to enhance 'earnings per share', which resulted in significant reduction of headcount and capital expenditures. IBM successfully significantly enhanced 'earnings per share' but produced a 'growth stall' and twenty quarters of declining revenues; pursuing 'earnings per share' decimated IBM's ability to innovate and compete in the consumer market (Hartung, 2018). Within German firms, the use of business ratios and financial control methods to evaluate innovation inhibited the development of a long-term view of innovative growth and also limited creativity and opportunities for failure (Hahn, 2019). Alternatively, German firms that funded innovation initiatives via internal cash flows were more future oriented, radial, exploratory and based not only on performance indicators, but also on the 'gut feeling' of higher management (Hahn, 2019). The ongoing centrality of short-term 'returns' in firm-level FoW investments is echoed by a survey of almost 400 chief financial officers (CFOs), who report they have increased firm-level investment primarily in the advanced technologies that promise 'real returns' in the form of 'increased efficiencies and cost savings' (Grant Thornton, 2019, p. 18). The same report states that technology and analytics will push the finance department to engage in scrutiny of 'talent' and to 'look for faster returns on the investments that are made and be a little less patient with those that are not showing the expected returns' (Grant Thornton, 2019,

p. 19). Financial market pressures for short-term returns are compounding the monopolistic drift of leading firms as markets tend to react positively to capital expenditure on exploratory new technologies only in already 'over-performing' firms (Gupta, 2012). Conversely, markets tend to punish, and sell stock of non-leading firms for investing in the same technologies (Gupta, 2012).

Worryingly, the same technologies driving the FoW are also expected to drive capital even further away from productive investments and towards inefficient skewed distributional outcomes that favour financial markets and not the 'real' economy. Algorithmic decision making is giving rise to a significant shift in assets from active to passive investment strategies; for example, over the past decade 40% of US equities are now under passive management by algorithms (Goldman Sachs, 2017). Referred to as 'the director's dilemma', the pronounced decline in active single-stock investing represents a fundamental shift in market movements with a company's share price becoming less correlated to a company's fundamentals (Goldman Sachs, 2017). Algorithms do not care why stock prices move, only that they do, and algorithms are causing firm equity increasingly to rise and fall en masse. In a high-profile report from US investment firm Sanford Bernstein, titled *The Silent Road to Serfdom: Why Passive Investing Is Worse than Marxism*, the authors argue that, while passive capital markets might be good for the short-term gains of an individual investment fund, algorithms cannot allocate capital efficiently throughout an economic system (Fraser-Jenkins et al., 2016). Passive, algorithmic investing heightens economic volatility and furthers the divide between a firm's operating performance and its financial market performance. This will particularly be the case if firm managers continue to prioritise what financial markets are pricing and rewarding in the short term and undermine fundamental long-term performance (Anadu et al., 2018; Fichtner et al., 2017).

The persistent orientation of firm strategies towards short-termism and weak internal expenditure raises questions about the 'market creating' growth potential of new technologies and how a firm's human resources deliver value.

NEW TECHNOLOGY AND RECONFIGURING EMPLOYEES' ROLES AND OBLIGATIONS

The technological advances associated with the FoW are thought to have the potential of general purpose technologies (GPTs). GPTs are the defining, pervasive technologies of a time that continuously improve to deliver vast complementary innovations and radically alter the economic environment (Brynjolfsson et al., 2018). The MIT 'Initiative on the Digital Economy' identifies the central role intangible assets play in shaping the potential of new technology.

> General purpose technologies (GPTs) have great potential from the outset, but realizing that potential requires larger intangible and often unmeasured investments and a fundamental rethinking of the organization of production itself. The extensive investment required to integrate GPTs into an organization is often forgotten . . . firms must create new business processes, develop managerial experience, train workers, patch software, and build other intangibles. (Brynjolfsson et al., 2018, pp. 2–3)

Effective HRM is considered an essential driver of innovation through productive, human activation of novel technological capabilities (Brynjolfsson and Mitchell, 2017; Syverson, 2011). More advanced and exploratory technologies require more expensive and sophisticated investments in human resource development to optimise labour productivity growth; namely economic output per labour hour (Andrews et al., 2016; Corrado et al., 2016; Moreira Vaz, 2013). In other words, HRM investments are required to derive productivity gains from new technology investments. However, labour productivity has been slowing for many of the world's largest economies since the late 1990s. An analysis of labour productivity across OECD firms shows that 'winner takes all' productivity dynamics are occurring whereby the largest firms are making consistent investments and deriving subsequent productivity increases while others have stagnated or declined (Andrews et al., 2016). Furthermore, the higher the productivity gains of industry leading firms, the lower the gains for the rest of that industry (Andrews et al., 2016). This has led to the OECD's claim that widespread technological diffusion, which sustained productivity growth in the OECD from 1950 to 1995, is breaking down (Andrews et al., 2016).

Innovation scholars claim polarising firm investments and subsequent uneven productivity gains serve to highlight the centrality of human resource-related intangibles, such as the cultivation of tacit knowledge, as a source of productive value that is out of reach for an increasing number of firms (Andrews et al., 2016). However, valuable intangible assets tend to have high fixed costs and firms are dissuaded from making the consistent internal investments in the employment systems that sustain firm productive capacities (Haskel and Westlake, 2017). Instead, employment systems across OECD countries are increasingly unequal, casualised, insecure and individualised, attributed largely to management's heightened tendency to *extract* value from employees through reductions in internal firm investment (Peters, 2011). As financial markets pressure firms to deliver returns via value extraction initiatives and inhibit widespread investment in exploratory technologies, the role and obligations of employees are likely to be reconfigured in two key ways. First, there are concerns regarding the increasing displacement and erosion of traditional, full-time permanent employment arrangements as firms increasingly turn to non-standard, platform and gig forms of disposable labour. For example, non-standard forms of employment accounted for 33% of the EU workforce in 2015 (Eurofound, 2018). The nomenclature of the 'crowd' and the 'core' has emerged to describe the FoW pools of labour that firms should cultivate and access (Boudreau and Lakhani, 2013). 'Crowd' labour is often depicted as a resource to enhance the innovative and productive capacities of a firm and demand for online gigwork has increased by roughly 20% year on year since emerging (Kässi and Lehdonvirta, 2018). However, while labour flexibility within firms is important for innovation and productivity, high external labour market flexibility often exists alongside low labour productivity and weak innovation (Preenen et al., 2017). Crowd work also relieves organisations of the obligations of traditional employment arrangements, reduces fixed costs and offloads risk (Howcroft and Bergvall-Kåreborn, 2019). For firms, rather than offshoring to lower-cost locations, work of varying complexity can be sporadically outsourced to and withdrawn from a board pool of virtual labour. Analysis of the impact of crowd work on labour providers has uncovered pervasive stress due to the punitive performance-ranking algorithms and financial insecurity as well as little opportunity for development (Eurofound, 2017a). The reduction of permanent employment is particularly concentrated amongst new entrants to the labour market. This leads into the second concern, regarding the erosion of job quality. While flexible work arrangements suit the needs of some, this work is associated with declining working conditions and job quality (Eurofound, 2017a, 2017b, 2018). Particularly, individuals forced into non-standard employment categories, such as solo self-employed, fixed-term and part-time work, have less job security, reduced access to training, poorer career prospects, less scope to exercise their skills and discretion, and a diminished social experience in the workplace (Eurofound, 2018). Non-standard workers are also more likely to experience punitive surveillance technologies and an age of 'Digital Taylorism' (Degryse, 2017). Wearable time and motion measurement devices remove employee autonomy and erode dignity, all the while yielding commercially valuable work process data identifying the 'one best way' of carrying out (Adler Bell and Miller, 2018; Chamorro-Premuzic et al., 2017). Ultimately, many of the labour market changes associated with FoW technologies appear to be more motivated by value extraction than by value creation. The weak and inconsistent investment in intangible assets for growth through innovation makes the route to firm growth unclear and, for HRM, this poses a question regarding the role HRM plays in contributing to firm value and growth.

CAN HRM PROTECT PRODUCTIVE GROWTH?

Primarily frontier firms are in a position to invest in cultivating human capital for innovation and productivity growth and this indicates the central role HRM plays in delivering sustainable firm success. Perhaps technological developments yielding the FoW will follow established cyclical trends whereby the more organisations routinise worker autonomy, the greater the opportunities for worker autonomy to be reconfigured as a source of productive competitive advantage. However, investments in innovation and development training are far from being the mainstream approach and, without it, trends associated with the 'low road' FoW will likely become commonplace for a growing portion of the labour market. Consequently, it seems the central FoW question for HRM will centre on the strategic role that an organisation's workforce is deemed to play in delivering value and whether this role is deemed worthy of consistent investment. The answer to this is likely to rest on HRM's ability to understand and protect the drivers of firm productive value and to argue for initiatives to stimulate sustainable employee productivity over the longer term. In other words, the FoW 'high road' requires a budget, and HRM will have to better argue its strategic importance to fund progressive human resource investment initiatives. HRM as a scholarly and professional discipline can protect the future quality of work largely through understanding the productive value of HRM investments such as re-skilling (Brown et al., 2017). For example, within some German car manufacturing firms, the elimination of physical manufacturing jobs prompted consultations with employee representatives with the goal of protecting secure, quality work for role-holders. The consultations resulted in investments in higher-skilled manufacturing occupations for which intellectual tasks involving ICT skills, information processing, quality control and problem solving became more common (Eurofound, 2017a).

A key challenge for HRM will be securing budgetary support for investments, particularly where the longer-term returns are unclear, amidst corporate processes that require clear financial metrics and certainty. For example, concerned about forecasts of mass employee displacement and erosion of quality of work, the founder of the world's largest and most successful hedge fund called for firms to invest in labour productivity, with one significant caveat:

He who lives by the crystal ball will eat shattered glass. [We need] metrics to come up with programs and measurements to make work productivity improvements that more than pay for themselves and measure the changes. I know of many cost effective ways that improvements that pay for themselves can be made and I'm sure that many others know of many more ways. We need leadership that can bring that about. Unfortunately, it is more likely that nothing along these lines will be done and, in the next economic downturn, the haves and have nots will be at each other's throats. (Dalio, 2018)

While Dalio supports investing in the development of a firm's human resources amidst technological disruption, he did not offer examples of self-financing productivity programmes, nor did he disclose the metrics that could help identify them. Nevertheless, Dalio's certainty that HR investments should be made on this transparent, self-financing basis is indicative of capital markets' need for clear and immediate 'returns'.

For their part, investors are reportedly interested in HRM; however, claims regarding adherence to HRM 'best practice' de jour are deemed meaningless (Krausert, 2018). At a practitioner level, the Chartered Institute of Personnel and Development (CIPD) UK has been instrumental in emphasising the need for HRM to engage with investors (CIPD, 2015, 2017b). HRM scholars are also highlighting the need for HRM to engage with capital markets, calling for quality HRM 'signals' for capital markets (Krausert, 2016) in order to have a 'strong human capital story to tell with numbers' (Creelman and Boudreau, 2015, p. 2). Human Capital Analytics (HCA), namely 'the systematic identification and quantification of the people-drivers of business outcomes', is often heralded as means to understanding and protecting HRM strategic contribution to value (van den Heuvel and Bondarouk, 2017, p. 130). For it to be effective, HCA must be logic driven and founded on a strategic understanding of how people contribute to firm success (Boudreau and Cascio, 2017). A handful of frontier firms actively promote and celebrate their strategic analytical approach to measuring HRM value. For example, Google's highly publicised 'Project Aristotle' and Apple's 'Apple U' initiatives track the impact of HR interventions on employees and subsequent successes and failures. However, HR practitioner publications reveal that, for most organisations, the range and use of HR performance measures is varied and disparate with no clear relationship between HR theory, analytics and value (CIPD, 2017a, 2018). Ultimately, the research and practice of HR performance points to a weak understanding of HRM contribution to firm value (Angrave et al., 2016). This is particularly problematic in the context of the FoW as this understanding is precisely what will be needed if HRM is to secure the internal investment required to sustain productive organisational employment systems.

CONCLUDING REMARKS

Commentaries on HRM's role in delivering the FoW often take a technologically deterministic approach whereby firm management innovates radically and human resources are restructured to strengthen the firm's ability to succeed in the consumer market. However, it is imperative that HRM scholars and practitioners grasp the role financial markets play in guiding the decisions and expenditure of firm leaders. The question about the impact of financialisation on firm investments in future innovation and employment is crucial as it reveals the resources available to firms to pursue the range of options before them. It seems innovation investment trends are prompting increasingly diverging and performative understandings of how a firm's human resources should best deliver value. On the one hand there are secure, valued employees working in frontier, monopolistic firms whose skills are invested in to enhance collective intelligence for the longer-term creation of firm value. On the other hand, standard employment arrangements are becoming less available and displaced employees increasingly pushed into lower-quality work in which security, autonomy and dignity are continually eroded. These diverging approaches to HRM and current uneven innovation investments pose a very real threat to HRM as a discipline, as the 'people advantage' and the investments required to achieve it will likely become less relevant for an increasing number of organisations. HRM and employee-related operational expenditure will remain as a cost centre, a drain on profits, and vulnerable within financial analyses and volatile financial markets. At the same time, longer-term firm productivity and the value-creating potential of exploratory technologies won't be realised until waves of complementary, intangible investments in people are implemented within firms. To retain strategic relevance, HRM will have to take a more active role in firm-level debates on internal investments to avoid being marginalised into a short-term implementation role. Responding to this threat requires an epistemic reflection on the part of HRM scholars and practitioners regarding HRM's role in delivering long-term productive value within firms. HRM can seek to position itself as a strategic guardian of firm productive value and strive to build employment systems and quality work that enable the creation of sustainable productive value. Or HRM can go further down a cul de sac of reactionary satisficing via unquestioning delivery of short-termist, value-extraction initiatives that diminish and marginalise the strategic relevance of the human resource advantage in the longer term.

Returning to the title question, HRM is poised to play a pivotal role in mediating whether firm-level technical changes will translate into employment systems that elevate sustainable value creation and the likelihood that the Future of Work pays off for all.

REFERENCES

Adler Bell, D. and M. Miller (2018). 'The datafication of employment: how surveillance and capitalism are shaping workers' futures without their knowledge'. The Century Foundation. Available at: https://tcf.org/content/report/datafication-employment-surveillance-capitalism-shaping-workers-futures-without-knowledge/?agreed=1. Last accessed May 10, 2019.

Anadu, K., M. Kruttli, P.E. McCabe, E. Osambela and C. Shin (2018). 'The shift from active to passive investing: potential risks to financial stability?' FEDS Working Paper No. 2018-060. Available at: https://papers.ssrn.com/sol3/papers.cfm?abstract_id=3242660. Last accessed May 10, 2019.

Andrews, D., C. Criscuolo and P. Gal (2016). 'The global productivity slowdown, technology divergence and public policy: a firm level perspective'. In: *Background Paper for OECD Global Forum on Productivity*. Available at: https://www.oecd.org/global-forum-productivity/events/GP_Slowdown_Technology_Divergence_and_Public_Policy_Final_after_conference_26_July.pdf. Last accessed May 10, 2019.

Angrave, D., A. Charlwood, I. Kirkpatrick, M. Lawrence and M. Stuart (2016). 'HR and analytics: why HR is set to fail the big data challenge'. *Human Resource Management Journal*, 26(1), pp. 1–11.

Arcand, J.L., E. Berkes and U. Panizza (2015). 'Too much finance?' *Journal of Economic Growth*, 20(2), pp. 105–148.

Bamber, G.J., T. Bartram and P. Stanton (2017). 'HRM and workplace innovations: formulating research questions'. *Personnel Review*, 46(7), pp. 1216–1227.

Batt, R. (2018). 'The financial model of the firm, the "future of work", and employment relations'. In: A. Wilkinson, T. Dundon, J. Donaghey, and Colvin, A. (eds), *The Routledge Companion to Employment Relations,* (pp. 465–479.) London: Routledge.

Boudreau, J. and W. Cascio (2017). 'Human capital analytics: why are we not there?' *Journal of Organizational Effectiveness: People and Performance*, 4(2), pp. 119–126.

Boudreau, K.J. and K.R. Lakhani (2013). 'Using the crowd as an innovation partner'. *Harvard Business Review*, 91(4), pp. 60–69.

Boyer, R. (2000). 'Is a finance-led growth regime a viable alternative to Fordism? A preliminary analysis'. *Economy and Society*, 29(1), pp. 111–145.

Braun, T.J., B.C. Hayes, R.L.F. DeMuth and O.A. Taran (2017). 'The development, validation, and practical application of an employee agility and resilience measure to facilitate organizational change'. *Industrial and Organizational Psychology*, 10(4), pp. 703–723.

Brown, J., T. Gosling, B. Sethi, B. Sheppard, C. Stubbings, J. Sviokla and D. Zarubina (2017). 'Workforce of the future: The competing forces shaping 2030'. *PwC*. Available at: https://www.pwc.com/gx/en/services/people-organisation/workforce-of-the-future/workforce-of-the-future-the-competing-forces-shaping-2030-pwc.pdf. Last accessed May 10, 2019.

Brynjolfsson, E. and T. Mitchell (2017). 'Profound change is coming, but roles for humans remain'. *Science*, 358(6370), pp. 1530–1534.

Brynjolfsson, E., D. Rock and C. Syverson (2018). *The productivity J-curve: How intangibles complement general purpose technologies* (No. w25148). National Bureau of Economic Research. Available at: https://siepr.stanford. edu/system/files/The%20Productivity%20J-Curve-%20How%20Intangibles% 20Complement%20General%20Purpose%20Technologies.pdf. Last accessed May 10, 2019.

Caulkin, S. (2014). 'Era of management-led growth held hostage by old ideas that refuse to die'. *Financial Times Business Education*. Available at: https://www. ft.com/content/cc4a40c4-085a-11e4-9afc-00144feab7de. Last accessed May 10, 2019.

Chamorro-Premuzic, T., R. Akhtar, D. Winsborough and R.A. Sherman (2017). 'The datafication of talent: how technology is advancing the science of human potential at work'. *Current Opinion in Behavioral Sciences*, 18, pp. 13–16.

Chandler, A.D. (1984). 'The emergence of managerial capitalism'. *Business History Review*, 58(4), pp. 473–503.

Chazan, G. (2018). 'German businesses under fire for low investment'. *Financial Times*. Available at: https://www.ft.com/content/0352b800-a517-11e8-8ecf-a7ae1beff35b. Last accessed May 10, 2019.

Christensen, C.M. and D. Van Bever (2014). 'The capitalist's dilemma'. *Harvard Business Review*, 92(6), pp. 60–68.

CIPD (2015). 'Human capital reporting: investing for sustainable growth', *Valuing Your Talent Research Report*. Available at: http://www.cipd.co.uk/binaries/ human-capital-reporting_2015-sustainable-growth.pdf. Last accessed May 10, 2019.

CIPD (2017a). *Human Capital Analytics and Reporting: Exploring Theory and Evidence*. Research report. London: Chartered Institute of Personnel and Development.

CIPD (2017b). *The Intangible Workforce: Do Investors See the Potential of People Data?* London: Chartered Institute of Personnel and Development.

CIPD (2018). *Creating and Capturing Value at Work: Who Benefits?* London: Chartered Institute of Personnel and Development.

Collings, D.G., H. Scullion and P.M. Caligiuri, eds. (2018). *Global Talent Management*. London: Routledge.

Corrado, C., J. Haskel, C. Jona-Lasinio and M. Iommi (2016). 'Intangible investment in the EU and the US before and since the Great Recession and its contribution to productivity growth'. EIB Working Papers 2016/08, European Investment Bank, Luxembourg.

Creelman, D. and J. Boudreau (2015). 'When investors want to know how you treat people'. *Harvard Business Review*, 10 February.

Cushen, Jean and Paul Thompson (2016). 'Financialization and value: why labour and the labour process still matter'. *Work, Employment and Society*, 30(2), pp. 352–365.

Dalio, R. (2018). 'Billionaire Ray Dalio: A.I. is widening the wealth gap, "national emergency should be declared"'. CNBC. Available at: https://www.cnbc. com/2018/07/06/bridgewaters-dalio-posts-on-ai-wealth-gap-capitalism-on-face book.html. Last accessed May 10, 2019.

Degryse, C. (2017). 'Shaping the world of work in the digital economy', ETUI

Research Paper – Foresight Brief #01-January 2017. Available at: http://dx.doi. org/10.2139/ssrn.2901937. Last accessed May 10, 2019.

Eurofound (2017a). *Non-standard forms of employment: Recent trends and future prospects.* Available at: http://eurofound.link/ef1746. Last accessed May 10, 2019.

Eurofound (2017b). *Sixth European Working Conditions survey – overview report (2017 update).* Available at: http://eurofound.link/ef1634. Last accessed May 10, 2019.

Eurofound (2018). *Does Employment Status Matter for Job Quality?* Luxembourg: Publications Office of the European Union.

Faust, M. and J. Kädtler (2017). 'Das (nicht nur) finanzialisierte Unternehmen – ein konzeptioneller Vorschlag'. In: M. Faust, J. Kädtler and H. Wolf (eds), *Finanzmarktkapitalismus. Der Einfluss von Finanzialisierung auf Arbeit, Wachstum und Innovation*, pp. 33–99. Frankfurt: Campus Verlag.

Fichtner, J., E.M. Heemskerk and J. Garcia-Bernardo (2017). 'Hidden power of the Big Three? Passive index funds, re-concentration of corporate ownership, and new financial risk'. *Business and Politics*, 19(2), pp. 298–326.

Fine, B. (2011). 'Financialization on the rebound?' London: SOAS.

Fraser-Jenkins, I., P. Gait, A. Harmsworth, M. Diver and S. McCarthy (2016). 'The silent road to serfdom: why passive investing is worse than Marxism'. *Sanford C. Bernstein*, Research Report.

Froud, J., A. Leaver, S. Johal and K. Williams (2006). *Financialization and Strategy: Narrative and Numbers.* London: Routledge.

Gimet, C., T. Lagoarde-Segot and L. Reyes-Ortiz (2018). 'Financialization and the macroeconomy: theory and empirical evidence'. *Economic Modelling*, 81, pp. 89–110.

Goldman Sachs (2017). 'Directors' dilemma: responding to the rise of passive investing'. Global Markets Institute Report January 2017. Available at: https:// www.goldmansachs.com/insights/public-policy/directors-dilemma-f/report.pdf. Last accessed May 10, 2019.

Grant Thornton (2019). 'All systems go: CFOs lead the way to a digital world'. Available at: https://www.grantthornton.com/CFOsurvey2019. Last accessed May 10, 2019.

Gupta, A. (2012). 'What the market likes: external learning and firm valuation'. In: *Academy of Management Proceedings.* Academy of Management Briarcliff Manor, New York, NY.

Hahn, K. (2019). 'Innovation in times of financialization: do future-oriented innovation strategies suffer? Examples from German industry'. *Research Policy*, 48(4), pp. 923–935.

Hartung, A. (2018). 'Warren Buffett's painful IBM lesson – have you learned it?' *Seeking Alpha*, February 28. Available at: https://seekingalpha.com/ article/4151587-warren-buffetts-painful-ibm-lesson-learned. Last accessed May 10, 2019.

Haskel, J. and S. Westlake (2017). *Capitalism without Capital: The Rise of the Intangible Economy.* Princeton, NJ: Princeton University Press.

Howcroft, D. and B. Bergvall-Kåreborn (2019). 'A typology of crowdwork platforms'. *Work, Employment and Society*, 33(1), pp. 21–38.

Kässi, O. and V. Lehdonvirta (2018). 'Online labour index: measuring the online gig economy for policy and research'. *Technological Forecasting and Social Change*, 137, pp. 241–248.

Krausert, A. (2016). 'HRM signals for the capital market'. *Human Resource Management*, 55(6), pp. 1025–1040.

Krausert, A. (2018). 'The HRM–capital market link: effects of securities analysts on strategic human capital'. *Human Resource Management*, 57(1), pp. 97–110.

Lazonick, W. and M. Mazzucato (2013) 'The risk–reward nexus in the innovation–inequality relationship: who takes the risks? Who gets the rewards?' *Industrial and Corporate Change*, 22(4), pp. 1093–1128.

Mazzucato, M. (2018). *The Value of Everything: Making and Taking in the Global Economy*. London: Hachette UK.

McKinsey and Company (2017). 'Digitally-enabled automation and artificial intelligence: shaping the future of work in Europe's digital front-runners'. Available at: https://www.mckinsey.com/featured-insights/europe/shaping-the-future-of-work-in-europes-nine-digital-front-runner-countries. Last accessed May 10, 2019.

Moosa, I.A. (2018). 'Does financialization retard growth? Time series and cross-sectional evidence'. *Applied Economics*, 50(31), pp. 3405–3415.

Moreira Vaz, R.A. (2013). *Job training determinants, R&D and effects on firms' productivity evidence from firm-level data in Latin America*. Católica-Lisbon School of Business and Economics.

OECD (2017). *The next production revolution: Implications for governments and business*. Paris: OECD Publishing. Available at: https://doi.org/10.1787/9789264271036-en. Last accessed on May 10, 2019.

Paauwe, J. and C. Boon (2018). 'Strategic HRM: a critical review'. In: D.G. Collings, G. T. Wood and L.T. Szamosi (eds) *Human Resource Management* (pp. 49–73). London: Routledge.

Peters, J. (2011). 'The rise of finance and the decline of organised labour in the advanced capitalist countries'. *New Political Economy*, 16(1), pp. 73–99.

Preenen, P.T., R. Vergeer, K. Kraan and S. Dhondt (2017). 'Labour productivity and innovation performance: the importance of internal labour flexibility practices'. *Economic and Industrial Democracy*, 38(2), pp. 271–293.

Robinson, J. (1952). 'The generalization of the general theory'. In: *The Rate of Interest, and Other Essays* (pp. 67–142). London: Macmillan.

Sawyer, M. (2013). 'What is financialization?' *International Journal of Political Economy*, 42(4), pp. 5–18.

Stewart, L.A. and R.D. Atkinson (2013). 'The greater stagnation: the decline in capital investment is the real threat to US economic growth'. *The Information Technology & Innovation Foundation*. Available at: http://www2.itif.org/2013-the-greater-stagnation.pdf. Last accessed May 10, 2019.

Syverson, C. (2011). 'What determines productivity?' *Journal of Economic Literature*, 49(2), pp. 326–365.

Thompson, P. and J. Cushen (2019). 'Value logics and labour: collateral damage or central focus?' In: P. Mader, D. Merten and N. Van der Zwan (eds), *The International Handbook of Financialization* (pp. 324–329). London: Routledge.

Tori, D. and Ö. Onaran (2018). 'Financialization, financial development and investment: evidence from European non-financial corporations'. *Socio-Economic Review*. Available online: https://doi.org/10.1093/ser/mwy044

van den Heuvel, S. and T. Bondarouk (2017). 'The rise (and fall?) of HR analytics: a study into the future application, value, structure, and system support'. *Journal of Organizational Effectiveness: People and Performance*, 4(2), pp. 127–148.

World Economic Forum (2018). *Eight futures of work: Scenarios and their implications*. Geneva, White Paper. Available at: https://www.weforum.org/whitepapers/eight-futures-of-work-scenarios-and-their-implications. Last accessed May 10, 2019.

8. Future of Work (FoW) and gender

Sarah Kaine, Frances Flanagan and Katherine Ravenswood

INTRODUCTION

The Future of Work (FoW) has become a ubiquitous topic of commentary as scholars and policy makers grapple with the economic and social challenges to accepted practice and understanding of employment caused by technological advancement. Key themes in academic research, grey literature and consultants' reports have emerged around automation (Acemoglu & Restrepo, 2018; Brynjolfsson & McAfee, 2014), artificial intelligence (AI) (Jarrahi, 2018; Manyika & Sneader, 2018) and the rise of on-demand electronically mediated work – often referred to as 'gig-work' (Commonwealth of Australia, 2018; Eurofound, 2018; ILO, 2018b). Significant concerns have been signalled about the potential for mass redundancy of human labour following the development of automation and artificial intelligence (Brynjolfsson & McAfee, 2014), the capacity and preparedness of labour to reskill (Points & Potton 2017), and the adequacy of existing social security frameworks to address such changes. Much of the debate around the impact of automation has not explicitly considered gender but rather looks at aggregate impact and, where it is more specific, has focused on areas of the labour market in which men predominate, such as manufacturing.

Automation and technological advances are a core focus of the FoW debates and theory. However, accompanying this is an increasingly obvious development of growing uncertainty and fracturing of the employment relationship. The development of the 'gig-economy', with its heightened work insecurity, automated and algorithmic management practices, embrace of AI, and the intensification of surveillance and control mechanisms exemplifies many of the more vexed labour-related issues in the broader 'future of work' debates. Of all of the aspects of the FoW, it is the gig economy that has drawn the greatest attention in employment relations and labour law scholarship. In particular, academic focus has been on the ambiguous nature of the employment relationship – notably the use of independent contracting rather than direct employment as a means to circumvent employment regulations and options for addressing this (Josserand & Kaine, 2019; Stewart & Stanford, 2017; Healy et al., 2017; Todolí-Signes, 2017). Gig work appears also to have sparked renewed interest in labour process theory (Gandini, 2019; Veen et al., 2019) as scholars examine how a 'shadow employer' creates a 'digital-based point of production' that also acts as the site of techno-normative control in the form of ratings systems (Gandini, 2019, p. 1040) and data collection.

While gender has largely been excluded from consideration of automation, technology and the gig economy, there have been some notable exceptions that consider the impact on women, and in doing so call into question some of the gendered assumptions around the future of work. An International Monetary Fund discussion paper suggested that in OECD countries, a slightly larger proportion of the female workforce than the male workforce are in jobs that are at risk of automation in the next twenty years. This estimate is based on the types of jobs most often undertaken by women, with these being 'more routine or codifiable tasks than men across all sectors and occupations – tasks that are more prone to automation' (Brussevich et al., 2018, p. 6). Counter to many of the negative forecasts, Howcroft and Rubery (2018) have suggested that, if the predictions about automation reducing the working week are accepted, there will be a benefit to women workers. Specifically, they argue that, if the reduced working week comes with a 'decent salary [it] could enable a more equal distribution of wage work'. As both men and women would have more free time, automation might theoretically allow men (for whom earlier norms had dictated should be out 'earning a family wage') to engage more equally in care work previously undertaken by women.

Likewise, there has been some consideration of gender and gig work, much of it focused on the gender pay gap in the gig economy (Renan Barzilay & Ben-David, 2017) and the negotiation capacity of women both as workers and employers in the gig economy (Galperin et al., 2017). A number of gig platforms have contended that their services offer the potential to accelerate economic opportunities for women (Shade, 2014). Such arguments rest on the premise that platforms facilitate labour market access for people who would be otherwise excluded from standard employment (as a consequence of caring duties, but also potentially due to disability, low mobility, or the absence of a formal work track record or training) and that the work they can perform is genuinely 'flexible', in that it can be readily co-ordinated around other life obligations. In assessing this claim, it is crucial that researchers attend to the lived experiences of gig workers, and grapple with the realities of performing gig work in co-ordination with care and household maintenance activities. Attendance to lived experience is crucial, too, in understanding the experiences of gig workers and clients affected by sexual harassment and assault, another gendered dimension of gig work that has received little published academic attention to date. That the studies investigating gender are few, and fail to consider the employment relationship at multiple levels, suggests that any research agenda should have gender at its core. This chapter seeks to consider our current understandings of this lived experience, gender discrimination, voice and prospects for gender equality in the electronically mediated 'gig economy'. Specifically, we point to a number of gaps in research that, combined, suggest an agenda for ongoing inquiry. We begin with a summary of how gender has been treated in industrial relations theory and research thus far.

GENDER IN EMPLOYMENT RELATIONS THEORY

Traditional employment relations (ER) research has been found wanting due to a lack of attention to the role that gender plays in how work and workers are researched and understood (Hansen, 2002; Rubery & Fagan, 1995). ER studies the institutions and actors that negotiate workplace conditions (Dunlop, 1993; Edwards, 2005). However, this analysis has often overlooked the gender of the actors, and the role that informal practices and processes contribute to the experience of women and men at work (Danieli, 2006; Wajcman, 2000). It is criticised for focusing on men and paid work (Hantrais & Ackers, 2005) and for often focusing on quantitative research in male-dominated industries (Danieli, 2006; Pocock, 1997). Kirton and Greene (2005) suggest that 'the dominant masculine construction of industrial relations has contributed to the invisibility of gender and equality' (p. 142). This may be because ER research assumes an anonymous, aggregate worker, which means that social processes that inform the meanings we bring to work are overlooked (Hansen, 2002; Holgate et al., 2006; Kirton & Greene, 2005; Wajcman, 2000). Forrest (1993) strongly stated that:

> the discipline has no interest in the doings of women, or men for that matter; the only 'actors' in the 'system', to use Dunlop's terminology, are workers, managers and trade unionists. So fixated are we on the employment relationship as the source of power and conflict at work that all other dimensions of power, most notably gender and race, are disregarded or dismissed as external to the 'system'. (p. 414)

Pocock (2011) points to ER's strong current of concern with power and how it impacts on the employment relationship, and highlights that gender, which is less recognised, plays an equally important role in how power is used, and who has power in the employment relationship. This is important to consider given Kaufman's (2008) conclusion that ER theory had begun to focus too much on unions and a 'labour-management paradigm' that had led to theory overlooking the employment relationship in general. This paradigm had become issue based, rather than theoretical. If, indeed, ER research has focused on the issue of 'unions' alone in the last few decades, this would pose problems for consideration of the future of work and the gig economy where one of the key debates is the fracturing of the 'traditional' employment relationship and decreasing union membership and representation. Power, and who wields it, in the employment relationship is critical to the 'demise' of unions.

Research on women in unions illustrates some of the gaps in mainstream ER research, theory and practice: that women are under-represented in union official and leadership positions (Cooper, 2012; Kirton & Healy, 2013), that unions often overlook issues seen as 'women's issues' (Gregory & Milner, 2009; Larsen & Navrbjerg, 2018; Ravenswood & Markey, 2011), and that women members may have more difficulty in exercising their union voice (Kirton, 2015; Parker, 2009). This is despite growing evidence that, when structures create space for women in unions, and their voices are heard, it is a powerful means of improving work conditions for all members, not just women. Indeed, it is well argued that increasing women's participation in and membership of unions could provide a boost to slow union decline (Kirton, 2018; Parker, 2009; Parker & Douglas, 2010).

The debate about gender in ER research and theory has led to discussions of whether gender analysis should be situated within the 'mainstream' or remain on the margins of ER work. Rubery and Hebson (2018) note that gender in ER research is much more prevalent in texts than twenty years ago, but often as an add-on of 'women's issues', for example, work–life balance and part-time work. Thus it leads to issues-based research that marginalises gender and women in ER research and theory. Such a generalised approach (McBride et al., 2015) obscures the power structures and does not allow room for the development of theory that can highlight the complexity of the employment relationship and power structures within it. It could be argued that a lack of theory and research on gender in ER, gender blindness, equates to a silencing of the real power relationships that privilege some over others in the employment relationship.

Although a gender lens can risk further marginalisation of gender research in ER, it can contribute to greater theoretical development. For example, examining care/work regimes and the power relationships within those (at the macro, meso and micro levels) can highlight how gender stereotypes have confined men and women to specific roles in the labour market (Baird, 2003; Baird et al., 2017). Indeed, Rubery and Hebson (2018) suggest that current models of ER omit social reproduction and are based on the male breadwinner model, thereby supporting our gendered norms of work. A model of ER analysis that attends to social reproduction would also extend our concepts beyond the binary 'employed' or 'unemployed', which might better suit research and theorising the future of work. Rubery and Hebson (2018) do not shy away from the challenges of transforming theory by using a 'gender' lens in research. Our norms of work, and contributors to the theory and practice of ER, are still very much based on the important 'forefathers' of ER research (cf. Dunlop, 1993; Hyman, 1981), therefore relying on male norms and theories of work, without adapting and extending the theory further to include gender and the changing employment relationship. In other words, there are compelling reasons to move away from single issues and from a focus on the technical employment relationship to encompass the wider social processes that make employment possible.

So, in order to progress ER research and theory in the future of work, making gender core to the analytical framework is necessary. However, this does not come without risks: we have already seen the use of 'flexibility' as a tool to wrest power from workers in a neoliberal paradigm, with the promise of making more family-friendly work for women. This is noted later in discussion of 'flexibility' and the future of work. In order to avoid such pitfalls as the flexibility argument, coming back to theory, it is necessary to question gendered assumptions and power within the employment relationship, from multiple perspectives (Kaufman, 2008; McBride et al., 2015; Rubery & Hebson, 2018).

Gig Work, Flexibility and Family Life

The empirical picture that presently exists concerning the co-ordination of gig work and family care responsibilities is largely broad brush and statistical, but it does indicate that gig work has a significant take-up for female caregivers. A 2018 International Labour Organization (ILO) study of crowdworkers (that is, individuals who perform work pursuant to platform-mediated requests issued to a geographically dispersed 'crowd') found that disproportionately large numbers of female crowdworkers reported paid caring work as their main activity prior to undertaking crowdwork (30% of women, compared with just 10% of men) (ILO, 2018b, p. 41). The same study found 21% of female workers in the sample had small children, with many respondents reporting that they preferred crowdwork to other forms of work as it enabled them to earn an income while caring for family. US respondents in particular noted the high cost of childcare as the factor that prevented them from taking up a job outside the home (ILO, 2018b, p. 69). The flexibility to work at night and in the evenings via platforms added to the appeal of such work, suggesting that gig work might be potentially operating as a new kind of 'second (or in some cases, third) shift' (Hochschild, 1989). Several other studies acknowledge the gendered context for conceptualisations of gig work as 'primary' or 'supplementary' income. Ipeirotis (2010) found that understandings of whether gig work was understood to be a primary or supplementary income source tended to correlate with the gender of the worker.

A worker's decision to undertake gig work is always one made in a bounded context, involving an evaluation of the quality and accessibility of gig work relative to the alternatives on offer, which may include standard employment, informal employment, reliance on the income of other household members, social security or any combination of the four. Worker perceptions of the benefits and weaknesses of gig work are thus always *relative*, and must be researched in a manner that is cognisant of the variable availability and cost of housing and childcare, and the cost of living expenses in different jurisdictions. It should not be assumed that standard employment forms will always and inevitably offer vastly superior conditions to those available in the gig economy. Even within the category of permanent employment, it is possible for work to be nevertheless 'on demand', in the sense that working hours are wholly or almost wholly dictated by business needs, rather than being within a regular (part- or full-time) schedule (Campbell et al., 2018). In Australia, it has been found that many permanent part-time workers are on zero-hours or minimum-hour arrangements that are, despite their technical 'permanent' status, substantively close to gig work in terms of working time. In other words, workers are required to respond to employer demands to work at short notice and to bear all the risk of low work demand. Moreover, they do not have a contract that evidences their true hours of work, something that might enable them to secure a mortgage or make life plans. Such on-demand working time patterns have been observed in a number of highly feminised industries, including relief teaching secondary schools, hospital nursing, domiciliary aged care and domiciliary disability care (Campbell et al., 2018). These studies, together with a number of articles on the burgeoning gig economy in care (Ticona and Mateescu, 2018; Flanagan, 2019), suggest an emerging picture of gig work as an extreme point within a continuum of insecure, 'on-demand', consumer-directed work arrangements within feminised care industries.

Just as standard employment may be less secure than it seems, so too gig employment may be less flexible than it initially appears. A variety of studies have found significant limitations to the idea that platform work facilitates high levels of worker autonomy in choosing working hours in practice. For instance, Lee et al. (2015) and Rosenblat and Stark (2015) found that, to be profitable, workers have to work at certain times to take advantage of surge pricing and have limited freedom to decline work. For those platforms where workers must spend extended periods of time 'out of life' waiting for potential 'gigs', how does this waiting time impact their capacity to undertake or plan for caring work? Empirical work is required to understand the practical impact of automated rostering on workers with caring obligations in particular. Are carers, for instance, disproportionately placed in low status groups as a consequence of their higher than average number of 'no-shows' and 'late-logins' and subsequently 'punished' through exclusion from desirable shifts[1] (Ivanova et al., 2018, p. 15)? What role does skill level play in workers' capacity to say no to shifts? Research from non-gig employment suggests that skill level is likely to be significant (many nurses, for instance, work under close to on-demand arrangements, but workers have a significant capacity to reject shifts without adverse consequences) (Allan, 1998).

There is a paucity of research, too, on the incidence and experience of households with 'dual-gig' earnings, and the consequences of such arrangements for the distribution of care and household maintenance work. Does the potential for performing (ostensibly gender-neutral) 'gigs' mean that women end up doing more, or less, of a relative proportion of this unpaid work?

The decision to engage in gig work should also be understood in the context of alternative possibilities to perform informal work. Informal work is work occurring outside legal regulation (including taxation laws) and makes up a significant portion of the economies of developing countries. In low- and low–middle-income countries informal workers are disproportionately female (ILO, 2018c, p. 20). Gig work shares many of the key features of work in the informal sector: easy entry, insecurity, lack of access to welfare, lack of union rights, ability to avoid taxes and retain social security benefits, flexibility to choose hours, sociability. Platform work, which partially formalises work relationships to some extent, may, in some circumstances, represent a relative *improvement* in work quality and formality. Care work is a particularly important industry to consider in this regard, given the historical (Flanagan, 2019) and present (Ticona & Mateescu, 2018) tendency for it to be performed 'off the books'. Ticona and Mateescu (2018) found that, while the carework platforms they analysed 'encouraged' workers' visibility to taxation authorities, and 'guided' parties toward a formally documented relationship, they did not go so far, however, as to *require* platform users to conform to legal standards, and did not make the provision of identity documents, minimum wages or tax payment a precondition of using the platform. Such studies raise the spectre of gig work as a phenomenon that, rather than acting as an agent for the incremental formalisation of work, may act to arrest such trends, and digitally 'encase' much of the work performed by women within an ongoing paradigm of semi-informality.

Gig work reflects a 'human capital' ethos of work, in which individuals are 'radically responsibilized' for their own skills and earning capacity, bear their own risks, and are expected to invest in their own economic value (Fleming, 2017, p. 692). Nevertheless, the question of how gig work intersects with a worker's entitlements to social security is highly salient to understanding the experience of female gig workers, given that women are, in general, more reliant on these, as a consequence of a range of factors including caring obligations and their relatively lower superannuation balances. Given the punitive conditions that attach to social security access in many countries (such as long mandatory waiting periods, heavy requirements for job applications, sanctions for breaches), it may be that women are turning to gig work as an alternative to accessing income support they may be entitled to (see Fleming, 2017 on entitlements).

As mentioned above, digital platforms are not constrained to traditionally masculine work. Carework is increasingly traded – building on traditional patterns whereby women fit informal or non-standard work around family care obligations. Research into the impacts of digital platforms into specific sectors, particularly highly feminised ones such as care, early childhood education and social assistance, is also required. Despite the centrality of human relationships to these industries, they are not immune to 'uberisation', and they are also workforces of large and growing importance. As Ticona and Mateescu (2018) observe, in 2014 Care.com had 5.3 million careworkers with profiles on its platform, while Uber had a mere 160 000 drivers actively working. Carework is already prone to being cast as 'nonwork' and viewed as 'invisibilized labour'. Digital platform mediation is unlikely to do anything to arrest these trends. Research to date suggests that the presence of gig platforms in these areas is likely to lead to a significant deterioration of work quality (Flanagan, 2019), but such theoretical arguments require empirical exploration too. Empirical study is also merited as to whether the intervention of platforms into these areas is changing the gender composition of the workforce.

Discrimination

It is tempting to assume that the anonymity afforded to some platform work means that the arrival of the gig economy marks a historic departure in the history of gender discrimination, in that it enables work to be performed in a truly 'gender-blind' manner. However, these arguments fail to place platform work into the context of the regulatory environment that constrains people's, and women's, choices to work in paid employment (McBride et al., 2015; Rubery & Hebson, 2018) and overlook who has control and power over these platforms and form of work. In the absence of a physically present supervisor, some might argue that it will be possible for gig platforms to usher in a new era of gender inclusion, in which human bias may be replaced by scientifically 'objective' automated processes for surveillance, collection of performance data, decision making and communication. Such assertions demand multi-faceted research that systematically breaks down the ways in which platforms potentially expand the range of ways in which discrimination might be practised and experienced, as well as foreclosing them.

The first, and perhaps most obvious, observation is that, despite the automation of management processes, human beings are still core to the functioning of digital platforms: it is humans who choose workers, negotiate pay and conditions, and code the software that sets the rules for how the work will proceed. Gender bias and discriminatory thinking can thus never be 'erased' from gig work through technical means. Understanding how it functions, however, within a gig context, will require an approach that goes beyond simply measuring the 'pay gap' between male and female gig workers (although initial empirical research on that question does reveal a significant gap – see Barzilay & Ben-David, 2017, as well as Graham et al., 2017 on discrimination against workers from certain geographical locations and Hannák et al., 2017 on ethnic backgrounds). The precise reasons behind the lower income share from gig work flowing to women are yet to be systematically dissected. Hannák et al. (2017) found that women, especially white women, received 10% fewer reviews compared with men of similar work experience on TaskRabbit. The desire to fashion a 'brave new gig world' of non-discrimination through platform work is not enough to prevent discriminatory practice: Weinberg and Kapelner (2018) found that online independent publishing platforms, despite the inclination of their users to greater gender equality, nevertheless largely replicate labour market segmentation in the traditional publishing industry.

Our understanding of gig platform discrimination must, necessarily, grapple with the distinctive changes of gender discrimination wrought by the operation of algorithmic management. Algorithms mine and analyse data, and thus have the potential to 'mechanically' reproduce discriminatory patterns without human intervention. It is the very 'blindness' of AI to context that is the source of this dynamic. AI-based decision making operates through a logic of correlation rather than causation: it is geared to ranking groups of workers who have in the past received higher pay or ratings more highly *regardless of the reason*. Lower-ranked and paid workers (likely to be disproportionately women of colour) are invisibly relegated, with no means of appeal, to a lower status, with no capacity to understand, contest or even be aware of this invisible 'sorting'. This lack of voice has potentially serious ongoing consequences for algorithmic management to be effectively challenged.

Algorithmically driven discrimination may prove to be more significant than more conventional, direct forms of human discrimination, given that some platforms are programmed to *limit* interactions between workers and clients (van Doorn, 2017, p. 898) and thus conceal the gendered and racial dimensions of their workforce as part of an effort to sell clients a 'post-domestic work fantasy' (Ticona and Mateescu, 2018, p. 4399). The effects of adverse ratings and rankings may influence future earnings a long time after the workers' engagement in the gig economy, compromising workers' ability to access standard employment in the future (Pallais, 2014).

To date there has been scant research into this dimension of gender discrimination in the gig economy. Ticona and Mateescu (2018) and Flanagan (2019) note that web-based reputation assessment mechanisms and background checks may readily create new forms of vulnerability, by preserving and publishing adverse data about work performance against which workers have no right of reply or review. In future, researchers may need to acquire new skills and develop novel research methodologies to get to grips with the nature and extent of these phenomena. Literacy in coding and data analysis will be necessary to understand how datasets and algorithms are programmed to 'handle' gender, and to dissect the ideas of 'neutrality' embedded in programmes. The secrecy that attaches to the intellectual property of most commercial digital platforms poses a further challenge to the performance of such research in the future.

Research is needed, too, to understand the ways in which algorithmic management shapes real-world behaviour. Not only do algorithms perpetuate and embed discrimination mechanically, they can also reinforce and place pressure on workers in real life who strive to 'perform' gender in their work with a view to increasing the likelihood of receiving high ratings and approval from existing and present clients. In one researcher's view, the discretionary emotional labour involved in undertaking gig work, which is largely speculative and unpaid, is tantamount to a form of 'neo-villeiny' (Harvey et al., 2016). Whether there is also a gendered element to the 'algorithmic imaginaries' proposed by Chan and Humphreys (2018), in which workers attempt to 'game' algorithmic management by manipulating the presentation of their gender or sexuality in some way, remains to be explored.

It seems likely, however, that involvement in the gig economy is likely to contribute to the pressure that workers feel to engage in gendered 'performance labour' in both real life and on social media generally. This is because, rather than relying on institutional mechanisms of accountability, many platforms instead look to major social media platforms such as Facebook and Twitter as a 'trust' mechanism. This interrelationship with large platforms not only effectively discriminates against workers who do not use these platforms (the profiles of such workers are displayed, in one major platform as greyed-out icons badged 'Twitter-unverified'), they also facilitate and normalise scrutiny from potential employers over workers' personal lives (Ticona & Mateescu, 2018, p. 4399), as well as imposing further labour on workers to manage and curate their digital social media profiles. How these reputational systems impact workers who do not conform to gender or sexual norms, or may face discrimination by virtue of their pregnancy or parental or marital status, will entail difficult, and innovative, research approaches.

Forms of discrimination may also occur against workers with caring responsibilities who are unable, due to their obligations to care for others, to accept shifts that it may be necessary to accept in order to improve rankings. The fact that most platforms do not enable workers to provide an explanation for why they cannot attend to a client or customer or might be late for one is also likely to disproportionately affect women. Where, in a formal employment relationship, a health emergency faced by a family member might trigger an entitlement to unpaid carers' leave, in gig work the consequence of such an event would be that the worker's rating would simply go down (or they would have to pay a penalty) if they were late, and their future earning potential would be reduced.

There has been little empirical examination of the experiences of female platform workers in relation to instances of harassment and work health and safety, despite the heightened vulnerabilities that are known to be present in work performed, as much gig work is, in people's homes, in isolated conditions, and in circumstances where there is minimal training and equipment (Huws, 2016).

Improving Work: Voice, Gender and the Gig Economy

The previous section highlighted the ways in which gender discrimination is made invisible in the gig economy. These are experiences and systems that could be resolved if attention to the voice of gig workers was allowed. Recent research has begun to consider changes and challenges to worker voice in the digital economy – particularly the gig economy (Johnston & Land-Kazlauskas, 2018; Zwick, 2018). Main areas to be examined have been how existing unions have responded to the challenges to traditional employment models posed by gig work. A common response by unions around the world has been to challenge the legal legitimacy of the 'independent contract' status that is the basis of engagement of work through most gig platforms. Other attempts to express collective voice have been through the development of less formal 'unions' or 'guilds' such as the Independent Drivers Guild (IDG) in New York and the Independent

Workers Union of Great Britain (IWGB) (Johnston & Land-Kazlauskas, 2018). These initiatives have met with varying degrees of success but have mostly been undertaken in areas in which women are the minority, for example ridesharing and bicycle food delivery.[2] A notable exception is the Freelancers Union (established in 1995 and representing 360 000 freelance workers in the US), which has a wide membership that ranges across professional contractors, entrepreneurs and what it describes as 'moonlighting' (Freelancers Union, 2019). However, it is not a 'traditional' union in that membership is free and it is philanthropically funded. While details of its membership by gender are not readily available, its founder and current CEO are women and its latest survey (conducted with the platform Upwork) suggests that 47% of freelancers in the US are female (Freelancers Union, 2017). Its focus is on advocacy for policy change and the provision of insurances for its members, rather than collective bargaining or grievance handling.

There is growing interest in the development of such 'alt-labor' organisations as the Freelancers Union, Coworker.org and Our Walmart and the necessity of these to work outside existing collective representation and bargaining frameworks (Kaine and Josserand, 2017; Walsh, 2018). However, there has been little research, to date, into the levels of female participation in these emerging organisations or in strategies to organise gig workers, or in the variety of other initiatives for improving gig work outlined by Graham et al. (2017), such as certification schemes, regulatory strategies or democratic control of online platforms. Although women make up the majority of members of traditional unions in Australia, only a handful of unions have substantively participated in organising or campaigning around workers in the gig economy. Little is known about the gender composition of microtask workers' initiatives such as Turker Nation, nor app-based drivers' associations or online professional task workers' initiatives. Research is required, not only into the participation of women in these groups, but also into the relative salience of gender issues in the matters they campaign on.

It has also been suggested that limiting consideration of worker dissatisfaction to observable 'voicing' of concerns through traditional avenues such as unions, obscures the phenomenon of worker 'silence' and what such silence means (Donaghey et al., 2011; Josserand & Kaine, 2016). Therefore, in some cases 'voice' may not prove the most appropriate explanatory idea, and indeed 'silence' may better convey how workers choose or are forced to navigate the vagaries of work. Silencing of marginalised groups within the labour market is not new. Extant literature emphasises how demographic difference such as gender and ethnicity (Sarikakis, 2012) and position within service and production networks (Kaine & Josserand, 2018) render some workers silent. Construction of silence or at least the manipulation of voice opportunities is a strategy that is frequently enacted to marginalise workers' voices, for example migrant women, who are exiled by schemas that locate authority and legitimacy elsewhere. Frazer observes that 'institutionalized patterns of cultural value recognize some categories of social actors as normative and others as deficient or inferior' (cited in Sarikakis, 2012, p. 802). Indeed, much of the literature on voice and silence is premised on managerialist assumptions, and its ideological lexicon, in which silence is viewed as representative of missed opportunities to improve productivity (or at least avoid problems) through the input of employees (Cullinane & Donaghey, 2014). Despite workers in the era of platform-mediated gig work not necessarily being employees who are bound to a 'workplace', managerial co-option of voice mechanisms (and, relatedly, the construction of silence on some issues and for some workers) is evident in frequent surveys of workers by platform service providers and other in-app mechanisms to provide feedback on specific aspects of working through that platform (Uber, 2015; Deliveroo, 2019). These structured 'voice' mechanisms represent a very small proportion of the data collected by platforms about the work practices. The technological mediation of work allows for continuous monitoring of workers. This is even the case for higher-skilled workers. Freelance professionals engaging in work through the platform Upwork have their keystrokes monitored and screenshots provided to their clients six times per hour (Upwork, 2019). Ironically, the capacity for such electronic surveillance produces a stronger imperative for research to investigate authentic worker voice to illuminate the lived experience of gig workers, which is in danger of being buried by the exponential growth in 'scientific' data on work performance and the selective collection of information on issues relating to poor worker experience. Specifically, the systems provided within platforms themselves for seeking redress against instances of gender discrimination, harassment or unfair treatment are severely circumscribed. In general, this is because platforms are structured around information asymmetries: clients are allowed to review and rate workers, and while in some cases workers are able to review and rate clients there is not always transparency around reviews (Flanagan, 2019; Ticona & Mateescu, 2018). For example, workers on Airtasker (a platform that provides a market for odd jobs and small tasks) can both review clients and see the reviews from clients, while Uber drivers can give a rating to riders but cannot see individual ratings and are instead provided with aggregate data on their overall rating. Access to an independent process for review or arbitration of unfair negative reviews has been the source of much contestation between gig workers and platforms, with access to a review panel of driver peers by the Independent Drivers Guild (IDG) in New York for rideshare drivers being seen as a major victory. Often, women will not even be aware that their exposure to potential clients has dropped, for reasons that may or may not be to do with entrenched gender bias, because of the speed and opacity of algorithmic decision making.

Anti-discrimination law is very poorly equipped to deal with this new era of algorithmically fuelled discrimination. In the first instance, such laws are based in national jurisdictions, which presents a challenge in the context of discrimination occurring in global peer-to-peer transactions. Second, they are premised on the actionability of individual acts of discrimination, rather than cumulative and embedded effects that occur as a consequence of the agglomeration of many thousands of anonymous instances of discrimination within enormous pools of data. Third, they require a human respondent. Algorithms are not persons: they cannot be the subject of legal proceedings for discrimination or harassment. Their designers and programmers are at many stages removed from instances of discrimination, and are unlikely to be found to possess the requisite intention or recklessness to a discriminatory outcome required at law. Finally, it is worth noting, that such laws are only of minimal impact within traditional, non-gig-based work contexts in any event. In jurisdictions with strong formal entitlements such as Australia, over thirty years after the passage of the *Sex Discrimination Act 1984*, one in ten women still report experiences of sexual harassment at work (Baird et al., 2018, p. 6).

The Gig Economy and the Wider Pursuit of Gender Equality

Although the FoW and the gig economy is only recently emerging as a research concern, this chapter has illustrated the ways in which concerns raised by scholars around gender in ER are essential as we consider the employment relationship in new ways of working. This chapter shows the pertinence of Rubery and Hebson's (2018) assertion that a gender lens, including social reproduction in ER theories, can and will transform ER theory. This was shown through empirical evidence of the pattern of women's work in the gig economy, balancing unpaid family care work with paid work. The gig economy and FoW research agenda must highlight the way in which social norms and formal and informal regulation constrain and free up individual and collective experiences of work. Taking a gender analysis of ER would also reveal the invisible and silent ways in which gender discrimination is already influencing women's choice and experience of employment in the gig economy. A gender analysis of ER and a re-evaluation of theory serves as a foundation for the transformation of practice. Discounting the experience of women in the FoW policy space risks exacerbating labour market inequality. Furthermore, consideration of social reproduction may prove necessary in the development of adequate policy responses to changing labour markets in which the increasing demand for care work has been identified as a global 'megatrend' (ILO, 2018a).

The rise of gig work must be understood as part of a broader unravelling of a social contract that existed in most developed nations over the three decades following the Second World War, that offered stable social reproduction to households on the basis of full-time, secure employment for the male breadwinner. The dismantling of that contract has included enormous gains for women in terms of granting formal equality of entitlements to wages and conditions, prohibiting discrimination, desegregating many industries, and implementing a range of policies that better enable both men and women to combine work with family life. The larger conceptual question for researchers and policy makers concerned with gender and the gig economy is whether platforms are agents for a new era of *de facto* male worker privilege, in which many of the equality gains of the last four decades are being quietly unwound. Such a new era will not be openly discriminatory; indeed, it may come in a form that foregrounds its claims to 'gender blindness' in historically novel ways. However, there are multiple ways, old and new, in which platforms may operate in such a context to perpetuate and entrench gender inequality. Such potential provides a compelling argument for the necessity to engage in ongoing research to monitor and document developments and their short-, medium- and long-term impact on women and for that evidence to form the basis of policy and practice cognisant of the economic and social benefits of gender equity.

NOTES

1. 'No-shows' and 'late-logins' are categories that are activated, in the case of Foodora, when a shift is cancelled less than 24 hours before it is due to begin ('no-show') and when a worker logs in 15 minutes late ('late-login') (Ivanova et al., 2018).
2. Uber is one of the largest ridesharing platforms by volume of rides and geographical coverage, and has a pledge to reach 1 million women drivers globally by 2020. However, in 2016 female drivers comprised 21% of Uber drivers in the US (Uber, 2016).

REFERENCES

Acemoglu, D. & P. Restrepo (2018). 'The race between man and machine: implications of technology for growth, factor shares, and employment'. *American Economic Review*, 108(6), pp. 1488–1542.

Allan, C. (1998). 'Stabilising the non-standard workforce: managing labour utilisation in private hospitals'. *Labour and Industry*, 8(3), pp. 61–76.

Baird, M. (2003). 'Re-conceiving industrial relations: 2003 AIRAANZ presidential address'. *Labour & Industry*, 14(1), pp. 107–116.

Baird, M., M. Ford, L. Hill & N. Piper (eds) (2017). *Women, Work and Care in the Asia-Pacific*. Oxford: Routledge.

Baird, M., R. Cooper, E. Hill, E. Probyn & A. Vromen (2018). 'Women and the Future of Work: Report 1 of the Australian Women's Working Futures Project'. Retrieved from https://sydney.edu.au/content/dam/corporate/documents/business-school/research/women-work-leadership/women-and-the-future-of-work.pdf (accessed 29 January 2019).

Barzilay, R. & A. Ben-David (2017). 'Platform inequality: gender in the gig-economy'. *Seton Hall Law Review*, 47(2), pp. 393–431.

Brussevich, M., E. Dabla-Norris, C. Kamunge, P. Karnane, S. Khalid & K. Kochhar (2018). 'Gender, technology, and the Future of Work'. IMF Staff Discussion Note SDN/18/07.

Brynjolfsson, E. & A. McAfee (2014). *The Second Machine Age: Work, Progress, and Prosperity in a Time of Brilliant Technologies*. New York, NY: W. W. Norton & Company.

Campbell, I., F. Macdonald & S. Charlesworth (2018). 'On-demand work in Australia'. In Michelle O'Sullivan, J. Lavelle, J. McMahon, L. Ryan, C. Murphy, T. Turner & P. Gunnigle (eds), *Zero-Hours and On-Call Work in Anglo-Saxon Countries*, Berlin: Springer Press, pp. 67–90.

Chan, N. & L. Humphreys (2018). 'Mediatization of social space and the case of Uber drivers'. *Media and Communication*, 6(2), pp. 29–38.

Commonwealth of Australia (2018). *Select Committee on the Future of Work and Workers: Hope is not a strategy – our shared responsibility for the future of work and workers*. Canberra.

Cooper, R. (2012). 'The gender gap in union leadership in Australia: a qualitative study'. *Journal of Industrial Relations*, 54(2), pp. 131–146.

Cullinane, N. & J. Donaghey (2014). 'Employee silence'. In A. Wilkinson, J. Donaghey, T. Dundon & R. Freeman (eds), *The Handbook of Research on Employee Voice*, Cheltenham, UK and Northampton, MA, USA: Edward Elgar Publishing, pp. 398–409.

Danieli, A. (2006). 'Gender: the missing link in industrial relations research'. *Industrial Relations Journal*, 37(4), pp. 329–343. doi:10.1111/j.1468-2338.2006.00407.x

Deliveroo (2019). 'Tech round-up: you say, we listen'. Retrieved from https://roocommunity.com/tech-round-up-feedback (accessed 8 October 2019).

Donaghey, Jimmy, Niall Cullinane, Tony Dundon & Adrian Wilkinson (2011). 'Reconceptualising employee silence: problems and prognosis'. *Work, Employment and Society*, 25(1), pp. 51–67.

Dunlop, J. T. (1993). *Industrial Relations Systems (Revised Edition)*. Boston, MA: Harvard Business School Press.

Edwards, Paul (2005). 'The challenging but promising future of industrial relations: developing theory and method in context-sensitive research'. *Industrial Relations Journal*, 36(4), pp. 264–282.

Eurofound (2018). 'Platform work: types and implications for work and employment – literature review'. Retrieved from https://www.eurofound.europa.eu/sites/default/files/wpef18004.pdf (accessed 29 January 2019).

Flanagan, F. (2019). 'Theorising the gig economy and home-based service work'. *Journal of Industrial Relations*, 61(1), pp. 57–78.

Fleming, P. (2017). 'The human capital hoax: work, debt and insecurity in the era of uberization'. *Organizational Studies*, 38(5), pp. 691–709.

Forrest, A. (1993). 'Women and Industrial Relations Theory: No room in the discourse'. *Relations Industrielles*, 48(3), pp. 409–439.

Freelancers Union (2017). 'Freelancing in America'. Retrieved from https://blog. freelancersunion.org/2017/10/17/freelancing-in-america-2017/ (accessed 8 October 2019).

Freelancers Union (2019). 'About Freelancers Union'. Retrieved from https://www. freelancersunion.org/about/ (accessed 8 October 2019).

Galperin, H., G. Cruces & C. Greppi (2017). 'Gender interactions in wage bargaining: evidence from an online field experiment'. Retrieved from https://papers. ssrn.com/sol3/papers.cfm?abstract_id=3056508 (accessed 10 December 2018).

Gandini, A. (2019). 'Labour process theory and the gig economy'. *Human Relations*, 72(6), pp. 1039–1056.

Graham, M., I. Hjorth & V. Lehdonvirta (2017). 'Digital labour and development: impacts of global digital labour platforms and the gig economy on worker livelihoods'. *Transfer*, 23(2), pp. 135–162.

Gregory, A. & S. Milner (2009). 'Trade unions and work–life balance'. *British Journal of Industrial Relations*, 47(1), pp. 122–146.

Hannák, Anikó, Claudia Wagner, David Garcia, Alan Mislove, Markus Strohmaier & Christo Wilson (2017). 'Bias in online freelance marketplaces: evidence from TaskRabbit and Fiverr'. *Proceedings of the 2017 ACM Conference on Computer Supported Cooperative Work and Social Computing*, 25 February, pp. 1914–1933.

Hansen, L.L. (2002). 'Rethinking the industrial relations tradition from a gender perspective: an invitation to integration'. *Employee Relations*, 24(2), pp. 190–210.

Hantrais, L. & P. Ackers (2005). 'Women's choices in Europe: striking the work–life balance'. *European Journal of Industrial Relations*, 11(2), pp. 197–212.

Harvey, G., C. Rhodes, S.J. Vacchani & K. Williams (2016). 'Neo-villeiny and the service sector: the case of hyper flexible and precarious work in fitness centres'. *Work, Employment and Society*, 31(1), pp. 19–35.

Healy, J., D. Nicholson & A. Pekarek (2017). 'Should we take the gig economy seriously?' *Labour and Industry*, 27(3), pp. 232–248.

Hochschild, A. (1989). *The Second Shift: Working Parents and the Revolution in the Home*. New York: Viking Penguin.

Holgate, J., G. Hebson & A. McBride (2006). 'Why gender and "difference" matters: a critical appraisal of industrial relations research'. *Industrial Relations Journal*, 37(4), pp. 310–328. doi:10.1111/j.1468-2338.2006.00406.x

Howcroft, D. & J. Rubery (2018). 'Automation has the potential to improve gender equality at work'. *The Conversation*, 11 June. Retrieved from https://theconversation.com/automation-has-the-potential-to-improve-gender-equality-at-work-96807 (accessed 10 December 2018).

Huws, U. (2016). 'A review on the future of work: online labour exchanges or crowdsourcing: implications for occupational health and safety', EU-OSHA Discussion Paper. Retrieved from https://oshwiki.eu/wiki/A_review_on_the_future_of_work:_online_labour_exchanges_or_crowdsourcing (accessed 29 January 2019).

Hyman, R. (1981). *Industrial Relations: A Marxist Introduction*. Hong Kong: Macmillan Press Ltd.

ILO (International Labour Organization) (2018a). *Care Work and Care Jobs for the Future of Decent Work*. Geneva: International Labour Office.

ILO (International Labour Organization) (2018b). *Digital Labour Platforms and the Future of Work: Towards Decent Work in the Online World.* Geneva: International Labour Office.
ILO (International Labour Organization) (2018c). 'Women and men in the informal economy: a statistical picture'. Retrieved from https://www.ilo.org/wcmsp5/groups/public/---dgreports/---dcomm/documents/publication/wcms626831.pdf (accessed 29 January 2019).
Ipeirotis, P. (2010). 'Analyzing the Amazon Mechanical Turk marketplace'. *XRDS*, 17(2), pp. 16–21.
Ivanova, M., J. Bronowicka, E. Kocher & A. Degner (2018). 'The App as a boss? Control and autonomy in application-based management'. Arbeit | Grenze | Fluss – Work in Progress interdisziplinä-rer Arbeitsforschung Nr. 2, Frankfurt (Oder): Viadrina, doi:10.11584/Arbeit-Grenze-Fluss.2. Retrieved from http://labourlawresearch.net/sites/default/files/papers/ArbeitGrenzeFlussVol02.pdf (accessed 8 October 2019).
Jarrahi, M. H. (2018). 'Artificial intelligence and the future of work: human–AI symbiosis in organizational decision making'. *Business Horizons*, 61(4), pp. 577–586.
Johnston, H. & C. Land-Kazlauskas (2018). 'Organizing on-demand: representation, voice, and collective bargaining in the gig economy', *Conditions of Work and Employment Series No. 94.* Geneva: Inclusive Labour Markets, Labour Relations and Working Conditions Branch, International Labour Office, pp. 1–42.
Josserand, E. & S. Kaine (2016). 'Labour standards in global value chains: disentangling workers' voice, vicarious voice, power relations, and regulation'. *Relations industrielles / Industrial Relations*, 71(4), pp. 741–767.
Josserand, E. & S. Kaine (2019). 'Different directions or the same route? The varied identities of ride-share drivers'. *Journal of Industrial Relations*, 61(4), pp. 549–573. doi:10.1177/0022185619848461
Kaine, S. & E. Josserand (2017). 'Alt-unionism: why businesses may be better with the devil they know'. *The Conversation*, 4 April. Retrieved from https://theconversation.com/alt-unionism-why-businesses-may-be-better-with-the-devil-they-know-75463 (accessed 6 December 2018).
Kaine, S. & E. Josserand (2018). 'Mind the gap: grass roots "brokering" to improve labour standards in global supply chains'. *Human Relations*, 71(4), pp. 584–609.
Kaufman, B. (2008). 'Paradigms in industrial relations: original, modern and versions in-between'. *Journal of Industrial Relations*, 46(2), pp. 314–339.
Kirton, G. (2015). 'Progress towards gender democracy in UK unions 1987–2012'. *British Journal of Industrial Relations*, 53(3), pp. 484–507.
Kirton, G. (2018). 'Anatomy of women's participation in small professional unions'. *Economic and Industrial Democracy*, 39(1), pp. 151–172. doi:10.1177/0143831X15606981
Kirton, G. & A. Greene (2005). 'Gender, equality and industrial relations in the "New Europe": an introduction'. *European Journal of Industrial Relations*, 11(2), pp. 141–149. doi: 10.1177/0959680105053960
Kirton, G. & G. Healy (2013). 'Commitment and collective identity of long-term union participation: the case of women union leaders in the UK and USA'. *Work, Employment & Society*, 27(2), pp. 195–212. doi: 10.1177/0950017012460304
Larsen, T.P. & S.E. Navrbjerg (2018). 'Bargaining for equal pay and work–life balance in Danish companies – does gender matter?' *Journal of Industrial Relations*, 60(2), pp. 176–200.

Lee, M.K., D. Kusbit, E. Metsky & L. Dabbish (2015). 'Working with machines: the impact of algorithmic and data-driven management on human workers'. *Human–Computer Interaction Institute*. Retrieved from https://www.cs.cmu.edu /~mklee/materials/Publication/2015-CHI_algorithmic_management.pdf (accessed 29 January 2019).

Manyika, J. & K. Sneader (2018). 'AI, automation and the future of work'. Retrieved from https://www.mckinsey.com/featured-insights/future-of-work/ ai-automation-and-the-future-of-work-ten-things-to-solve-for (accessed 10 December 2018).

McBride, A., G. Hebson & J. Holgate (2015). 'Intersectionality: are we taking enough notice in the field of work and employment relations?' *Work, Employment and Society*, 29(2), pp. 331–441.

Pallais, A. (2014). 'Inefficient hiring in entry-level labor markets'. *American Economic Review*, 104(11), pp. 3565–3599.

Parker, J. (2009). 'Women's collectivism in context: women's groups in UK trade unions'. *Industrial Relations Journal*, 40(1), pp. 78–97.

Parker, J. & J. Douglas (2010). 'Can women's structures help New Zealand and UK trade unions' renewal?' *Journal of Industrial Relations*, 52(4), pp. 439–458.

Pocock, B. (1997). 'Gender and Australian industrial relations theory and research practice'. *Labour & Industry*, 8(1), pp. 1–18.

Pocock, B. (2011). 'Rethinking unionism in a changing world of work, family and community life'. *Relations Industrielles*, 66(4), pp. 562–584. doi:10.7202/1007633ar

Points, L. & S. Potton (2017). 'Artificial intelligence and automation in the UK'. House of Commons Briefing Paper Number 8152, House of Commons Library.

Ravenswood, K. & R. Markey (2011). 'The role of unions in achieving a family-friendly workplace'. *Journal of Industrial Relations*, 53(4), pp. 486–503.

Renan Barzilay, A. & A. Ben-David (2017). 'Platform inequality: gender in the gig-economy'. *Seton Hall Law Review*, 47, pp. 393–431.

Rosenblat, A. & L. Stark (2015). 'Algorithmic labor and information asymmetries: a case study of Uber's drivers'. *International Journal of Communication*, 10(27), pp. 3758–3784.

Rubery, J. & C. Fagan (1995). 'Comparative industrial relations research: towards reversing the gender bias'. *British Journal of Industrial Relations*, 33, pp. 209–236.

Rubery, J. & G. Hebson (2018). 'Applying a gender lens to employment relations: revitalisation, resistance and risks'. *Journal of Industrial Relations*, 60(3), pp. 414–436.

Sarikakis, Katharine (2012). 'Access denied: the anatomy of silence, immobilization and the gendered migrant'. *Ethnic and Racial Studies*, 35(5), pp. 800–816.

Shade, L. R. (2014). '"Give us bread, but give us roses": Gender and labour in the digital economy'. *International Journal of Media & Cultural Politics*, 10(2), pp. 129–144.

Stewart, A. & J. Stanford (2017). 'Regulating work in the gig economy: what are the options?' *Economic and Labour Relations Review*, 28(3), pp. 1–18.

Ticona, J. & A. Mateescu (2018). 'Trusted strangers: carework platforms' cultural entrepreneurship in the on-demand economy'. *New Media & Society*, 20(11), pp. 4384–4404.

Todolí-Signes, A. (2017). 'The "gig economy": employee, self-employed or the need for a special employment regulation?' *Transfer: European Review of Labour and Research*, 23(2), pp. 193–205.

Uber (2015). 'New survey: drivers choose Uber for its flexibility and confidence'.

Retrieved from https://www.uber.com/newsroom/driver-partner-survey/ (accessed 8 October 2019).

Uber (2016). 'This International Women's Day, women take the wheel'. Retrieved from https://www.uber.com/newsroom/driven-women (accessed 8 October 2019).

Upwork (2019). 'How it works'. Retrieved from https://www.upwork.com/i/how-it-works/client/ (accessed 8 October 2019).

van Doorn, N. (2017). 'Platform labor: on the gendered and racialised exploitation of low-income service work in the "on-demand" economy'. *Information, Communication & Society*, 20(6), pp. 898–914.

Veen, A., T. Barratt & C. Goods (2019). 'Platform-capital's "app-etite" for control: a labour process analysis of food-delivery work in Australia'. *Work, Employment and Society*. doi:10.1177/0950017019836911

Wajcman, J. (2000). 'Feminism facing industrial relations in Britain'. *British Journal of Industrial Relations*, 38(2), pp. 183–201.

Walsh, D. (2018). 'Alt-labor, explained'. *MIT Management Sloan School*, 29 October. Retrieved from https://mitsloan.mit.edu/ideas-made-to-matter/alt-labor-explained (accessed 6 December 2018).

Weinberg, D. & A. Kapelner (2018). 'Comparing gender discrimination and inequality in indie and traditional publishing'. *PLoS ONE*, 13(4). Retrieved from https://journals.plos.org/plosone/article?id=10.1371/journal.pone.0195298 (accessed 29 January 2019).

Zwick, A. (2018). 'Welcome to the Gig Economy: neoliberal industrial relations and the case of Uber'. *Geojournal*, 83(4), pp. 1–13.

9. Biotechnological change and its implications

David Peetz and Georgina Murray

Most of the public debate about technology and robots to date has focused on what technological change means for job loss (Elliott 2017, Ip 2017, Kasriel 2017), or (in some cases) the character of jobs (O'Connor 2017, Preston 2017). Some academic literature—less so than popular concern—has focused on the role of technology in managerial control (Bain and Taylor 2000).

Always, though, the academic debate assumes that, while the form of technology may change, it is essentially the same relationship to the production process and class.

However, this need not be the case for all future *bio*technology—in particular, 'cyborg work'—which may raise questions about who controls the individual physically enhanced by a machine: the organisation or the individual? A paradigm shift will occur when cyborg technology becomes 'cyborg work' and 'digital humans' come into existence. Research into the future of work needs to encompass biotechnological change and the impact of the emergence and rise of digital humans.

CYBORG WORK

What are digital humans and cyborg work? 'Digital human' is a slightly creepy-sounding (but unintentionally so) term we use to describe a person who combines features of natural biology and implanted digital ('cybernetic') technology—technologies that become embedded within the body itself, linked to the ear, the brain or other parts of the body. So, by cyborg work we are referring to work undertaken by such people—by digital humans or what science fiction has sometimes called 'cyborgs'. Cyborg work is the performance of work or holding of skills that is related to cybernetic devices in a human. The technologies that are relevant here are those that enable individuals to think or process information substantially faster, perceive matters substantially more efficiently or work more quickly. They concern situations where humans and machines to some extent merge.

Although this may seem like it is a long way into the future, the time frame may actually be less than a century, well within that considered relevant for critical issues like climate change policy.

A glimpse as to what may come is given us by one of the earliest high-technology examples—the Cochlear implant—that now enables otherwise deaf people to hear. Other cyborg technologies have been used in the past to improve the lives of people. That implant in turn was far from the first example of technology being incorporated into the human body. Heart pacemakers are more recent, and these days can also be connected to external electronic sources. While artificial limbs are purely mechanical, Cochlear implants have a digital component. Perhaps most importantly for our discussion, they send a message to the brain.

Recent developments provide more vivid examples of how machines could be integrated into people. In 2015 a paraplegic man was able to walk again after being fitted with an electrode cap that relayed brain signals to devices in his knees, telling his legs to walk (Sample 2015). In 2016, researchers restored movement to a quadriplegic man in a paralysed limb using an implanted microelectrode array that bypassed his spinal injury (Healy 2016, Bouton et al. 2016). A 2016 television series showed how a youth with severe quadriplegia, who only had control over his eye movements, could be wired up to autonomously operate household devices such as electric lights and even to drive a form of motor vehicle (Nguyen 2016). The potential benefits for individuals with disabilities or severe injuries are enormous, and this is a factor that will continue to drive research in this field.

In time, machines will develop that will be able to be implanted in the head (or wherever in the body is convenient), enabling the relevant individuals to combine the lateral thought capacity of the human brain with processing speeds currently beyond comprehension. Initially this might be limited by the processing speed and temperature of the chip or device embodied within the human, but eventually this can be overcome by connectivity, and individuals will be able to combine the lateral thought capacity of the human brain with processing speeds of the world's (at that point in time) fastest computer. Individuals will ultimately be able to include within their body a massive amount of stored 'memory', comprising much of what is already known to science. As it is, hard disk drives are becoming slowly redundant, with many computers (including the one on which most of this chapter was written) storing information on solid state drives that require no ongoing energy or cooling and are more compatible with low-waste principles (Murugesan 2008, Coughlin 2016). The technical limits will be set by atomic structures. The social limits will be set by cost and power structures, to which we return shortly.

Eventually, people might merge with machines—in the very long run, measured in say millennia, this seems highly likely to us. Individuals might mostly comprise machines with only a minority of biological parts—or perhaps more accurately, they might be biotechnological machines. The whole concept of 'individuals' may be questionable. Eventually sexual reproduction may be unnecessary—but these questions, though fascinating, are outside the scope of this chapter.

In the meantime, however, we are concerned with questions as to what happens when people integrate parts of machines into their bodies to massively increase their capabilities as individuals—in particular, what happens to work and the research on it. Facebook's Mark Zuckerberg envisages an external brain sensor that 'lets you communicate using only your mind' (Stibel 2017). The most important development is research into neural implants or 'neural lace'. Tesla and SpaceX founder Elon Musk in 2017 announced the establishment of a company, Neuralink, to develop an interface between human brains and computers (Unknown 2017). The idea has been controversial, with some suggesting it would not happen—or at least, that it 'is not as close at hand' as Musk suggests (Regalado 2017). Musk claims that the timeframe could be 8 to 10 years, though this seems rather optimistic. Still, the technology itself appears very possible. It is rather difficult but likely to come to fruition. In 2015, scientists reported the invention of an 'ultra-fine mesh that can merge into the brain [of mice] to create what appears to be a seamless interface between machine and biological circuitry' (Newitz 2015). The mesh was 'syringe injectable' (Liu et al. 2015). Others have announced the launching of projects to identify 'neural code', arguing that 'the market for implantable neural prosthetics including cognitive enhancement and treatment of neurological dysfunction will likely be one of if not the largest industrial sectors in history' (Johnson 2016).

This is not a chapter about artificial intelligence and the debate about whether computers will one day achieve consciousness (Cadwalladr 2014). That AI debate hinges on speculation of what it would be like to be a machine endowed with AI. Rather, *our* interest focuses on the implications of reaching towards, but not beyond, the limits of technological capability and its insertion into or integration with the human body. Whether AI will achieve sentience is a debate for others, though it seems to us that any 'consciousness' by computers would regardless be pre-empted or superseded by the emergence of the 'super consciousness' that cyborg technology would permit.

While developments in robot technology and AI have transfixed some in policy debate, and in the case of AI raised important questions about the roles of robots and machines as separate entities in relation to each other, little thought has been given to what happens when the two are *not* separated—that is, when technology is embedded *within* humans, and how that relates to social structures and forces.

BIOTECHNOLOGY AND WORK ORGANISATION

We commence by looking at how biotechnological changes may affect work organisation. At first glance, this may seem like a niche question. Surely, only a small portion of occupations would need to be altered by the availability of cyborg technology. But look at it another way: what occupations would be *enhanced* by the availability of cyborg technology? And then, what would be the cost of such biotechnology, both in financial terms? It will not be introduced where the costs exceed the benefits either financially or in terms of coping with resistance by workers. There are not many jobs that have been unaffected by technological change over the past half century, and of those there are few that are not influenced by computer network technology. Any job that is enhanced by computer network technology would be further enhanced by cyborg technology that is linked to computer networks. Any job that involves decisions that can be learnt, replicated and accelerated by artificial intelligence would be further enhanced by cyborg technology that is linked to artificial intelligence. Whether and when these jobs are, in practice, enhanced by cyborg technology will depend in turn on the relative costs and benefits for employers of doing so. Even if the technology is available for a particular occupation, the cost may be too high for widespread or limited application, at least initially. The potential, however, will be there, and it will increase as the cost comes down.

A medical practitioner, for example, would be in a much better position to diagnose and treat a patient if they had access to a global network of information about every illness that had ever been catalogued, and instantaneous access to a machine-learning algorithm that led to the optimal outcome for patients based on a series of decisions arising from questions the doctor could ask or just make observations on.

That is, the doctor would *think* about what information was needed. Instead of having to click or swipe on a pad or screen, they would be able to call up the information they needed by thinking about it. Then, instead of having to ponder a series of decisions to help them decide what the diagnosis was, they could access an AI algorithm that would, almost instantly, determine the most likely ailment, perhaps with probabilities attached to scenarios. The treatment would then also be resolved by AI. All this would happen, as far as the doctor and patient were concerned, in the doctor's head. The doctor could, if they wished, override the AI diagnosis and pre-scribe a different treatment—but it would take some courage to do so, as the risk of a malpractice suit would probably loom if that treatment failed and the decision tree was traceable, which it likely would be. The doctor would still have full autonomy in the formal sense, but the practical room for discretion would probably be much smaller due to the potential need to explain how their judgment outperformed the AI.

There would be applications across all sorts of professional occupations. A tax accountant would be able to instantly access information about and give advice on ways to minimise the tax associated with any commercial activity. A human resource manager could instantaneously make decisions about hiring and firing—after a separate machine has scanned any number of applications. Much of this has already been done: someone has already been sacked from their job by a computer, acting in error, but it was too difficult for mere humans to override that decision (Ross and Carrick 2018, O'Neill 2016).

The application of this technology goes well beyond professional occu-pations, however. A prison officer could always know where all the other guards and prisoners were—and what instructions they were receiving from the prison commander. A sales assistant would know what was in stock in any store in the country, and what was the best technique for getting a sale from a particular customer given their age, gender, cloth-ing and whatever other characteristics they and thousands of other shop assistants were able to visually record. A bus driver—if buses exist in an Uberised world (see Salinas 2018)—would know not only all the traffic conditions and scenarios, but also all the financial and criminal records of all their passengers.

For some occupations, with heavy emotional labour content or high creativity demands, this technology might seem irrelevant. But would it be? Even now, technology exists by which agencies can profit by sending carers to clients with minimal travel costs and maximum control over their time. Photographers or artists would perhaps benefit from accessing globally net-worked information, even if the use of AI is low. The Cyborg Foundation, an organisation that defends cyborg rights, defends people who wish to become cyborgs and encourages cyborg art, was established in 2010 by Neil Harbisson and Moon Ribas, both artists, the former colour-blind. Probably the only occupation in which it is difficult to see any advantage in cyborg technology is labourers—and even here, there might be advantages in terms of surveillance for employers, an issue we come back to later.

As mentioned, the implementation of all these applications depends crit-ically on cost. That, in turn, has major interactions with class and power, to which we now turn. We necessarily discuss how technology relates in general terms to productivity and the reproduction of class and class relations, before discussing the likely impact of biotechnology developments on those.

TECHNOLOGY, PRODUCTIVITY AND CLASS

Let us look at the present relationship between technology and class. To date, technology has in effect been embodied within the circuit of capital. In whatever goods are produced, the owners of capital have sought to increase their market shares. They might use new technologies to create new products or gain some other competitive advantage over rivals. Increased profitability may have been through simply greater volume of sales, or through a combination of increased volume and an increased rate of surplus value permitted by the new technology.

Higher productivity has also enabled the possibility of increased wages and therefore lifted living standards. Whether those improvements in wages (and living standards) have occurred has depended on the relative bargaining power of labour and capital. Through the post-war period to the 1970s, higher productivity was, in most developed countries, linked to higher wages. The wages share of national income, at least relative to the profits share, moved within a moderately narrow range in the context of (relatively) high and stable trade union membership (Chang and Sorrentino 1991), and the post-war Keynesian compromise (Maier 1987, Cahill 2014).

Since the 1980s, the emergence of financialisation and 'neoliberalism' have seen weaker unions, a lowering in the labour share of national income (Ellis and Smith 2007, Cahill 2014, Peetz 2018), a polarisation of inequality (Claeys 2018, Denniss 2018, Dunlop 2018, MacLean 2018), and a decoupling of wages and productivity (Cowgill 2013). The lesser power of labour has sometimes been due to collective labour law changes, but has often been due to the greater influence of 'markets' and the political power of their advocates (Salas-Porras and Murray 2017).

Reproduction of Class Relations

Through these periods, *class relations* (here referring to the relations between those involved in production: capital and labour) were reproduced and the dominance of capital over labour entrenched through mechanisms that varied between countries. One of these was barriers to labour organisation. While freedom of association and the right to strike were recognised in international law and embodied in core conventions of the International

Labour Organization, in a number of countries there have been limitations in one or more ways on the right to strike (Visser 2013). Most limitations on labour organisation, however, have taken other forms: state facilitation or corporate actions of individual or non-union contracting (Peetz 2006); corporate resistance to unionisation including through threatening, disadvantaging, dismissing or intimidating activists (Bronfenbrenner 2009); capital mobility (Bronfenbrenner 2001); or fragmentation of labour, making collective organisation unfeasible or unattractive for workers (Kalleberg 2009, Quinlan et al. 2001). Often labour unions failed to modernise or adequately respond in the face of these challenges (Pocock 1998). At times, violence has been used to suppress labour (International Trade Union Confederation 2017).

Since the 1980s, barriers to labour organisation appear to have intensified. For example, fragmentation of labour has worsened and employer resistance has intensified (Peetz 2006, Quinlan 2016, Quinlan et al. 2001). Explicitly anti-union legislation (promoting individual contracting or weakening union security) is mostly a phenomenon of Anglophone countries—in most industrialised countries, the 'right to strike' has either been unchanged or slightly strengthened (Peetz 2016). Most of the damage to labour's bargaining power has been done through other aspects of market liberalism—for example, impacts through budgetary policy including 'austerity' policies, privatisation, other ways of 'exposing' public sector decision making to market forces, and the deregulation of product markets.

Second, ideology and culture have helped reproduce class relations. These are not independent of class but often embedded within the class structure. They might be influenced by the media (mostly owned or controlled by powerful interests in capital), 'think tanks', education, the family, and other forces of socialisation tied to existing power structures (Connell 1977, Salas-Porras and Murray 2017, Bagdikian 2000).

Third, technological change has played a role in the reproduction of class relations, albeit a less powerful one, through facilitating greater managerial control of labour. For example, bar code and scanning technology enables greater monitoring of workers' performance in retailing and wholesale warehouses (Wright and Lund 1996, Price 2015). Digital tracking enables monitoring of time use by workers in call centres to the millisecond (Townsend 2005). Indeed, surveillance technology in general has become widespread, albeit used more prominently by governments (Sullivan 2013) than employers to date, constrained in the latter regard by privacy legislation in some jurisdictions.

Often, increased control has also enabled management to increase its control over the *timing* of labour. Hence there has been an increased use of peripheral labour, contractors, labour hire or permanent part-time work.

This also requires low power of labour, as labour has resisted such casu-alisation in the past. Indeed, there is nothing historically new about casual labour—it harks back to the way labour was used in the early parts of the industrial revolution or even in the 19th century (Lee and Fahey 1986, Marx 1887, ch. XXI). The same thing applies to the fragmentation of tasks via platforms like Taskmaster. Organised labour successfully resisted much of this control in the 20th century, but its ability to do so has waned.

While technological advances have often been used to combat the gains of organised labour, technology's effects have not always been uniform. Social media have been used with good effect in some political and even industrial campaigns (Caro 2013), and their potential for use by unions has already been highlighted (White 2010). Indeed, social media or the inter-net have been described by some as a 'democratising' influence on society (Loader and Mercea 2011). On the other hand, reliance on time-eating smart devices grows and we see increasing concentration in technology-related sectors, led by firms like Facebook and Amazon. Comparisons are made with the oil monopolies or 'robber barons' of the 19th century and there are resultant calls for anti-trust legislation (Taplin 2017, Baker 2017).

Reproduction of Classes

More important for this discussion is the reproduction of *classes* themselves—that is, the people who collectively comprise the ruling class and the working class. What is it that enables the members of the ruling class to stay in that class, and the children of the ruling class to also stay in that class? While countries vary in the degree of inter-generational mobility, with the USA the worst industrialised country in these terms (at the most immobile end of the 'Gatsby curve', Krueger 2012), in all countries there is some tendency for reproduction of classes—for the children of people in a particular class to themselves end up in that class. Three explanatory factors probably stand out.

The first is inherited wealth. When the wealthy can pass their wealth on to their children, it stands to reason that the children will themselves end up wealthy. Data on class continuity bear this out. UBS in 2016 estimated that 'fewer than 500 people (460 of the billionaires in the markets we cover) will hand over USD 2.1trn, equivalent to India's GDP, to their heirs in the next 20 years' (UBS and PWC 2016, p. 15). Inherited wealth is one of the major predictors of being a billionaire. Alvaredo et al. (2017) estimated that in 2010 inherited wealth accounted for 60 per cent of total wealth in Europe, up from 30–40 per cent in the post-war period, and was likely a similar proportion in the US.

The second factor is education. Higher education leads to higher productivity and incomes (Norris et al. 2005), and people from wealthier backgrounds are often better prepared than poor children before entering school, more oriented towards the benefits of education, and have more resources to continue through and complete their education (Willis 1977). Probably more important for us is the 'signalling' role served by education (Psacharopoulos 1974). Where private resources enable 'better' education to be purchased, the school or university one attended becomes a signalling device that is used to facilitate entry into high-paying jobs in finance and elsewhere and lay the groundwork for further wealth accumulation (Skattebol and Redmond 2018).

A third factor is geography. Cities are segmented into wealthier and poorer areas. Wealthier children have wealthier peers, more materially endowed networks, and greater access to skills and social resources that will enable them to advance further (Grabar 2015). Fewer resources in poorer areas increases the likelihood that their inhabitants will remain poor. The geographical segregation of cities appears to be increasing over time, with growing gaps in average incomes between the richest and the poorest areas in cities (Bradbury 2017).

CYBORG WORK, TECHNOLOGY AND CLASS REPRODUCTION

Cyborg work changes some key aspects of the reproduction of classes and raises important questions for researchers on that issue.

Productivity and the Distribution of the Benefits from Productivity Growth

In an era of cyber work, by contrast with earlier technological epochs, increased productivity would no longer be embodied within the technology that is owned by the owners of capital, to be fought over with labour. Instead, the technology would be a characteristic of individuals themselves.

You might initially think that this would increase the power of labour vis-à-vis capital. That is, if we take technology out of the hands of capital and place it in the hands of labour, this could markedly change the balance of power in the employment relationship in favour of labour. Labour would no longer have to fight over the distribution of benefits from technology that capital owned—it would own and control the technology, and dictate the terms under which it was rewarded.

But would it? The workplace is a collective location where, even if capital holds the upper hand, contestation between labour and capital over the appropriation of the benefits of new technology can occur. The human body is an individualistic location. Who would really gain the benefits of productivity growth when there is a shift from, in effect, collective to individual location of new technology? And how large might the gains in personal productivity from cyborg technology be?

Timing in such matters is everything, and it would be a mistake to imagine that an expensive beneficent technology would be simultaneously, universally available. The *reverse* of the above scenario might be the case, because of the cost of cyborg technology, especially in the initial stages. It is these initial stages that may be crucial in determining the winners and losers from cyborg technology.

The likely high cost of cyborg technology could mean that, under the existing social order, only a very wealthy minority of people would be initially able to afford it. Thus only those that have permanently higher productivity and those able to enjoy a permanently higher performance or the profits there-of—an elite group—may be advantaged.

True, the cost will likely eventually decline after a technology has been around for a while, thereby enabling a wider group to afford it—though it is unlikely that the cost would be so low that the bulk of the population, or at least many in the working class, could afford it. However, by the time the price of some neural implant technology has come down, a new neural technology will be available that will be rare and very expensive and, again, only able to be afforded by an elite wealthy few. So, as different waves of cyborg technology are released, the individual productivity advantages that they create will only be available to a small wealthy group that will enjoy a permanently higher performance than the vast majority of people. What, if anything, would stop the appropriation of the benefits of cyborg technology by a ruling class of digital humans? Under what conditions might those benefits be shared more equitably? What would be the implications for inter-generational mobility? What would be the implications for the distribution of income—between labour and capital, between digital humans and purely biological humans, between the 'one per cent' and the rest?

Gender and Labour Market Disadvantage

There are important questions about the gender dimensions of this technology. Since the driving force behind the move to cyborg work is innovation in the information and communications technology (ICT) sector, and that sector is *increasingly* male dominated (Keane 2016a, 2016b, 2016c, Naughton 2017, Levin 2017, Zarya 2016, Kessler 2015), would the technology be designed to favour men? We have seen the examples of an artificial heart being designed to suit male rather than female bodies (suitable for 86 per cent of men but only 20 per cent of women), simply because it would be too costly to separately design one for women (Broad 2018). Would cyborg technology designed predominantly by men generate similar, or perhaps distinct, gendered limitations? Against whom would cyber-harassment be directed, by what methods and with what effects? How would instant links via those websites presently advertising how to 'be powerful and get inside a woman's head' affect male–female behaviour? If ruling-class children are as likely to be female as male, would the former be equally likely to be gifted with cyborg technologies to maintain advantages over (male and female) people from other classes? What would be the likely incomes achieved by workers in the ICT sector, and would this have implications for the gender income gap?

Would other existing fissures in the labour market, such as the disadvantages facing migrants, disabled people or young people, be narrowed or worsened? Much of the impetus for the march of cyborg technology arises from the benefits it promises for persons presently disabled: the ability to move limbs that were previously frozen, to see things previously invisible, to do things previously undoable. Would it work that way?

Control, Cyborg Technology and the Reproduction of Class Relations

Another important set of questions about cyborg technology and the emergence of digital humans concerns implications for the reproduction of *class relations*, in particular through the implications for *control*.

The opportunity for greater control of workers arises from the networking of neural technology if the technology is not owned by the commons. But this only applies when neural implant technology is widespread. In the initial phases, as discussed above, neural implant technology would likely only be available to a select, wealthy few. Over time, it would become available to more, outside the initial groups of the core of the ruling class. Overall, it seems likely that, at some time in the future, *networked* neural technology will be available to, and used by, all members of the population, even though that used by the majority is likely to be far inferior to that used by the elite. The profits to its producers would potentially be enormous through popularisation.

What opportunity, then, would the widespread adoption of neural implant technology open up for greater surveillance? We already know of the ways in which mobile phone locations or more explicitly bespoke monitoring devices enable the locations of drivers or other workers to be continuously tracked. But neural implants cannot be separated from the body. Could employers insist all potential employees have one, and that they leave them turned 'on'? What policy approaches would be required to deal with this? What opportunities would there be for 'hacking' or external control, by external entities, or even by employers themselves? What would be the implications of that? How could policy respond? How could workers act collectively in such circumstances—how could unions organise, even survive?

RESEARCH IMPLICATIONS

The preceding discussion has already raised a number of important research questions. Others are forms of the question: what is likely to happen? Some will be issues that will emerge later. From the earlier discussion we can already envisage a major research agenda on the implications of biotechnology for work and work organisation. In it, emotional labour, autonomy, stress, health and wellbeing may loom large. What are the implications for workers of the potential reduction in discretion that cyborg technology and its links with AI might bring? What risk and emotional labour will be involved in overriding the decision that is presented to them via AI? If a finance worker almost instantly knows the financial and personal circumstances and demographic, attitudinal and behavioural characteristics of the person to whom they are talking, and they are themselves subjected to certain performance-based pay standards, how does that shape the behaviour of the finance worker and the rights of the consumer, and influence the stress and health of the finance worker? How does emotional labour come into play when a carer considers the rules of the algorithm do not allow them enough time with a needy client—a matter that has already been the subject of some limited research (Kirchhoff and Karlsson 2013)? What are the implications for health, safety and wellbeing of reduced worker autonomy in this context? Many other questions will be variations on a long-standing issue in labour process research: exactly how will control of the labour process be exerted and resisted? What is the potential for successful resistance? Already it appears that, just with new platform technologies, the forms of control are complex and varied (Veen et al. 2019, Wood et al. 2018).

Further research issues are forms of the question: what is to be done? What policy options are available? For example, should the intellectual property for cyborg technologies be part of the commons—like water? What are the requirements for, and prospects of, genuine ethical input not only into AI (as has already being considered, e.g. Boden et al. 2017, Vamplew et al. 2018) but also into implant technology? Could these protect future generations from elite control of this intimate technology? When power is already unevenly distributed these research questions may be especially difficult to investigate.

Our questions are not meant to suggest that this march towards cyborg technology is inherently bad. For some, its effects on people with acute or chronic illnesses, injuries or disabilities will likely create possibilities that were otherwise imaginable and lift some from misery. That is, indeed, one of the reasons why the movement of technology in this direction is probably unstoppable. But that makes it no less necessary to research and understand its full implications, both positive and negative, and to devise policy that can maximise the positive and minimise the negative implications.

One thing that is clear is that the traditional way of responding to policy questions in the world of work—wait till a problem is very evident, argue about it for a long time, and then do something—will not work. By the time that problems have become very evident (and the problems should not be expected to reveal themselves all at once) it will be too late as there will likely be little or no opportunity to enact policies that take power away from those who benefit most from cyborg technology. Whatever else happens it seems unlikely that, in the absence of some very conscious policy interventions, the rise of cyborg technology will be a force for equalising the distribution of income and power. Most likely, it seems, it will have very much the opposite effect.

The rise of neural implant technology and other forms of cyborg technology poses some major challenges—probably the greatest challenges society will have faced since the emergence of capitalism, with the possible exception of climate change. There are potentially enormous consequences if current patterns continue. But nothing is inevitable in this area. In the end, we choose what outcomes will arise from the development of neural technology: whether it will be a force for overcoming injury, illness and disability and for bringing about unprecedented improvements in living standards; or for ushering in a period of inequality and suppression as great as that envisaged in any of the dystopian science fiction novels; or both.

REFERENCES

Alvaredo, Facundo, Bertrand Garbinti and Thomas Piketty. 2017. 'On the share of inheritance in aggregate wealth: Europe and the United States, 1900–2010.' *Economica* 84, pp. 237–260.

Bagdikian, Ben H. 2000. *The Media Monopoly.* 6th edn. Boston, MA: Beacon Press.

Bain, P., and P. Taylor. 2000. 'Entrapped by the electronic panopticon? Worker resistance in the call centre.' *New Technology, Work and Employment* 15 (1), pp. 2–18.

Baker, Dean. 2017. 'Monopoly power: is it time to bring back anti-trust?' Centre for Economic and Policy Research. At http://english.hani.co.kr/arti/english_edition/e_editorial/792919.html. Last accessed 30 April 2019.

Boden, Margaret, Joanna Bryson, Darwin Caldwell, Kerstin Dautenhahn, Lilian Edwards, Sarah Kember, Paul Newman, Vivienne Parry, Geoff Pegman, Tom Rodden, Tom Sorrell, Mick Wallis, Blay Whitby and Alan Winfield. 2017. 'Principles of robotics: regulating robots in the real world.' *Connection Science* 29 (2), pp. 124–129. doi: 10.1080/09540091.2016.1271400.

Bouton, Chad E., Ammar Shaikhouni, Nicholas V. Annetta, Marcia A. Bockbrader, David A. Friedenberg, Dylan M. Nielson, Gaurav Sharma, Per B. Sederberg, Bradley C. Glenn, W. Jerry Mysiw, Austin G. Morgan, Milind Deogaonkar and Ali R. Rezai. 2016. 'Restoring cortical control of functional movement in a human with quadriplegia.' *Nature* 533, pp. 247–250.

Bradbury, Bruce. 2017. 'What did the rich man say to the poor man? Why spatial inequality in Australia is no joke.' *The Conversation*, 31 March.

Broad, Ellen. 2018. *Made By Humans*. Melbourne: Melbourne University Press.

Bronfenbrenner, Kate. 2001. 'Uneasy terrain: The impact of capital mobility on workers, wages and union organizing.' Paper to Union Renewal Symposium, Universite Laval, Quebec, 26 May.

Bronfenbrenner, Kate. 2009. *No Holds Barred: The Intensification of Employer Opposition to Organizing*. Washington, DC: Economic Policy Institute.

Cadwalladr, Carole. 2014. 'Are the robots about to rise? Google's new director of engineering thinks so....' *The Guardian*, 23 February.

Cahill, Damien. 2014. *The End of Laissez Faire? On the Durability of Embedded Neoliberalism*. Cheltenham, UK and Northampton, MA, USA: Edward Elgar Publishing.

Caro, Jane, ed. 2013. *Destroying the Joint: Why Women Have to Change the World*. Brisbane: University of Queensland Press.

Chang, Clara, and Constance Sorrentino. 1991. 'Union membership statistics in 12 countries.' *Monthly Labor Review*, December, pp. 46–53.

Claeys, Gregory. 2018. *Marx and Marxism*. London: Penguin.

Connell, Raewyn. 1977. *Ruling Class, Ruling Culture*. Cambridge: Cambridge University Press.

Coughlin, Tom. 2016. '3D NAND enables larger consumer SSDs.' *Forbes*, 7 June.

Cowgill, Matt. 2013. *A Shrinking Slice of the Pie*. Melbourne: Australian Council of Trade Unions.

Denniss, Richard. 2018. 'Dead Right: how neo liberalism ate itself and what comes next.' *Quarterly Essay*.

Dunlop, Tim. 2018. *The Future of Everything: Big Audacious Ideas for a Better World*. Sydney: New South Books.

Elliott, Larry. 2017. 'Robots to replace 1 in 3 UK jobs over next 20 years, warns IPPR.' *The Guardian*, 15 April.

Ellis, Luci, and Kathryn Smith. 2007. 'The global upward trend in the profit share.' In *BIS Working Paper No 231*. Basel: Bank for International Settlements.

Grabar, Henry. 2015. 'The devious paradox of American inequality: How the rich get richer by staying hidden.' *Salon.com*, 4 January.

Healy, Melissa. 2016. 'Leaping over spinal cord injury, researchers teach a quadri-plegic's hand to move again.' *Los Angeles Times*, 13 April. At http://www.latimes.com/science/sciencenow/la-sci-sn-spinal-cord-hand-movement-20160413-story.html. Last accessed 15 October 2019.

International Trade Union Confederation. 2017. *The 2017 ITUC Global Rights Index: The World's Worst Countries for Workers.* Brussels: ITUC.

Ip, Greg. 2017. 'Robots aren't destroying enough jobs.' *Wall Street Journal*, 10 May.

Johnson, Bryan. 2016. 'Kernell's quest to enhance human intelligence.' At https://medium.com/@bryan_johnson/kernels-quest-to-enhance-human-intelligence-7da5e16fa16c. Last accessed 20 October 2017.

Kalleberg, Arne L. 2009. 'Precarious work, insecure workers: employment relations in transition.' *American Sociologial Review* 74 (1), pp. 1–22.

Kasriel, Stephane. 2017. 'As long as we have problems to solve, we won't run out of jobs.' In *World Economic Forum*: Quartz. At https://www.weforum.org/agenda/2017/04/as-long-as-we-have-problems-to-solve-we-wont-run-out-of-jobs. Last accessed 25 April 2019.

Keane, Bernard. 2016a. 'Rape fears and harassment, but bright spots for women in tech, too.' *Crikey!*, 18 March.

Keane, Bernard. 2016b. 'The looming crisis for women in Oz tech.' *Crikey!*, 16 March.

Keane, Bernard. 2016c. 'What's driving women out of tech industries?' *Crikey!*, 17 March.

Kessler, Sarah. 2015. 'Tech's big gender diversity push, one year in.' At http://www.fastcompany.com/3052877/techs-big-gender-diversity-push-one-year-in. Last accessed 29 November 2015.

Kirchhoff, Jörg W., and Jan C. Karlsson. 2013. 'Expansion of output: organizational misbehaviour in public enterprises.' *Economic and Industrial Democracy* 34 (1), pp. 107–122.

Krueger, Alan B. 2012. *The Rise and Consequences of Inequality.* Washington, DC: Council of Economic Advisers.

Lee, Jenny, and Charles Fahey. 1986. 'A boom for whom? Some developments in the Australian labour market, 1870–1891.' *Labour History – A Journal of Labour and Social History* 50, pp. 1–27.

Levin, Sam. 2017. 'Accused of underpaying women, Google says it's too expensive to get wage data.' *The Guardian*, 27 May.

Liu, Jia, Tian-Ming Fu, Zengguang Cheng, Guosong Hong, Tao Zhou, Lihua Jin, Madhavi Duvvuri, Zhe Jiang, Peter Kruskal, Chong Xie, Zhigang Suo, Ying Feng and Charles M. Lieber. 2015. 'Syringe-injectable electronics.' *Nature Nanotechnology* 10, pp. 629–636. doi: doi:10.1038/nnano.2015.115.

Loader, Brian D., and Dan Mercea. 2011. 'Networking democracy? Social media innovations in participatory politics.' *Information, Communication and Society* 14 (6), pp. 757–769.

MacLean, Nancy. 2018. *Democracy in Chains.* Chicago, IL: Penguin Random House.

Maier, Charles S. 1987. *In Search of Stability: Explorations in Historical Political Economy.* Cambridge: Cambridge University Press.

Marx, Karl. ([1887] 1998). *Capital, Volume 1.* London: The Electric Book Company.

Murugesan, S. 2008. 'Harnessing green IT: principles and practices.' *IT Professional*, 10(1), pp. 24–33.

Naughton, John. 2017. 'Want to succeed in tech? Try not to be a woman....' *The Guardian*, 11 June.

Newitz, Annalee. 2015. 'Scientists just invented the neural lace.' At https://www.gizmodo.com.au/2015/06/scientists-just-invented-the-neural-lace/. Last accessed 29 March 2017.

Nguyen, Jordan. 2016. 'Becoming superhuman part 2'. In *Catalyst*: Australian Broadcasting Corporation. At https://www.abc.net.au/catalyst/becoming-super-human-part-2/11016544. Last accessed 31 May 2019.

Norris, Keith, Ross Kelly and Margaret Giles. 2005. *Economics of Australian Labour Markets*, 6th edn. Sydney: Pearson Education.

O'Connor, Sarah. 2017. 'Never mind the robots; future jobs demand human skills.' *Financial Times*.

O'Neill, Cathy. 2016. *Weapons of Math Destruction: How Big Data Increases Inequality and Threatens Democracy*. New York, NY: Crown Publishing Group.

Peetz, David. 2006. *Brave New Workplace: How Individual Contracts are Changing Our Jobs*. Sydney: Allen & Unwin.

Peetz, David. 2016. 'Industrial action, the right to strike, ballots and the Fair Work Act in international context.' *Australian Journal of Labour Law* 29, pp. 133–153.

Peetz, David. 2018. 'The labour share, power and financialisation.' *Journal of Australian Poliical Economy* 81, pp. 33–51.

Pocock, Barbara. 1998. 'Institutional sclerosis: prospects for trade union transformation.' *Labour & Industry* 9 (1), pp. 17–33.

Preston, John. 2017. 'The tyranny of competence: why it is bad for us to be "good enough".' *The Conversation*, 23 May.

Price, Robin. 2015. 'Controlling routine front line service workers: an Australian retail supermarket case.' *Work, Employment and Society* 30 (6), pp. 915–931.

Psacharopoulos, G. 1974. 'The screening hypothesis and the returns to education.' *Journal of Political Economy* 82 (5), pp. 985–998.

Quinlan, Michael. 2016. 'FactCheck: do better pay rates for truck drivers improve safety?' *The Conversation*, 13 April. At https://theconversation.com/factcheck-do-better-pay-rates-for-truck-drivers-improve-safety-57639. Last accessed 15 October 2019.

Quinlan, Michael, Claire Mayhew and Philip Bohle. 2001. 'The global expansion of precarious employment, work disorganization, and consequences for occupational health: placing the debate in a comparative historical context.' *International Journal of Health Services* 31 (3), pp. 507–536.

Regalado, Antonio. 2017. 'With Neuralink, Elon Musk promises human-to-human telepathy. Don't believe it.' *MIT Technology Review*, 22 April.

Ross, Monique, and Damien Carrick. 2018. 'A robot didn't take Ibrahim's job, but it did fire him.' *ABC News*, 16 August. At http://www.abc.net.au/news/2018-08-14/ibrahim-diallo-man-who-was-fired-by-a-machine-law-ai/10083194. Last accessed 14 August 2018.

Salas-Porras, A., and G. Murray, eds. 2017. *Think Tanks and Global Politics: Key Spaces in the Structure of Power*. Singapore: Palgrave Macmillan.

Salinas, Sara. 2018. 'Uber and Lyft are racing to own every mode of transportation—they're getting close.' *MSNBC Tech*, 9 June.

Sample, Ian. 2015. 'Paraplegic man walks with own legs again.' *The Guardian*, 24 September.

Skattebol, J., and G. Redmond. 2018. 'Troubled kids? Locational disadvantage, opportunity structures and social exclusion.' *Children's Geographies*. doi: 10.1080/14733285.2018.1487031.

Stibel, J. 2017. 'Hacking the brain: the future computer chips in your head.' *Forbes*, 10 July. At https://www.forbes.com/sites/jeffstibel/2017/07/10/hacking-the-brain/#45dc2b782009. Last accessed 15 October 2019.

Sullivan, John L. 2013. 'Uncovering the data panopticon: the urgent need for critical scholarship in an era of corporate and government surveillance.' *The Political Economy of Communication* 1 (2). Available at http://polecom.org/index.php/polecom/article/view/23/192. Last accessed 15 October 2019.

Taplin, Jonathan. 2017. 'Is it time to break up Google?' *New York Times*, 22 April.

Townsend, Keith. 2005. 'Electronic surveillance and cohesive teams: room for resistance in an Australian call centre?' *New Technology, Work and Employment* 20 (1), pp. 47–59.

UBS and PWC. 2016. *Billionaires—Insights: Are Billionaires Feeling the Pressure?* London and Zurich: Union Bank of Switzerland and PricewaterhouseCoopers.

Unknown. 2017. 'Elon Musk wants to connect brains to computers with new company.' *The Guardian*, 28 March.

Vamplew, Peter, Richard Dazeley, Cameron Foale, Sally Firmin and Jane Mummery. 2018. 'Human-aligned artificial intelligence is a multiobjective problem.' *Ethics and Information Technology* 20 (1), pp. 27–40.

Veen, Alex, Tom Barratt and Caleb Goods. 2019. 'Platform-capital's "App-etite" for control: a labour process analysis of food-delivery work in Australia.' *Work, Employment and Society*. doi: 10.1177/0950017019836911.

Visser, Jelle. 2013. *Database on Institutional Characteristics of Trade Unions, Wage Setting, State Intervention and Social Pacts, 1960–2011 (ICTWSS)*, Version 4.0. Amsterdam: Amsterdam Institute for Advanced Labour Studies AIAS, University of Amsterdam.

White, Alex. 2010. *Social Media for Unions*. Melbourne: Aletheia Media and Communications.

Willis, Paul. 1977. *Learning to Labour: How Working Class Kids Get Working Class Jobs*. Farnborough: Saxon House.

Wood, Alex. J., Mark Graham, Vili Lehdonvirta and Isis Hjorth. 2018. 'Good gig, bad gig: autonomy and algorithmic control in the global gig economy.' *Work, Employment and Society* 33 (1), pp. 56–75. doi: 0950017018785616.

Wright, Christopher, and John Lund. 1996. 'Best practice Taylorism: "Yankee Speed-Up" in Australian grocery distribution.' *Journal of Industrial Relations* 38 (2), pp. 196–212.

Zarya, Valentina. 2016. 'Female programmers make nearly 30% less than their male counterparts.' *Fortune.com*, 16 November.

10. Work and wages in the gig economy: can there be a high road?

Joshua Healy and Andreas Pekarek[*]

1. INTRODUCTION

The rise of digital platforms and the 'gig economy' is a central topic in debates about the future of work. As new platform companies have emerged in a range of markets, including transport, food delivery, and home and personal services, established business models and employment arrangements have come under increasing pressure. The hallmark of 'gig work' is precarity; platform companies rely on contract workers and subject them to new forms of algorithmic management and control (Goods *et al.*, 2019; Wood *et al.*, 2018). The contract-based nature of gig work is an enduring source of controversy and a basis for recurring legal challenges to platform companies around the world.

While the line between contractors and employees is yet to be definitively drawn in the gig economy, efforts to improve workers' wages and conditions can also be advanced in other ways that have heretofore received less attention. In this chapter, we discuss three avenues for accomplishing this improvement that do not hinge on how gig work is legally classified: workers organising, consumer behaviours, and changing labour market conditions. Building on Osterman's (2018) aspirational model of the 'High Road', we consider how these three levers might be used to achieve better outcomes for workers in the evolving gig economy.

2. PLATFORM COMPANIES, THE GIG ECONOMY AND THE FUTURE OF WORK

Digital platforms have spread quickly into many parts of the economy. Platform companies combine multiple technologies and systems – including global positioning systems, machine-learning algorithms, and payment facilities – to connect workers and consumers in markets for both online tasks (e.g., data entry) and person-to-person services (e.g., meal delivery).

In this chapter, we focus on the latter type of 'locally-delivered' work (Wood *et al.*, 2018).

Platform-based work represents a departure from the model of regular employment inside firms. Instead of recruiting employees, platform companies register prospective workers as independent contractors and allocate them tasks according to variable customer demand. The new workforce segment that has emerged as a result of platforms' growth has a variety of names that reflects its inherent irregularity; we refer to it as the 'gig economy' in keeping with common parlance, while acknowledging that term's descriptive limitations (Nunberg, 2016). The notion of a 'gig' implies work that is short lived or one off – and initial evidence shows that gig workers are, indeed, often supplementing their main earnings from another job (Hall and Krueger, 2018). This feature of the work has important rhetorical and political ramifications for how the gig economy is understood, structured, and regulated.

At their simplest, platform companies are mediators. Their technologies 'sit between' – and limit the interactions between – those requesting a service and those who can provide it. In exchange, platforms claim a portion of each transaction as revenue, while the service nature of gig work means that labour is a major cost (Boxall and Purcell, 2016). Survival depends on transaction volumes, and how successfully platforms can build and maintain their user base.

The gig economy is a flashpoint in debates about contemporary work and inequality. Critics contend that it reverts to exploitative labour conditions that predate today's minimum standards (Stanford, 2017). From this view, platforms threaten to further erode established worker protections. Proponents of the gig economy, instead, emphasise the benefits of new platforms for consumer convenience and wider economic activity (Pasquale, 2016). They argue that, by drawing in new market participants and reducing search costs, the benefits afforded by new platforms outweigh the disruption to established firms, workers, and jobs.

Reflecting these divergent perspectives, arguments about the gig economy are increasingly polarised. The patchy and sometimes partisan nature of the evidence exacerbates this problem. Few national statistical agencies have attempted to measure gig work in a representative way. Progress is hampered by scoping, definitional, and measurement problems stemming from the practical difficulties of distinguishing 'gigs' from other forms of work (BLS, 2018a). As a result, consistent and impartial evidence is lacking on basic issues, such as gig workers' demographics, working hours, and earnings (Bajwa *et al.*, 2018).

The platforms' engagement of gig workers as contractors is highly controversial. Critics in the labour movement object to this practice because it allows platform companies to evade certain obligations tied to regular employment, including minimum wages, superannuation, minimum shift lengths, and unfair dismissal laws. Platforms have thus become a target for union campaigns, such as that of the Australian Council of Trade Unions, to 'Change the Rules' (Gahan *et al.*, 2018). Yet, platform companies insist that contracting is benign, or even preferred by gig workers. They have strenuously resisted mounting challenges, on the streets and in the courts, to their labour practices (Deakin and Markou, 2017; Tassinari and Maccarrone, 2017).

At a deeper level, contract-based gig work enables other, more insidious forms of worker control. Formulas setting pay rates can be altered by platform companies, and workers can be 'deactivated' (i.e., disbarred) as users for minor or alleged transgressions in performance (van Doorn, 2017). Lacking fixed schedules, workers may be tempted to work long hours at times of peak demand, jeopardising their own or others' safety (Scheiber, 2017). Finally, because platforms are *technologies* (software) rather than *physical systems* (hardware), they are often developed and operated by off-shore companies, which can prove hard to reach in legal claims. These risks are aggravated by the attributes of typical gig workers: many are young or from vulnerable population groups (Balaram *et al.*, 2017).

The platforms' business model nonetheless depends on preserving a 'clean' and legitimate legal distinction between contractors and employees, which is increasingly being tested in multiple legal claims and jurisdictions. If this distinction was compromised, and if employees were found to have been wrongly classified as contractors, the current labour practices of leading platforms would be seriously threatened.[1] This explains why the status of gig work has become such a legal battleground. A definitive ruling against their reliance on contract workers would be a major 'win' for the gig economy's detractors and an existential crisis for many platform companies (Prassl and Risak, 2016; Taylor *et al.*, 2017).

The question of whether gig workers are contractors or employees dominates the debate. While we recognise the genuine economic and moral consequences of this distinction (e.g., for taxation revenue and the treatment of workers), the ongoing wrangling over legal status has, in our view, focused attention too narrowly on one contentious issue. It has, we argue, led to inadequate scrutiny of other prospective ways to improve the conditions of gig work.

Our concern is that there may never be a legal decision of universal application, given the complex tests to be applied, and the likelihood that specific practices of specific platforms would need to be examined case by case. Even if a definitive ruling is possible, it may be years away. Until then, an uneasy *status quo* exists, in which platform companies continue to use contractors while opponents decry the illegitimacy of this use. Without a ruling that resolves workers' status, we face a deadlock. Meanwhile, gig workers are at ongoing risk of low pay and job insecurity (Commonwealth of Australia, 2018, pp. 73–81).

In this chapter, we explore three other promising avenues for improving gig work that do not hinge on workers' conversion to employee status. To do this, we apply the 'High Road' perspective in industrial relations, which offers a normative ideal to which platforms could aspire – or could be held – until the legal question of workers' status is resolved. Our use of the High Road extends the analytical range of this influential framework while enriching the analysis of 'gig work relations' (Healy *et al.*, 2017).

3. APPLYING THE HIGH ROAD CONCEPT TO THE GIG ECONOMY

Industrial relations scholars have long been concerned with studying different employment practices and their outcomes for firms and workers. The High/Low Road dichotomy is one major approach that has been developed to classify and critique these differences (Wilkinson *et al.*, 2018). The criteria that distinguish High Road and Low Road firms vary, but often include dimensions of human resource management, such as compensation schemes, training, and the nature of labour–management relations, along with a business strategy 'driven by values other than the quest for short-term stock prices' (Kochan, 2016, pp. 70–75).

In an authoritative recent contribution, Osterman (2018) draws the boundaries of the High Road more narrowly, based on the wages–profits nexus. He argues that, for workers, the defining feature of the High Road is adequate wages. 'Adequacy' implies that the wages of High Road firms are superior to their competitors, above the minimum required to attract workers, and high enough to keep workers from poverty. In Osterman's (2018) formulation, adequate wages are the only non-negotiable ingredient of the High Road – its *sine qua non*. Other practices still matter, but changing these without raising wages would betray the High Road ideal.

For firms, however, 'adequate' wages may detract from profits. The evidence cited by Osterman (2018) is ambiguous about whether the benefits of taking the High Road *offset*, let alone *exceed*, the associated higher wage costs, which may be why this approach is not more widespread (Kochan, 2016). Business models that emphasise profitability do not seem naturally aligned with High Road employment practices. Osterman (2018) shows that many celebrated High Road firms are idiosyncratic, such that profitability is not their singular goal. For most firms, however, 'market discipline' may make the extra costs of the High Road harder to justify and sustain. Indeed, Osterman (2018) suggests that few firms will tolerate these additional costs unless they have already adopted – or can be compelled to adopt – a broader 'stakeholder view' of their constituents and responsibilities. Discouraging pure profit-making appears to be a prerequisite for the wider adoption of High Road practices.

The High/Low Road dichotomy is a fitting framework for analysing work in the gig economy. It provides a basis for interrogating and seeking to improve the conditions of gig workers that is quite different from testing their employment status. Depending on how future legal cases are decided, platform companies might ultimately be vindicated in using contractors. This would affirm that their labour practices are legal, but not necessarily that they are fair, responsible, or adequate. These are quite different tests of legitimacy, which the High Road model introduces. It compels us to look beyond the contractual *form* of gig work and focus instead on the *substance* of platforms' practices and their consequences for workers.

Further, low-wage industries are the primary target of High Road initiatives, because wages are inadequate for many workers in these industries. Osterman (2018, p. 6) defines High Road firms as those 'paying or providing a path to an adequate wage *in a low-wage industry*' (our emphasis). This criterion readily applies to the gig economy, where low wages and job insecurity are prevalent (Ashford *et al.*, 2018; ILO, 2018).

Given that High Road practices may affect profits, platform companies are unlikely to follow this path naturally – with its connotation of adequacy above minimal compliance – and the law alone cannot compel them to. We should therefore ask what other sources of external pressure might help to move platforms towards the critical (broader) 'stakeholder view'. As Osterman (2018) recognised, this involves new sources of power that change the mixture of costs and incentives facing platforms, thereby encouraging them to pursue goals other than profits alone.

We next consider three avenues for exerting this pressure in the gig economy.

4.   AVENUES FOR IMPROVING LABOUR PRACTICES IN THE GIG ECONOMY

4.1   Workers Organising

The primary mechanism for raising awareness of, and challenging, the labour practices of platform companies to date is workers organising.

Countervailing labour power has often been necessary to propel firms towards the High Road (Kochan, 2016).

The individualised and arm's-length nature of gig work does not, at first, seem conducive to collective action, and yet we observe increasingly fervent activity, occurring spontaneously at a grassroots level and through more conventional means. In short time, the gig economy has become a lightning rod for the wider labour movement's campaigning around workers' rights. This engagement is motivated by the core concern that gig work represents the 'thin edge of the wedge' and that the platforms' model of contracting and job fragmentation will soon colonise other sectors.

We discern three main forms of worker activism in the gig economy, which are related and arguably mutually reinforcing, but which differ in their sophistication, scope, and purpose.

At an elementary level, this activism can be characterised as a form of 'mutual aid' (Nissen and Jarley, 2005). It involves largely informal contact and exchange of knowledge between workers about task performance and expectations. Picture here a group of delivery-riders gathering before the dinner rush in a popular urban food precinct. Or, its online equivalent: a social media forum or messaging app. These types of contact foster an awareness and a sharing of common experiences (and grievances), which not only empower the individuals but can also stimulate the development of collective identities that pre-figure the more ambitious expressions of solidarity discussed below (Ford and Honan, 2019). Notably, even these rudimentary manifestations of collectivism have provoked responses from platform companies that suggest hostility towards meaningful worker voice (Chau and Kontominas, 2018).

Beyond mutual aid, the establishment of dedicated new collective organisations entails a more formalised commitment to advancing gig workers' interests. In Australia, the leading example is RideShare Drivers United (RSDU). A further extension involves campaigning by other smaller, grassroots unions, whose focus is not solely on gig workers but who seek to represent them alongside other marginalised and precarious groups. Prominent examples internationally are the Independent Workers of Great Britain (IWGB) and United Voices of the World (UVW). Common strategies of these fledgling and 'quasi-union' organisations include a mix of public relations campaigns and direct action against platform companies over Low Road working conditions. Their emergence has enabled more coordinated action in pursuit of claims, as exemplified by the new tactic of 'log-off strikes' in which gig workers voluntarily disconnect from platforms for a designated period, sometimes in multiple countries (Leonhardt, 2019; RSDU, 2018).

Because of its perceived threat to wider labour standards, gig work is now also a rallying point for some traditional unions. In Australia, the Transport Workers Union has taken the lead in opposing the labour practices of ride-share and courier platforms, through research, advocacy, lobbying, and legal action. Less frequently, this extends to direct negotiations between unions and platforms. In Australia, the peak body in one State, Unions New South Wales, reached a deal with the platform company Airtasker to instate voluntary guidelines and other procedural measures that encourage, but do not mandate, its compliance with minimum standards (Minter, 2017). As well as lending institutional support to nascent efforts to organise gig workers, these developments broaden the workforce coverage, and expand the toolkit of, established unions, offering them new possibilities for revitalisation.

Although these are distinctive approaches, we expect them to be complementary in their contribution to promoting High Road practices in the gig economy. This process works both by overcoming shortcomings and amplifying strengths. For instance, mutual aid provides fertile ground for organising efforts, while mobilising by established unions within more mature, institutionalised arenas encourages further grassroots activism. Together, these efforts have the potential to spark a 'virtuous circle' of gig work organising (Figure 10.1), which accelerates progress towards the High Road.

To date, there are promising signs of momentum building towards better-organised worker responses to the gig economy. There have been some important developments, partly for their significance as symbolic 'wins' for organisers, and because they help to keep gig work relations in the public eye. However, it remains to be seen whether there is sufficient

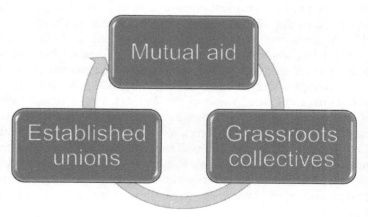

Figure 10.1   The virtuous circle of gig work organising

force in these initiatives to instigate a wider, sustained 'raising of the bar' for platform companies.

4.2 Consumer Behaviours

While our focus is on the conditions of gig work, we recognise that the gig economy emerged not as a vehicle for workforce participation but to meet consumer needs. This puts consumers into focus as a key stakeholder group for platform companies and, by extension, their potential role as a conduit for exerting pressure to improve gig work.

Notwithstanding intermittent attention (Bellemare, 2000; Heery, 1993), the consumer as actor has not been a sustained focus for industrial relations scholarship (Kessler and Bach, 2011). However, the potential to leverage consumer behaviour in pursuit of better working conditions is illustrated by more recent studies of 'consumption relations' and how these can influence labour standards in global supply chains (Donaghey *et al.*, 2014; Wright, 2016). This work suggests that consumers factor in ethical considerations when making purchasing decisions, and can therefore be mobilised, either to withhold their support for certain products ('boycotts') or to actively direct their support to others ('buycotts') (Kimeldorf *et al.*, 2006). These more deliberate ethical decisions can then precipitate deeper political engagement beyond the narrow realm of markets (Barnett *et al.*, 2005).

These issues are echoed in a strand of the marketing literature that examines 'ethical consumption' (Newholm and Shaw, 2007). It shows that consumer behaviours are shaped by a range of ethical considerations, including the environment, treatment of animals, and workers' rights. A key finding is that, in certain circumstances, consumers will pay more for ethical production, particularly when it benefits other people (Tully and Winer, 2014). Put simply, ethical labour practices can command a premium price from consumers.

This evidence is pertinent for encouraging High Road practices in the consumer-centric gig economy, given the trade-offs involved and the potential effects on profit (Osterman, 2018). While Osterman's critique implicitly assumes that firms cannot raise their prices in taking the High Road, this constraint may not apply if ethical consumers are willing to pay more for sustainable practices. To date, there is no research specifically evaluating whether consumer sentiments can be marshalled to improve working conditions in the gig economy. Yet, it has several characteristics that lead us to believe consumers will be critical in shifting platform companies towards the High Road.

First, because of the hyper-competitive markets in which platform companies are operating, they are highly attuned to customer perceptions. In the most prominent segments of the gig economy (e.g., ride-sharing), it is easy for customers to switch providers at negligible cost. This means that relatively minor points of perceived differences between platforms' brands may be influential in customer decisions. There is already evidence that newer operators in the Australian ride-sharing market, such as Ola and Muve, are attempting to set themselves apart from their established rival, Uber, by advertising that drivers' earnings are 'fairer' (Ola) or 'the highest in the market' (Muve). The attempt to draw in ethically minded consumers is taken a step further by Muve, which allocates 10 per cent of the company's share from each transaction to a charity supported by its drivers.[2]

Second, the gig economy is labour intensive. Given that consumers' ethical sympathies are most affected by how other people are treated, the nature of gig work should readily evoke these sentiments. Further, because gig work is often done locally, there is a clear 'line of sight' between workers and consumers. Other research shows that 'process transparency' matters: customers are more appreciative of workers when they can observe their labour (Buell *et al.*, 2017). The visibility of gig work might therefore prompt greater empathy from consumers, inclining them to support those platforms that adhere to High Road principles.

Third, the limited evidence available on the attributes of those who consume gig services indicates that they may have both a greater readiness to prioritise ethical concerns, and the capacity to pay premium prices for them. In Australia, gig work consumers are more affluent and better educated, suggesting they could afford to pay for High Road practices (Goggin *et al.*, 2017).

In other contexts, unions and labour rights campaigners are already leveraging consumer demand for ethical production to encourage firms to adopt High Road practices. A common model involves non-governmental certification authorities that establish ethical criteria and conduct periodic audits of firms' practices; the Fairtrade Foundation and Rainforest Alliance are well-known examples (Bartley, 2007). Building on earlier initiatives, the 'Fairwork certification scheme' is a recent attempt to extend this model to the gig economy (Oxford Internet Institute, 2018). Its aim is to rank platform companies' work processes and certify those that are sustainable. Several European trade unions, including Germany's IG Metall and Sweden's Unionen, have also collaborated to start 'Fair Crowd Work', a website that publishes ratings of pay and conditions at leading platforms, based on worker survey data and assessments of companies' terms of service (De Stefano, 2016).[3] As well as informing prospective workers, such ratings can also guide consumers' choices.

An important obstacle is that consumer sentiments can also be mobilised in opposition to change. For example, when Uber's licence to operate in London was revoked in 2017 by the city's transport authority, the company started a petition and urged customers to sign it in opposition to the loss of 'consumer choice' (Dave and Schomberg, 2017). Uber had used the same tactic before, in resisting regulatory challenges to its operations in other major cities. These actions are evidence that platform companies have the capacity to exploit their large customer databases for political purposes. Within 24 hours of starting its petition against Transport for London, Uber had amassed more than half a million signatures in its support (Dave and Schomberg, 2017). Their customer databases, which are extensive and 'targeted', give the major platforms a significant natural advantage in countering any attempts to shift them towards High Road practices via the lever of sustained consumer pressure. At minimal cost, platforms can target their own consumers with messages to which they are likely to be receptive and sympathetic.

This access is a valuable resource that is difficult for workers and regulators to match. If they want to win consumers' support for improved gig work conditions, they must overcome this information disadvantage – and the pro-platform sentiments that accompany it. One way to do this may be by targeting sections of the community that are not already active platform users, and crafting messages that engage them emotively. Most Australians, for instance, have not used either Uber or Deliveroo, two of the leading platforms (Goggin *et al.*, 2017); as such, they are likely to be 'uncommitted' in their views about the gig economy. Effective marketing campaigns could sway how these consumers' views develop (Irwin, 2015).

4.3 Labour Market Conditions

The state of the wider labour market is an important tertiary influence on how the gig economy develops. While less visible than workers organising or consumers changing their behaviours, the labour market is a key background factor that will serve to either reinforce or undermine other efforts to promote the High Road.

A favourable market for workers is one in which labour demand is strong relative to supply, jobs are plentiful, and jobseekers have work opportunities outside the gig economy. Such a labour market would intensify the pressure on platform companies to offer better pay and conditions, in order to prevent workers from leaving the gig economy to take more attractive jobs elsewhere. This additional market pressure could induce some platforms to offer pay rates that are higher than their immediate competitors, and nearer to the level of 'adequacy' that characterises the High Road (Osterman, 2018).

An unfavourable labour market would have the opposite effects on workers' prospects and platform companies' practices. As alternative work opportunities dwindle, more jobseekers will be drawn into the gig economy, creating a flood of choice for platforms. This effect has been quantified for one major platform, Freelancer: it experienced a 6 per cent increase in new user registrations for each 1 per cent rise in unemployment (Huang *et al.*, 2017). Faced with long queues of willing workers, platform companies would have little incentive in this scenario to accede to High Road demands.

Superficially, current labour market conditions appear to favour workers. In Australia, the unemployment rate has declined for the past four years, to its present 5.1 per cent, while the number of unfilled job vacancies has risen sharply (ABS, 2018a, b). In the United States, the current unemployment rate is even lower: 3.7 per cent, a level not seen in five decades (BLS, 2018b). This seemingly tighter labour market should benefit workers, by forcing firms to compete more actively for a smaller pool of labour. Strategies for appealing to workers include raising wages or offering better conditions (Healy *et al.*, 2015; Maestas *et al.*, 2018).

This process by which firms must 'bid higher' to find and retain workers in a tighter labour market has particular benefits for more marginalised jobseekers. As labour shortages bite, one way that firms can respond is by recruiting from 'non-traditional groups', including ethnic minorities and people with a disability (Henkens *et al.*, 2008). The tightening United States labour market of the late 1990s, for instance, disproportionately benefited workers from 'more disadvantaged groups', including teenagers, minorities, and those with lower education levels (Lerman and Schmidt, 1999). This experience is relevant for anticipating how platform companies might respond to a tighter labour market today, since so many workers in the gig economy come from more vulnerable population groups.

The prospect of workers being drawn out of the gig economy by an improving labour market is plausible, given how most gig work is done today. Put simply, few workers do gigs as their main income-earning activity. Instead, many are participating in ways that are episodic and supplementary (Hall and Krueger, 2018; Mishel, 2015). These are not conditions that nurture strong mutual ties of reciprocity between workers and platforms; nor, by insisting that workers are contractors, do platforms seek closer ties. Hence, when the labour market improves and workers can more easily find better jobs elsewhere, many may opt out of the gig economy (Borchert *et al.*, 2018). Irrespective of whether these workers trim their hours or drop out entirely, both amount to a reduction in platforms' labour supply, which would adversely affect customer service. Their need to maintain a ready supply of workers would then necessitate improving wages and/or conditions.

The labour market could thus help to 'tip the balance' for platform companies towards High Road practices. Yet, there are also several reasons why this might not occur in today's circumstances. What matters is whether the apparent tightness in the labour market is 'real' enough to threaten the labour supply, and thus the labour practices, of platform companies.

Other measures of labour market performance highlight the persistence of under-utilisation and considerable 'slack' in demand. Under-utilisation means that employers retain access to willing workers, despite a low unemployment rate. For the past four years in Australia, even as the unemployment rate has fallen, the under-employment rate (a measure of those who want more work) has been stuck above 8 per cent – its highest sustained level for 30 years (ABS, 2018b). Young workers, who are over-represented in the gig economy, notably also have an under-employment rate that is more than twice the national average (Healy, 2016).

Platform companies are thus in the fortunate position of drawing labour from a part of the market with little 'real' tightness and much unmet demand for hours. Indeed, cultivating an image of gig work as an easy source of discretionary hours – the now-fashionable trope of a 'side hustle' (Quart, 2019) – is a favoured marketing strategy of the platform behemoths. Buoyed by these favourable underlying labour market conditions, and without contrary evidence and resonant counter-narratives (Gahan and Pekarek, 2013), platform companies are unlikely to feel an urgent imperative to shift towards the High Road to avert the threat of labour shortages.

The impact of under-employment on gig work conditions is also exacerbated by continuing strong growth in low-skill labour migration to Australia, which has occurred because of the large numbers of temporary migrants arriving here as students or 'working holiday-makers' (Boucher, 2016). Their lack of local contacts and experience will mean that joining the gig economy is one of the easiest ways for many of these migrants to find work while building their credentials and local networks. And, while platform companies can continue to source ample numbers of inexperienced jobseekers from this flow of temporary migrants, they are further insulated from pressures to raise wages in an otherwise-tightening labour market.

A final issue is that economic and labour market conditions are cyclical. Even if there is tightness in the market that could be exploited to accomplish a shift in platform companies' practices today, there is no guarantee that those gains would be secure in the future, when the cycle turns. At least, this is true while platforms maintain their preferred, highly individualistic and contract-based model of worker engagement. So long as there is scope for platforms to unilaterally adjust their default contracts with workers, there is no assurance that gains achieved in a market upswing will not be immediately rescinded in a downturn. A different outcome would be possible, however, if gains made in a favourable market were formalised in agreements or regulations, which cannot then be revoked at the platforms' behest. These prospects are unlikely to be realised without continuing efforts by workers and unions, perhaps supported by consumer behaviours, as previously discussed.

5. CONCLUSION

Much remains to be done in understanding the shape and operations of the gig economy. In this chapter, we have argued for a modest reorientation of researchers' and policymakers' focus, away from the still-contested legal question of gig workers' employment status, and towards the slightly different question of what could be done within existing constraints to deliver better wages and working conditions.

Our analysis rests on the notion of adequate wages that Osterman (2018) identified as the lynchpin of High Road practices. This issue takes precedence in the gig economy, where low wages and prevailing job insecurity are causing mounting controversy. We have considered how three pressure points (workers organising, consumer behaviours, and changing labour market conditions) could encourage platform companies to prioritise and institute adequate wages as an essential first step towards a more sustainable workforce–management model. Once this foundation of wage adequacy has been realised, more comprehensive High Road practices could conceivably be pursued and adopted in the gig economy. However, central to our argument is that other High Road practices should be seen as conditional on workers first securing adequate pay.

While the High Road concept provides a tractable normative benchmark for assessing gig work, it is clear that little *evaluative* progress can be made in determining how far platform companies have to go to meet this standard without better evidence on a range of issues. We have previously set out an ambitious gig economy research agenda (Healy *et al.*, 2017) that ties in with the themes of this chapter. With the High Road as a guiding framework, we can now further extend and refine this agenda.

There is a fundamental need for more detailed, consistent, and representative data about gig workers and their earnings. Until we have better evidence about issues such as average earnings, variability in earnings, and what other sources of income gig workers have, it is difficult to meaningfully advance the adequacy agenda that is central to the High Road.

Work has begun, and more is needed, on studying the different avenues used by workers and unions (old and new) to force changes in the labour practices of platform companies. We have discussed three of the most prominent mechanisms in this chapter, ranging from mutual-aid-type arrangements to more formalised bargaining directly between unions and platforms. Exploratory and comparative case studies are needed to study the effectiveness of these different measures and how they develop over time. A critical question is whether certain approaches are more successful than others in promoting a *sustained* shift onto the High Road by platform companies.

We have argued that consumers represent an important but largely untapped constituency that could be used to exert greater leverage for High Road practices on platform companies. With some exceptions (e.g., Goggin *et al.*, 2017), little is known about consumers in the gig economy. Research in adjacent fields shows that there are possibilities for using notions of 'ethical consumption' to motivate actions in workers' favour from gig economy consumers, but at the same time we know that platform companies often hold considerable sway. How attached are consumers to the convenience and low cost on which most platforms' business models are founded? What sensitivity would different consumers have to a small increase in price – if this is seen to support better outcomes for workers? One exciting prospect here is the use of experimental designs to tease out consumers' appetite for alternative models.

Finally, useful progress could be made in studying the strategies of platform companies. While there are some features that most platforms have in common, interesting differences are starting to emerge, even between companies competing for similar customer segments. Researchers can study the origins of these differences and evaluate whether they make any lasting difference to the dominant platforms' strategies or the adequacy of workers' wages. As in the High Road literature more broadly (Osterman, 2018), better evidence is needed on the *long-term viability* of platform labour practices that are not solely motivated by profits.

Separate from these empirical questions, there is also much conceptual work to be done in applying the idea of wage adequacy to the gig economy, and perhaps modifying it for that context. What level of wages is 'adequate' when workers are paid by piece-rates and those rates are highly variable? What account should be taken of the fact that many gig workers are supplementing another source of income? How can longer-term 'adequacy' be judged, given that few gig workers are covered by compulsory superannuation arrangements?

In considering all of these issues, researchers must of course continue to be mindful of the shifting legal terrain on which the gig economy rests. Changes to the legal treatment of gig workers are being carefully weighed by authorities in many countries, and developments in this area may reorder the priority given to some of the key topics we have identified. In the meantime, however, there is much useful research to do. Although it is still small, the gig economy is likely to occupy the attention of many industrial relations and human resource management scholars for years to come.

NOTES

*   We are grateful to Diarmuid Cooney-O'Donoghue for research assistance undertaken to support this chapter.
1. A recent case concerns Foodora, a food-delivery platform that ceased trading in Australia in controversial circumstances in 2018. Earlier that year, the workplace 'watchdog' had brought legal action against Foodora, alleging that it 'engaged in sham contracting activity that resulted in the underpayment of workers' (FWO, 2018). Foodora's administrator subsequently admitted that workers on the platform were likely to have been misclassified as contractors, leaving potential debts of more than $5 million in unpaid wages and entitlements (Workplace Express, 2018).
2. Further information is available at: https://www.muve.com.au/charity (accessed 6 December 2018).
3. Further information is available at: http://faircrowd.work/platform-reviews/ (accessed 4 December 2018).

REFERENCES

ABS (Australian Bureau of Statistics) (2018a) *Job Vacancies, Australia, Aug 2018*. Catalogue no. 6354.0. Canberra: ABS.
ABS (Australian Bureau of Statistics) (2018b) *Labour Force, Australia, October 2018*. Catalogue no. 6202.0. Canberra: ABS.
Ashford, S., B. Caza and E. Reid (2018) 'From surviving to thriving in the gig economy: A research agenda for individuals in the new world of work.' *Research in Organizational Behavior*, 38, pp. 23–41.
Bajwa, U., L. Knorr, E. Di Ruggiero, D. Gastaldo and A. Zendel (2018) *Towards an understanding of workers' experiences in the global gig economy*. Toronto: Global Migration and Health Initiative. Available at: https://www.glomhi.org/gigs.html (accessed 27 November 2018).
Balaram, B., J. Warden and F. Wallace-Stephens (2017) *Good gigs: A fairer future for the UK's gig economy*. London: The RSA (Royal Society for the encouragement of Arts, Manufactures and Commerce). Available at: https://www.thersa.org/globalassets/pdfs/reports/rsa_good-gigs-fairer-gig-economy-report.pdf (accessed 27 November 2018).
Barnett, C., N. Clarke, P. Cloke and A. Malpass (2005) 'The political ethics of consumerism.' *Consumer Policy Review*, 15, pp. 45–51.
Bartley, T. (2007) 'Institutional emergence in an era of globalization: The rise of transnational private regulation of labor and environmental conditions.' *American Journal of Sociology*, 113, pp. 297–351.
Bellemare, G. (2000) 'End users: Actors in the industrial relations system?' *British Journal of Industrial Relations*, 38, pp. 383–405.
BLS (Bureau of Labor Statistics) (2018a) 'Electronically mediated work: New

questions in the Contingent Worker Supplement.' *Monthly Labor Review*, September. Washington, DC: United States Department of Labor. Available at: https://doi.org/10.21916/mlr.2018.24 (accessed 27 November 2018).

BLS (Bureau of Labor Statistics) (2018b) *Labor Force Statistics from the Current Population Survey*. Washington, DC: United States Department of Labor. Available at: https://www.bls.gov/cps/ (accessed 27 November 2018).

Borchert, K., M. Hirth, M. Kummer, U. Laitenberger, O. Slivko and S. Viete (2018) 'Unemployment and online labor.' Unpublished manuscript, Centre for European Economic Research. Available at: http://dx.doi.org/10.2139/ssrn.3178692 (accessed 27 November 2018).

Boucher, A. (2016). 'Australia's de facto low skilled migration program.' In *Migration: The Economic Debate*, Committee for Economic Development of Australia, pp. 43–54. Melbourne: CEDA.

Boxall, P. and J. Purcell (2016) *Strategy and Human Resource Management*, 4th edition. London: Palgrave.

Buell, R., T. Kim and C. Tsay (2017) 'Creating reciprocal value through operational transparency.' *Management Science*, 63, pp. 1673–1695.

Chau, D. and B. Kontominas (2018) 'Foodora loses unfair dismissal case and is ordered to pay former delivery rider $16,000.' *ABC News*, 16 November.

Commonwealth of Australia (2018) *Hope is not a strategy – Our shared responsibility for the future of work and workers*. Report of the Select Committee on the Future of Work and Workers. Canberra: The Senate.

Dave, P. and W. Schomberg (2017) 'More than 500,000 people sign Uber petition to overturn London ban.' *The Sydney Morning Herald*, 24 September.

Deakin, S. and C. Markou (2017) 'London Uber ban: Regulators are finally catching up with technology.' *The Conversation*, 26 September.

De Stefano, V. (2016) 'The rise of the «just-in-time workforce»: On-demand work, crowdwork, and labor protection in the «gig-economy».' *Comparative Labor Law Policy Journal*, 37, pp. 471–504.

Donaghey, J., J. Reinecke, C. Niforou and B. Lawson (2014) 'From employment relations to consumption relations: Balancing labor governance in global supply chains.' *Human Resource Management*, 53, pp. 229–252.

Ford, M. and V. Honan (2019) 'The limits of mutual aid: Emerging forms of collectivity among app-based transport workers in Indonesia.' *Journal of Industrial Relations*, 61, pp. 528–548.

FWO (Fair Work Ombudsman) (2018) *Fair Work Ombudsman commences legal action against Foodora*. Melbourne: FWO. Available at: https://www.fairwork.gov.au/about-us/news-and-media-releases/2018-media-releases/june-2018/20180612-foodora-litigation (accessed 6 December 2018).

Gahan, P. and A. Pekarek (2013) 'Social movement theory, collective action frames and union theory: A critique and extension.' *British Journal of Industrial Relations*, 51, pp. 754–776.

Gahan, P., A. Pekarek and D. Nicholson (2018) 'Unions and collective bargaining in Australia in 2017.' *Journal of Industrial Relations*, 60, pp. 337–357.

Goggin, G., A. Vromen, K. Weatherall, F. Martin, A. Webb, L. Sunman and F. Bailo (2017) *Digital Rights in Australia*. The University of Sydney. Available at: http://hdl.handle.net/2123/17587 (accessed 4 December 2018).

Goods, C., A. Veen and T. Barratt (2019) '"Is your gig any good?" Analysing job quality in the Australian platform-based food-delivery sector.' *Journal of Industrial Relations*, 61, pp. 502–527.

Hall, J. and A. Krueger (2018) 'An analysis of the labor market for Uber's driver-partners in the United States.' *Industrial and Labor Relations Review*, 71, pp. 705–732.

Healy, J. (2016) 'The Australian labour market in 2015.' *Journal of Industrial Relations*, 58, pp. 308–323.

Healy, J., K. Mavromaras and P. Sloane (2015) 'Adjusting to skill shortages in Australian SMEs.' *Applied Economics*, 47, pp. 2470–2487.

Healy, J., D. Nicholson and A. Pekarek (2017) 'Should we take the gig economy seriously?' *Labour & Industry: A Journal of the Social and Economic Relations of Work*, 27, pp. 232–248.

Heery, E. (1993) 'Industrial relations and the customer.' *Industrial Relations Journal*, 24, pp. 284–295.

Henkens, K., C. Remery and J. Schippers (2008) 'Shortages in an ageing labour market: An analysis of employers' behaviour.' *International Journal of Human Resource Management*, 19, pp. 1314–1329.

Huang, N., G. Burtch, Y. Hong and P. Pavlou (2017) 'Unemployment and worker participation in the gig economy: Evidence from an online labor platform.' Unpublished manuscript. Available at: http://dx.doi.org/10.2139/ssrn.3105090 (accessed 27 November 2018).

ILO (International Labour Office) (2018) *Digital Labour Platforms and the Future of Work: Towards Decent Work in the Online World*. Geneva: ILO.

Irwin, J. (2015) 'Ethical consumerism isn't dead, it just needs better marketing.' *Harvard Business Review*, 12 January. Available at: https://hbr.org/2015/01/ethical-consumerism-isnt-dead-it-just-needs-better-marketing (accessed 6 December 2018).

Kessler, I. and S. Bach (2011) 'The citizen–consumer as industrial relations actor: New ways of working and the end–user in social care.' *British Journal of Industrial Relations*, 49, pp. 80–102.

Kimeldorf, H., R. Meyer, M. Prasad and I. Robinson (2006) 'Consumers with a conscience: Will they pay more?' *Contexts*, 5, pp. 24–29.

Kochan, T. (2016) *Shaping the Future of Work: What Future Worker, Business, Government, and Education Leaders Need to Do for All to Prosper*. New York, NY: Business Expert Press.

Leonhardt, D. (2019) 'Take today off from Uber and Lyft.' *The New York Times*, 8 May. Available at: https://www.nytimes.com/2019/05/08/opinion/uber-lyft-drivers-strike.html (accessed 10 May 2019).

Lerman, R. and S. Schmidt (1999) *An Overview of Economic, Social, and Demographic Trends Affecting the US Labor Market*. Washington, DC: Urban Institute for the United States Department of Labor.

Maestas, N., K. Mullen, D. Powell, T. von Wachter and J. Wenger (2018) 'The value of working conditions in the United States and implications for the structure of wages.' Unpublished manuscript. Available at: https://www.nber.org/papers/w25204 (accessed 27 November 2018).

Minter, K. (2017) 'Negotiating labour standards in the gig economy: Airtasker and Unions New South Wales.' *The Economic and Labour Relations Review*, 28, pp. 438–454.

Mishel, L. (2015) 'Uber is not the future of work.' *The Atlantic*, 16 November. Available at: http://theatln.tc/2m6QICq (accessed 28 November 2018).

Newholm, T. and D. Shaw (2007) 'Studying the ethical consumer: A review of research.' *Journal of Consumer Behaviour*, 6, pp. 253–270.

Nissen, B. and P. Jarley (2005) 'Unions as social capital: Renewal through a return to the logic of mutual aid?' *Labor Studies Journal*, 29, pp. 1–26.

Nunberg, G. (2016) 'Goodbye jobs, hello "gigs": How one word sums up a new economic reality.' *Fresh Air*, 11 January. Washington, DC: NPR (National Public Radio).

Osterman, P. (2018) 'In search of the High Road: Meaning and evidence.' *Industrial and Labor Relations Review*, 71, pp. 3–34.

Oxford Internet Institute (2018) *Fairwork*. Available at: http://fair.work/certifications/ (accessed 4 December 2018).

Pasquale, F. (2016) 'Two narratives of platform capitalism.' *Yale Law & Policy Review*, 35, pp. 309–319.

Prassl, J. and M. Risak (2016) 'Uber, Taskrabbit, and co.: Platforms as employers – rethinking the legal analysis of crowdwork.' *Comparative Labour Law and Policy Journal*, 37, pp. 604–619.

Quart, A. (2019) 'The con of the side hustle.' *The New York Times*, 6 April. Available at: https://www.nytimes.com/2019/04/06/opinion/sunday/tax-day-side-hustle.html (accessed 10 May 2019).

RSDU (RideShare Drivers United) (2018) 'Strike Results – Fast 4 Uber Log-OFF, 5th September 2018.' Available at: http://ridesharedriversunited.com/strike-results-fast-4-uber-log-off-5th-september-2018/ (accessed 6 September 2018).

Scheiber, N. (2017) 'How Uber uses psychological tricks to push its drivers' buttons.' *The New York Times*, 2 April. Available at: https://nyti.ms/2nMmDtc (accessed 27 November 2018).

Stanford, J. (2017) 'The resurgence of gig work: Historical and theoretical perspectives.' *The Economic and Labour Relations Review*, 28, pp. 382–401.

Tassinari, A. and V. Maccarrone (2017) 'The mobilisation of gig economy couriers in Italy: Some lessons for the trade union movement.' *Transfer: European Review of Labour and Research*, 23, pp. 353–357.

Taylor, M., G. Marsh, D. Nicol and P. Broadbent (2017) *Good Work: The Taylor Review of Modern Working Practices*. London: Department for Business, Energy and Industrial Strategy.

Tully, S. and R. Winer (2014) 'The role of the beneficiary in willingness to pay for socially responsible products: A meta-analysis.' *Journal of Retailing*, 90, pp. 255–274.

van Doorn, N. (2017) 'Platform labor: On the gendered and racialized exploitation of low-income service work in the "on-demand" economy.' *Information, Communication & Society*, 20, pp. 898–914.

Wilkinson, A., M. Barry, R. Gomez and B. Kaufman (2018) 'Taking the pulse at work: An employment relations scorecard for Australia.' *Journal of Industrial Relations*, 60, pp. 145–175.

Wood, A., M. Graham, V. Lehdonvirta and I. Hjorth (2018) 'Good gig, bad gig: Autonomy and algorithmic control in the global gig economy.' *Work, Employment and Society*, Online First. Available at: https://doi.org/10.1177/0950017018785616 (accessed 27 November 2018).

Workplace Express (2018) 'ATO's Foodora report could be ticking bomb: Academic', 9 November. Available at: https://www.workplaceexpress.com.au/ (accessed 12 November 2018).

Wright, C. (2016) 'Leveraging reputational risk: Sustainable sourcing campaigns for improving labour standards in production networks.' *Journal of Business Ethics*, 137, pp. 195–210.

11. The growing disruptive impact of work automation: where should future research focus?

Victor Gekara and Darryn Snell

INTRODUCTION TO THE KEY DEBATES

This chapter examines the emerging technology of work automation and proposes various questions for research in the next few years. There is little doubt that new digital and automation technologies are expected to cause major industrial transformations and far-reaching disruptions to people's working lives. The nature and extent of impact has, however, been the subject of policy and academic debate for many years (Mokyr et al., 2015). Historically the debate has taken a form that Dunlop (2016) characterises as a mindless back and forth between technology sceptics and advocates, noting key celebrants of the benefits of workplace technological advancements, such as Autor (2013) and Brynjolfsson and McAfee (2014) on the one hand, and those who see more negative disruption, in the form of job loss and socio-economic disadvantage, than any positive change, such as Dunlop (2016) and Acemoglu and Robinson (2012), on the other.

The sceptics have often anchored their concerns on what they see as the increasing employment displacement capacity of new technologies. They observe that, unlike the situation in the 19th and 20th centuries, when Luddite and the Captain Swing riots were taking place, between 1811 and 1832, and the earlier 20th-century waves of advanced mechanisation across many sectors, including agriculture, manufacturing and transport (see Mokyr et al., 2015), 21st-century automation possesses highly transformative capacities with far-reaching implications for occupations, job roles and entire industries (Acemoglu and Robinson, 2012; Mokyr et al., 2015). They argue that earlier technologies were more complementary with labour and, whilst there was some employment displacement, an almost equivalent number emerged within existing and emerging sectors, which were readily accessible to displaced workers subject to minimal retraining and reskilling. Furthermore, technology did enhance workers' skills, leading to enhanced performance and productivity (Mokyr et al., 2015; Berg, 1980). In this regard, Mokyr et al. explain that,

> In the end, the fears of the Luddites that machinery would impoverish workers were not realized . . . the magnitude of technological unemployment and labour displacement turned out to be relatively small during this time period . . . (p. 36)

They further propose that there was an increase in workers' wages overall (Allen, 2005; Mokyr, 1988), although, as Voth (2004) explains, such increase brought with it 'longer hours of more intensive work, performed in more dangerous and unhealthy workplaces' (p. 33).

The fast rate and global scale of adoption and implementation of new workplace technologies in the 21st century, as well as the level of sophistication and capability of such technologies as Machine Learning, Artificial Intelligence and smart robotics (e.g. Ford, 2015; Rid, 2016) has, however, led to heightened levels of concern for not just the massive labour substitution being predicted in recent studies, but also increasing employment casualisation under the emerging gig economy, declining wages, growing workplace surveillance and monitoring, and increased work intensity and stress (Frey and Osborne, 2013; Arntz et al., 2016; Moore et al., 2018). Thus, although some have argued that nothing is new in the current debate (e.g. Autor, 2013), the discussion is no longer just about such issues as de-skilling the workforce (Braverman, 1974), or just about a few occupational areas of impact, i.e. the low skills, manual and repetitive jobs. Rather, what is observed is swift, large-scale and total transformation of occupations and jobs, with the effect that entire occupational skills are rendered redundant (Charles et al., 2013; Jaimovich and Siu, 2012; Edwards and Ramirez, 2016; Roos and Shroff, 2017; Smith, 2016). This observation informs Arntz et al.'s (2016, p. 9) strong conclusion that

> the technological capabilities to perform tasks that have until recently been considered genuinely human are increasing rapidly [and] since the current speed with which human labour becomes potentially obsolete is high and even increasing, attempts to upgrade skills and education may no longer suffice to win the 'Race Against the Machines' as titled by Brynjolfsson and McAfee (2014).

In addition, in response to the tech-enthusiasts and doubters of the socio-economic impacts who question the validity of earlier predictors of the destructive impact of technology on employment and jobs like Keynes (1930) and Leontief (1952), Acemoglu and Restrepo (2017, p. 1) explain that

> [t]hough these predictions did not come to pass in the decades that followed, there is renewed concern that with the striking advances in automation, robotics, and artificial intelligence, we are on the verge of seeing them realized.

The nature of the impact, however, needs to be examined at two levels: the national economy level and the individual level. At the national economy level there are growing concerns regarding the short-term impacts on employment, with fears of growing retrenchments and unemployment, leading to questions about employment transition for displaced workers. Long-term concerns, however, relate to the impacts on overall economic productivity and growth, with not just prolonged employment displacement but also falling consumer incomes. Concerns at the individual level relate to the effect on individual workers forced out of employment and their re-employment opportunities. These two levels of impact are intimately integrated and cannot be examined and understood in isolation. As suggested earlier, there is already evidence to show that technologies are displacing employment at a fast rate across different countries (Ford, 2015) and that in these countries there are growing policy concerns about how to ensure that these workers are successfully transitioned into gainful employment to minimise the socio-economic impact. Research is also predicting a future of growing job loss, a trend that is predicted for many countries, particularly but not restricted to advanced industrial economies of the OECD (Arntz et al., 2016; Manyika et al., 2017; Acemoglu and Restrepo, 2017). It is predicted that, by 2030, 60 percent of jobs globally will be lost to automation. In China as many as 118 million jobs will be lost, while India will lose 57 million. The US will lose 39 million, Japan 16 million, and Mexico and Germany 9 million each (see Manyika et al., 2017). This is just an illustrative selection of a mix of countries from developed and developing regions.

This introduction notwithstanding, we engage little with the question of whether technology is destroying more jobs than it creates. Instead, we concern ourselves more with the fate of workers being displaced by technology now and into the future. As research has focused more on the so-called future of work, little attention is paid to the presently unfolding situation. We suggest that research is required on several important questions to inform effective policy and practice on work and employment under emerging technologies. The remaining sections of the chapter will outline and discuss the key areas that should form the research agenda over the next five to ten years.

THE MOST AFFECTED AND THE MOST AT RISK FROM AUTOMATION TECHNOLOGIES

The impact of automation technologies, with regard to who is most at risk, is commonly studied from two perspectives: an occupational perspective and a geographical perspective (Centre for Progressive Policy, 2018; Munro, 2019). The literature dating back several decades seems to imply a foregone conclusion that the jobs most at risk of automation are those in low-skill occupations characterised by low-skill, dirty, physical, manual, repetitive tasks. Those at the higher cognitive level, involving a degree of evaluation and judgement, are considered less automatable (Frey and Osborne, 2013). This is certainly the view with earlier technologies, whose emergence and impact was described by Keynes (1930, p. 3) as 'a new disease . . . namely, technological unemployment', which would become more prominent with time. Leontief, a little later (1952), similarly predicted that more and more workers [would] be replaced by machines. This view of technology's impact on employment at the lower-end occupational levels seems to have persisted among the techno-enthusiasts even when growing evidence suggests that more and more jobs at the higher end of the occupational scale are being displaced as the technologies become more sophisticated and implemented in large scale and at an increasingly fast pace (Ford, 2015; Roos and Shroff, 2017; Manyika et al., 2017; Mokyr et al., 2015). The McKinsey study (Manyika et al., 2017), for example, shows that:

> The impact [of technology] will be felt not just by factory workers and clerks but also by landscape gardeners and dental lab technicians, fashion designers, insurance sales representatives, and even CEOs. (p. 2)

Like Acemoglu and Robinson (2012) the McKinsey study finds that, whether occupations are categorised as high risk or not, a large number of tasks and job roles within them are likely to be automated in the near future, suggesting that the scale of jobs at risk is much higher than commonly represented. Nevertheless, the notion of only, or predominantly, unskilled, semi-skilled workers doing physical, dirty, repetitive work being technologically displaced is often invoked by the techno-enthusiasts in an attempt to under-represent the impact of work automation (Jenkins and Sherman, 1979; Rifkin, 1995). However, the debate, in our view, misses the important point: it is not about where, on the occupational level, the jobs at risk are located. Rather, it is enough of a concern that jobs are being displaced, so that the important policy concern is how displaced workers can and should be assisted.

A geographical perspective may be applied at a national or international scope in order to examine how workers in different geographical locations are likely to be impacted by automation. Regional areas that commonly depend on traditional manufacturing, heavy industries and agriculture, for instance, are far more likely to suffer job loss due to rapid technological change in these industries. These also often tend to be localities characterised by socio-economic disadvantage and low educational attainment, which presents challenges for capturing new high-tech high-skill growth industries. Much of the research on geographical impacts has centred on advanced economies in North America and Europe with little consideration for what the implications are for emerging nations. Given the high concentration of labour-intensive industries in emerging economies, which are ripe for technological disruption, one would expect these economies to be unjustly burdened with technological-induced job loss. In this regard, Ford (2015) observes that China is the fastest automating economy, which supports Manyika et al.'s (2017) estimation that China will lose up to 118 million jobs to automation by 2030. The fact that India is also up there, with a predicted 57 million jobs on the line by 2030, suggests a serious emerging crisis for poorer economies.

This situation presents additional policy challenges insofar as many of the local authorities, and national governments, in these regions are often not well resourced to tackle the challenges of mass retrenchments through some of the proposed welfare approaches like guaranteed basic wage or labour market approaches such as reduced hours of work. They are also not well positioned, economically, to generate alternative employment. Whereas a lot of research work has been done on the occupational aspect of this question, the geographical aspect is yet to be well researched and articulated. Trends and patterns of geographical technological disruption need to be studied and understood to enable the provision of effective policies for sustainable employment.

STRATEGIES FOR ASSISTING TECHNOLOGICALLY DISPLACED WORKERS

How best to assist employees, when displaced by technological change, is emerging as a new and significant policy concern for many countries. Job loss is often considered a negative 'life transition' development (McKee-Ryan and Kinicki, 2002), and the financial hardship (loss of wages and benefits) and psychological distress (loss of self-esteem, self-regard and dignity, and powerlessness) experienced by workers, following company closures or major industrial restructuring, is well documented (Ross and Mirowsky, 2013; Burgard et al., 2007). The impact of retrenchment, however, does not stop with displaced workers but impacts on spouses, family members and, often, entire communities and local economies (Westman et al., 2004). The nature and extent of the impact of technological unemployment is yet to be fully understood.

Given this situation, years of research into job loss through structural adjustment, downsizing, outsourcing and factory closures provides important insights with regards to the challenges that technologically displaced workers are likely to confront. It also provides insight into the kinds of policy responses that might be needed to assist these workers in finding alternative employment. Research on displaced workers has identified a range of barriers that make finding alternative employment difficult, including declining demand for the types of skills they possess, limited credentials, incomplete understanding of the diversity of their skills and their relationship to jobs in the local labour market, narrow access to the social networks operating within labour markets, and inadequate job-seeking skills and experiences, as well as age discrimination (see Callan and Bowman, 2015; Beer and Evans, 2009; Blyton and Jenkins, 2012; Snell et al., 2016).

A broad range of academic and policy-oriented research has concluded that, for retrenched workers to overcome these individual barriers, they need retraining and labour market assistance (see OECD, 2013; OECD, 2012; Callan and Bowman, 2015; Brenner et al., 2007). Government-supported 'worker in transition' assistance and structural adjustment programmes are now mainstream policy responses to retrenchment scenarios across a range of OECD countries (see OECD, 2015). Unlike previous periods, however, where government departments and agencies performed the principal role in assisting disadvantaged and unemployed workers to find employment, neo-liberal policy approaches, embraced by governments in recent decades, have transformed the way assistance is delivered and redefined the composition and role of the key labour market intermediaries (see Autor, 2009). Some research suggests this is resulting in practices that may not be delivering the most desirable outcomes. Australian research conducted by Agllias et al. (2016), for example, found that employees of privatised job service agencies were committed to providing 'formulaic, routinized, "simple solutions"' (p. 304) to job-seekers, which were consistent with their organisational interests but not necessarily in the best interest of job-seekers.

Increasingly governments are overlooking not-for-profit labour market intermediaries or those that have performed this role in the past, such as trade unions, which are often more familiar with local labour markets and employer networks important to connecting the unemployed to work, in favour of corporate recruitment and workforce management firms such as Manpower or Hays (see Brenner et al., 2007). Many of these organisations operate according to private sector management models but are dependent on government funding to deliver 'worker in transition' services with the primary mission of supporting disadvantaged workers. However, little is known about how this government-financed and market-led employment assistance industry conducts its operations and delivers services to clients. How its performance against government objectives is measured is not clear, leading to important questions about the quality of its services and the outcomes. Given this situation there is an increased need to better understand the role, approaches and effectiveness of third-party organisations in delivering government intervention programmes aimed at assisting displaced workers and their families.

Retraining is by far the most common policy response to assisting displaced workers. As noted by Goldstein (2017), 'even among people who disagree over almost everything else about the economy, the common wisdom is that workers who lose a job, without much likelihood of finding another in the same field, should go back to school to retrain for a different one' (p. 311). This 'common wisdom' is also prolific in academic as well as policy-oriented literature on how workers can best respond to the negative impacts of technological disruption (see Centre for Progressive Policy, 2018; Menkhoff and Yue, 2008; Munro, 2019). Technologically displaced workers are often told that retraining will provide them with 'opportunities to move into jobs with higher functions and better salaries' (Oxford Economics and CISCO, 2018, p. 26). Evidence, however, suggests that, even when displaced workers undertake retraining, they are not always successful.

In Goldstein's study (2017) of autoworkers displaced in Janesville, Wisconsin following the closure of the General Motors factory, it was found that laid-off workers who undertook retraining were less likely to have a job than those who had not retrained. In 2006, the UK Government conducted an audit of the re-employment of retrenched workers, following the closure of the MG Rover factory in the West Midlands. The audit found mixed outcomes from retraining and ultimately concluded that training was not always what most benefited workers (UK National Audit Office, 2006). Other studies have demonstrated that displaced workers, even after retraining, often struggle to find stable full-time employment and are often working for lower pay and in worse conditions (see Beer and Evans, 2009; Blyton and Jenkins, 2012; Bailey et al., 2008; Leana and Feldman, 1995; Rocha, 2001).

What digital disruption certainly tells us is that digital skills development is a priority for all workers in many countries confronting a current or future digital skills shortages. Emerging economies confront the most significant digital skills challenges. According to research conducted by Oxford Economies and CISCO (2018), 6.6 million Southeast Asian workers will be made redundant because of AI by 2028 with 41 percent of these workers 'acutely lacking' necessary IT skills. The experience and treatment of displaced older workers is of particular concern. It is generally acknowledged that older workers confront significant challenges when competing in the labour market and there is the additional danger that these workers may be perceived as less digitally literate, contributing to further discrimination and marginalisation. A better understanding of the changing nature of skills requirement, with workplace technology change and being able to predict the nature of industrial change, will help design policy for more effective training programmes taking into consideration socio-demographic and occupational perspectives (see Gekara et al., 2019; European Commission, 2011).

Some countries are responding to these concerns with improved policies (see OECD, 2019). The Singapore Government, for example, is offering funding to all its citizens aged 25 years and older, consisting of $400 financial support for training to ensure mid-career and older workers have the skills they need to thrive in a competitive labour market, under the SkillsFuture Singapore Program (see Osman-Gari and Jacobs, 2005). Australia has also recently introduced similar financial support for workers between the ages of 15 and 44 to acquire the skills needed for employment in the digital economy, under the Delivering Skills for Today and Tomorrow Package in the 2019/20 budget (Australian Government, 2019). Nevertheless, across many countries public funding for skills development and job training programmes is falling. As noted by Manyika et al. (2017),

> between 1993 and 2015, spending on workforce training programs, as a percentage of GDP, fell from 0.08 percent to 0.03 percent in the United States, while Japanese spending dropped from 0.03 percent to 0.01 percent. In Germany— still one of the larger spenders—outlays for training fell from 0.57 percent of GDP to 0.2 percent. (p. 107)

This trend will need to be reversed if countries are truly serious about addressing digital skills shortages and better preparing workers for the real prospect that they may lose their jobs due to technological disruption. Yet, without a clear research-driven understanding of the developments, technology trends, and work and employment impact patterns, any new policy changes are tantamount to shots in the dark.

RESPONSIBILITY FOR ACTION

The question of who, between the state and employers, is responsible for assisting workers to prepare for, and survive, the impact of changing technologies of work is an important one. In this regard, there are two forms of response to be considered. One relates to equipping workers, and the general population, with appropriate training and skills for jobs in the emerging economy, while the other relates to impact response, i.e. assisting victims of technological displacement to find work and continue productive and gainful employment. Ultimately, however, it boils down to a question of investment in education and training, and in employment transition programmes for displaced workers.

Basic logic would suggest that, if businesses are introducing advanced labour-saving technologies that displace large numbers of workers in an economy, they should also take the responsibility for assisting affected workers to find new employment. Employers, and the pro-technology policy and academic commentators, however, argue that technologies are creating new jobs so that, in the end, it is a win–win outcome for employers, workers and the economy (Autor, 2015; Brynjolfsson and McAfee, 2014). Others, however, argue that the number of new jobs created is often far less than the disappeared, and that these new jobs are rarely created at the same location and accessible to the same workers (Dunlop, 2016). They explain that most of the displaced workers have little opportunity to acquire these new jobs, raising the critical questions of where and to whom these new jobs are available, and what happens to the displaced (Acemoglu and Robinson, 2012; Dunlop, 2016). Furthermore, 'user pays' logic would mean that if, in the emerging highly automated and digitalised world of work, employers rely on a highly digitally skilled workforce, they must bear the greater responsibility to adequately resource appropriate training and education programmes.

Surprisingly, however, the role and responsibility of business in managing the introduction of technologies and its impacts on workers is not widely debated despite business being the leaders in the development, and implementation, of these technologies. Research is needed, for example, on the intersections between corporate social responsibility (CSR) and how technological innovation and change is handled by firms. Should technological change, for example, which has such significant impact on working lives, be included in CSR obligations? Why do some corporations appear to be more supportive than others in assisting their workforce to adjust to technological change?

While corporate decisions to introduce technological innovations are typically made on the basis of a 'business case', there is often great diversity in how firms manage technological change, assist employees to develop new digital competencies and assist those detrimentally impacted. At face value, these divergent corporate behaviours force us to question approaches that treat firms as a 'black box' that is 'conceptualised as a profit-maximising entity which reacts to external pressures and structural constraints' (Brown et al., 2010, p. 25). The influence of CSR on business ethics and practices is often invoked to explain why some firms would approach restructuring in a more socially responsible manner (Cascio and Wynn, 2004; Edwards and Wajcman, 2005; Freeman, 2009; Forde et al., 2009). Technological innovation and adoption by firms, which has significant impacts on working lives, would certainly align with these social responsibility concerns.

In these contexts, therefore, the disruption brought on by a firm's technological innovation is potentially subject to CSR that is often legislated by the state or negotiated between firms, employees and unions, and the state. In liberal market economies, however, where CSR is treated as something firms do beyond legal responsibilities, technologically impacted and disadvantaged workers will have to rely much more extensively on a firm's voluntary commitment to managing technological change in a socially responsible manner. In countries like the UK, US and Australia, for example, businesses are likely to expect government and individuals to bear the responsibility for acquiring new skills as well as finding new work post retrenchment. Notwithstanding, responsibility so far has largely remained with government to develop and resource initiatives for appropriate educational programmes, including science, technology, engineering, maths (STEM) education, as well as funding employment transition programmes for the displaced. Appropriate allocation of responsibility is perhaps best summed up in the Oxford Economics/CISCO (2018) report: 'governments, businesses, institutions, and individuals will need to work together to smooth the transition to these new, digitally-led economies and labour forces' (p. 42).

The need for, and the drive in, such collaborative working is only possible through extensive studies synthesising different policies, practices and approaches, for managing new technology implementation, in different economies around the world. Such analysis is required to establish workable and best-practice frameworks for different economies, since the wide diversity of geo-economic circumstances negates the notion of a one-size-fits-all approach.

CONCLUDING STATEMENT

As new technologies increasingly enter the workplace, increase in the scale of adoption and implementation, and advance in their capability and sophistication, their nature and potential impact is becoming much clearer. A lot of research, in the past few decades, has focused on trying to understand not only the technologies themselves, but also their impact. In addition to showing the potential to displace large numbers of workers, research has revealed increasing work pressure and stress, resulting from work intensification, as fewer workers are expected to perform more work in a shorter time, as well as increasing surveillance, monitoring and micro-control by employers.

What is less understood, as research and the policy and academic debate focuses more on the nature of technology and its potential impact, is how technology adoption and the impacts can, and should, be managed and by whom. The central focus of this chapter has been a call for more research and greater debate on some of the key questions relating to impact management. The discussion shows that future research is required focusing on three broad questions. First, who is most affected and/or most at risk in the unfolding workplace technological change? More empirically driven understanding is required on the occupational progression of job destruction, the speed of this progression and locations where the impact is likely to be most felt. For a long time, industry mantra has been that only jobs at the lower-skill end will disappear, leaving room for new, cleaner and well-paid jobs. How true does this still hold, with the increasing sophistication of technologies? In this regard, further research, which builds on Frey and Osborne (2013), is essential to revisit the question of which jobs are susceptible to automation. This will inform policy and practice on preparing workers for new jobs, new workplaces, and a new way of thinking about work and employment.

The second broad question relates to how those affected can be assisted and what systems of mitigation can be introduced to protect workers from the impacts experienced and envisaged. What approaches are being implemented in different countries and to what effect? Ultimately, such research is required to develop a comprehensive framework for (1) enhancing our understanding of the nature of technology's impact on work and jobs in different settings, (2) developing frameworks to assist industry training stakeholders in designing better skills programmes for workers in the emerging world of work, and (3) helping workers better appreciate their skills and their transferability potential.

The third question relates to who is, and should be, responsible for the above tasks. As in most areas of national socio-economic management, there is strong contention regarding allocation of responsibility for adverse impacts of economic transition. A review of the literature reveals different approaches in different countries to managing the unfolding situation, but there are very few conclusions on the success or failure of those measures. Consolidating this literature and identifying best practice should be an important part of the research agenda for the next decade, as different economies try to come to terms with the changes and the implications as well as examining policy needs. Due to the speed and complexity of the developments, governments require clear, empirically driven guidance on effective policies to manage technological change and associated economic transition. Similarly, industry requires informed strategies to effectively manage technological change while maintaining an appropriately skilled, engaged and motivated workforce.

REFERENCES

Acemoglu, D. and P. Restrepo (2017) *Robots and Jobs: Evidence from US Labor Markets*. National Bureau of Economic Research Working Paper 23285.

Acemoglu, D. and J.A. Robinson (2012) *Why Nations Fail: The Origins of Power, Prosperity, and Poverty*. New York, NY: Crown Publishing.

Agllias, K., A. Howard, L. Schubert and M. Gray (2016) 'Australian workers' narratives about emergency relief and employment services clients: complex issues, simple solutions', *Australian Social Work*, 69(3), pp. 297–310.

Allen, R.C. (2005) 'Capital accumulation, technological change, and the distribution of income during the British Industrial Revolution', Department of Economics Discussion Paper 239, Oxford University.

Arntz, M., T. Gregory and U. Zierahn (2016) 'The risk of automation for jobs in OECD countries: a comparative analysis', OECD Social, Employment and Migration Working Papers, No. 189, OECD Publishing, Paris. At http://dx.doi.org/10.1787/5jlz9h56dvq7-en [accessed 25/03/19].

Australian Government (2019) *Skills and Training Budget Overview 2019–20*, Department for Education and Training. At https://www.education.gov.au/skills-and-training-budget-overview-2019-20 [accessed 08/10/19].

Autor, D.H. (2015) 'Why are there still so many jobs? The history and future of workplace automation', *Journal of Economic Perspectives*, 29(3), pp. 3–30.

Autor, D.H. (2013) 'The "task approach" to labor markets: an overview', *Journal of Labour Market Research*, 46(3), pp. 185–199.

Autor, D.H. (2009) *Studies of Labor Market Intermediation*. Chicago, IL: University of Chicago Press.

Bailey, D., C. Chapain, M. Mahdon and R. Fauth (2008) *Life after Longbridge: Three Years On. Pathways to Re-employment in a Restructuring Economy*. London: The Work Foundation.

Beer, A. and H. Evans (2009) *The Impacts of Automobile Plant Closures*. London: Routledge.

Berg, M. (1980) *The Machinery Question and the Making of Political Economy, 1815–1848*. Cambridge: Cambridge University Press.

Blyton, P. and J. Jenkins (2012) 'Life after Burberry: shifting experiences of work and non-work life following redundancy', *Work, Employment and Society*, 26(1), pp. 26–41.

Braverman, H. (1974) *Labor and Monopoly Capital: The Degradation of Work in the Twentieth Century*. New York, NY: Monthly Review Press.

Brenner, C., L. Leete and M. Pastor (2007) *Staircases or Treadmills? Labor Market Intermediaries and Economic Opportunities in a Changing Economy*. New York, NY: Russell Sage Foundation.

Brown, D., A. Vetterlein and A. Roemer-Mahler (2010) 'Theorizing transnational corporations as social actors: an analysis of corporate motivations', *Business and Politics*, 12(1), pp. 1–37.

Brynjolfsson, E. and A. McAfee (2014) *The Second Machine Age: Work, Progress, and Prosperity in a Time of Brilliant Technologies*. London: W. W. Norton & Company.

Burgard, S., J. Brand and J. House (2007) 'Towards a better estimation of the effect of job loss on health', *Journal of Health and Social Behaviour*, 48, pp. 369–384.

Callan, V.J. and K. Bowman (2015) *Industry Restructuring and Job Loss: Helping Older Workers Get Back into Employment*. Adelaide: NCVER.

Cascio, W.F. and P. Wynn (2004) 'Managing a downsizing process', *Human Resource Management*, 43(4), pp. 425–436.

Centre for Progressive Policy (2018) *Skills for Inclusive Growth*. London: Centre for Progressive Policy.

Charles, K.K., E. Hurst and M.J. Notowidigdo (2013) *Manufacturing Decline, Housing Booms, and Non-employment*. Technical report, NBER Working Paper No. 18949, National Bureau of Economic Research.

Dunlop, T. (2016) *Why the Future is Workless*. Sydney: NewSouth Publishing.

Edwards, P. and P. Ramirez (2016) 'When should workers embrace or resist new technology?', *New Technology, Work and Employment*, 31(2), pp. 99–113.

Edwards, P. and J. Wajcman (2005) *The Politics of Working Life*. Oxford: Oxford University Press.

European Commission (2011) *Transferability of Skills across Economic Sectors*. Brussels: European Commission, European Union Programme for Employment and Social Solidarity Progress (2007–2013).

Ford, M. (2015) *The Rise of the Robots: Technology and the Threat of Mass Unemployment*. London: Oneworld Publications.

Forde, C., M. Stuart, J. Gardiner, I. Greenwood and R. Mackenzie (2009) 'Socially responsible restructuring in an era of mass redundancy', Working Paper 5. Centre for Employment Relations Innovation and Change, Leeds University Business School.

Freeman, K.W. (2009) 'The right way to close an operation', *Harvard Business Review*, 87(5), pp. 45–51.

Frey, C.B. and M.A. Osborne (2013) *The Future of Employment: How Susceptible are Jobs to Computerization?*, University of Oxford. At https://www.oxfordmartin.ox.ac.uk/downloads/academic/The_Future_of_Employment.pdf [accessed 25/03/19].

Gekara, V., D. Snell, A. Molla, S. Karanasios and A. Thomas (2019) *Skilling the Australian Workforce for the Digital Economy*. Adelaide: NCVER.

Goldstein, A. (2017) *Janesville: An American Story*. New York, NY: Simon and Schuster.

Jaimovich, N. and H.E. Siu (2012) 'The trend is the cycle: job polarization and jobless recoveries', National Bureau of Economic Research. At https://www.nber.org/papers/w18334 [accessed 25/03/19].

Jenkins, C. and B. Sherman (1979) *The Collapse of Work*. London: Methuen.

Keynes, John Maynard (1930) 'Economic possibilities for our grandchildren', in *Essays in Persuasion*, pp. 321–332. London: Macmillan.

Leana, C. and D. Feldman (1995) 'Finding new jobs after a plant closing: antecedents and outcomes of the occurrence and quality of reemployment', *Human Relations*, 48(12), pp. 1381–1401.

Leontief, Wassily (1952) 'Machines and man', *Scientific American*, pp. 150–164.

Manyika, J., M. Chui, A. Madgavkar and S. Lund (2017) 'Technology, jobs, and the future of work', McKinsey Global Institute. At https://www.mckinsey.com/

featured-insights/employment-and-growth/technology-jobs-and-the-future-of-work [accessed 08/10/19].

McKee-Ryan, F. and A. Kinicki (2002) 'Coping with job loss: a life-facet perspective', *Industrial and Organisational Psychology*, 17, pp. 1–30.

Menkhoff, T. and W. Yue (2008) 'Technological change management strategies in Asian small-scale businesses: trends in Singapore', *Internationales Asien Forum. International Quarterly for Asian Studies*, 39(3–4), pp. 305–324.

Mokyr, J. (1988) 'Is there still life in the pessimistic case? Consumption during the Industrial Revolution, 1790–1850', *Journal of Economic History*, 48(1), pp. 69–92.

Mokyr, J., C. Vickers and N.L. Ziebarth (2015) 'The history of technological anxiety and the future of economic growth: is this time different?', *Journal of Economic Perspectives*, 29(3), pp. 31–50.

Moore, P.V., M. Upchurch and X. Whittaker (2018) *Humans and Machines at Work: Monitoring, Surveillance and Automation in Contemporary Capitalism.* Cham: Springer.

Munro, M. (2019) *Countering the Geographical Impacts of Automation: Computers, AI, and Place Disparities.* Washington, DC: Brookings Institution.

OECD (2019) *Adult Learning in Italy: What Role for Training Funds?* Paris: OECD Publishing.

OECD (2015) *Back to Work. Sweden: Improving the Re-employment Prospects of Displaced Workers.* Paris: OECD Publishing.

OECD (2013) *Activating Jobseekers: Lessons from Seven OECD Countries.* Paris: OECD Publishing.

OECD (2012) *Activating Jobseekers: How Australia Does It.* Paris: OECD Publishing.

Osman-Gani, A. and R. Jacobs (2005) 'Technological change and human resource development practices in Asia: a study of Singapore-based companies', *International Journal of Training and Development*, 9(4), pp. 271–280.

Oxford Economics and CISCO (2018) *The Impact of AI on Workers in ASEAN's Six Largest Economies. Technology and the Future of ASEAN Jobs.* At https://www.oxfordeconomics.com/recent-releases/dd577680-7297-4677-aa8f-450da197e132 [accessed 09/10/19].

Rid, T. (2016) *Rise of the Machines: The Lost History of Cybernetics.* Brunswick, Australia: Scribe Publications.

Rifkin, J. (1995) *The End of Work: The Decline of the Global Labor Force and the Dawn of the Post-market Era.* New York: ERIC.

Rocha, C. (2001) 'From plant closure to reemployment in the new economy: risks to workers dislocated from the declining garment manufacturing industry', *Journal of Sociology and Social Work*, 28(2), pp. 53–74.

Roos, G. and Z. Shroff (2017) 'What will happen to the jobs? Technology-enabled productivity improvement – good for some, bad for others', *Labour & Industry*, 27(3), pp. 165–192.

Ross, C. and J. Mirowsky (2013) 'The sense of personal control: social structural causes and emotional consequences', in C.S. Aneshensel, J.C. Phelan and A. Bierman (eds), *Handbook of the Sociology of Mental Health, 2nd edition.* Dordrecht: Springer Science+Business Media, pp. 379–402.

Smith, A. (2016) 'Public predictions for the future of workforce automation', *Pew Research Centre*. At http://www.pewinternet.org/2016/03/10/public-predictions-for-the-future-of-workforce-automation/ [accessed 08/10/2019].

Snell, D., V. Gekara and K. Gatt (2016) *Cross-occupational Skill Transferability: Challenges and Opportunities in a Changing Economy*. Adelaide: NCVER.

UK National Audit Office (2006) *The Closure of MG Rover*. London: National Audit Office.

Voth, Hans-Joachim (2004) 'Living standards and the urban environment', in Roderick Floud and Paul Johnson (eds), *The Cambridge Economic History of Modern Britain: Volume I*. Cambridge: Cambridge University Press. At https://www.cambridge.org/core/books/cambridge-economic-history-of-modern-britain/living-standards-and-the-urban-environment/B6115E693C9FB1DEC10D4111008D9DFB [accessed 05/03/19].

Westman, M., D. Etzion and S. Horovitz (2004) 'The toll of unemployment does not stop with the unemployed', *Human Relations*, 57(7), pp. 823–844.

12. Governing Global Production Networks in the new economy

Huw Thomas

1. INTRODUCTION

In recent years, the employment relations implications of Global Production Networks (GPNs)[1] have hit the headlines. Children are found to be stitching our clothes, the shrimp sold by supermarkets is peeled by forced labourers, modern day slavery is associated with our favourite sporting events and numerous tragedies have occurred, causing appalling loss of life. Whether this is the fall of the Rana Plaza factory in 2013, killing over 1,100 workers, or when commercial pressure from Apple for short lead times at Foxconn led to the attempted suicides of 18 workers in 2010, these disasters signal that our understanding of production networks is essential for researching the future of work.

GPNs, which now account for 80 per cent of world trade (UNCTAD 2013), pose a significant challenge but also an opportunity for the promotion and protection of decent work (ILO 2016). With over 450 million workers employed in these networks (ILO 2015, p. 132), GPNs have obvious implications for employment relations research. There has been a long tradition of international employment relations research into the effects of globalisation and, more recently, a greater focus on the inter-connectedness of actors and inter-firm structural relations coordinated globally by (primarily Northern) lead firms. However, most theories of employment relations are based at the level of the firm and within specific national institutional contexts (Reinecke et al. 2018). Short shrift has been paid to the interaction between the multi-scalar activities of (transnational) capital and the governance mechanisms promoted by a whole range of strategic actors, with a much greater focus on the agency of labour in determining their conditions of work in these networks.

The purpose of this chapter is to evaluate current forms of global labour governance in the new economy and its implications for the objectives of the employment relationship: efficiency, equity and voice (Budd 2004). The focus is then shifted to reflect on some current exciting areas of research and forward into areas that are critical to continue to push the investigation of GPNs forward. The argument is that it is high time for employment relations scholars to take GPNs seriously as a theoretical tool with the recognition that workers are not at the mercy of structural inter-firm economic relationships and some have the agency to improve their relative position in the network. The subsequent focus on contestation, multi-scalarity and voice serve as potentially useful areas to help inform practice and policy.

Today, much of the discussion around the future of work and GPNs has been dominated by the assumption that technological change will have a significant impact on the international division of labour and result in 'reshoring' and the displacement of workers in these networks (ILO 2018, p. 2). However, these contemporary accounts stake a claim to a singular future of work where workers are inert to change that may (or may not) arrive. Technology for example can make it easier for workers to monitor working conditions and labour law compliance in GPNs and can facilitate cross-border solidarity that can galvanise the support of complementary institutions and civil society. In other words, as I and others have argued elsewhere,[2] focussing on only one future of work, in which workers are no more than victims to inter-firm relationships and the restructuring processes of transnational capital, obscures the work that needs to be done in understanding how labour can shape and resist these changes through experimental forms of organisation, regulation and governance. This is an area that employment relations scholars, informed by GPN theory, have a lot to offer.

2.   FROM HORIZONTAL TO VERTICAL GOVERNANCE

GPNs, 'an organizational arrangement comprising interconnected economic and noneconomic actors coordinated by a global lead firm and producing goods or services across multiple geographic locations for worldwide markets' (Yeung and Coe 2015, p. 32), influence the structure of labour markets across the world and have led to significant changes in the international division of labour (Rainnie et al. 2011). The rise of GPNs has been associated with the rapid expansion of outsourcing by lead firms in the global North to suppliers in the developing South. Driven by intensive cost competition, many have argued that a 'race-to-the-bottom' in labour standards has started (Donaghey et al. 2014). Given what is happening in the world of work it is not surprising that many have concluded that the traditional (horizontal) system of national labour regulation, such as labour laws and collective bargaining, is under strain in the globalised economy (Lakhani et al. 2013; Meardi and Marginson 2014). In the absence of a 'hard' system of global social justice, the declining power of organised labour and given the capacity or (un)willingness of national governments to enforce labour standards (Levi et al. 2013), a global labour governance 'regime' that prioritises soft-law over hard-law combined with a shift from the (horizontal) nation state to the (vertical) production network has emerged (Thomas and Turnbull 2018).

Historically, the ILO played a central role in setting the 'rules of the game' for (inter)national labour governance. According to Polanyi (1944, pp. 27–8), the ILO was set up 'to equalize conditions of competition among the nations so that trade might be liberated without danger to standards of living'. ILO Conventions and Recommendations provided a 'social floor' for national labour markets in Western Europe and North America under the Keynesian social democratic model. However, the ratification of many ILO Conventions is disappointingly low, and recent Conventions designed to reflect the changing world of work have seen very limited uptake and even less impact for the workers or industrial sectors concerned (Thomas and Turnbull 2018). Under the voluntarist framework for implementing ILO labour standards, governments are 'at liberty' to ratify Conventions they agree with, ignore those they do not care for, and de-ratify those they dislike, limiting the ILO's standard-setting role and impairing its supervisory mechanisms (Standing 2008, p. 356). Whilst the ILO maintains that public horizontal governance is the foundation of workplace compliance in GPNs and that 'national legislation is a prerequisite for decent work' (ILO 2016, p. 39), 'the simple fact that violations remain so widespread, and compliance with the ILO's core labour standards so uneven, suggests that costs of protection and benefits of violation often dominate' (Levi et al. 2013, p. 12).

Persistent labour rights violations by Transnational Corporations (TNCs) have been represented as products of a 'governance gap' whereby the capacity of national governments to steer and constrain transnational business activity has diminished and the (vertical) power and capabilities of TNCs has expanded. Of particular importance is the 'spatial–juridical fix' of global capital (Rainnie et al. 2011) and the exploitation of 'spaces of exception', in which certain workers are stripped of their decency and the normal rule of law does not apply (Lillie 2010). By moving spatially, capital is able to 'dis-embed' itself from particular national (horizontal) regulations and established class compromises. As a result, whilst even the most 'flighty' of capital must 'come to ground' at some point and 're-embed' itself in a particular place (Herod et al. 2007, p. 253), production systems and social relations will be reconfigured in the process, enhancing the control of capital over labour. In effect, 'capital removes specific work spaces, contexts and categories of people from the protection they would normally enjoy within sovereign states' (Lillie 2010, p. 688). Export processing zones (EPZs), conservatively estimated to employ at least 66 million workers worldwide (ILO 2014, p. 4), are the most blatant example of a spatial–juridical fix in which territorial sovereignty is 'little more than a convenient fiction' (Lillie 2010, p. 683). Such 'spaces of exception' now extend well beyond EPZs and certainly reach into the lower echelons of GPNs.

Whilst the tripartite (horizontal) actors were the traditional driving force of labour governance, nowadays 'new' (vertical) governance actors have emerged such as consumer groups, civil society organisations (CSOs) and (grudgingly) TNCs. Given the challenges that these regulatory gaps or 'spaces of exception' pose, much employment relations research on GPNs has focussed on the operation and attempted (re)regulation of these networks at the global scale (Meardi and Marginson 2014; Reinecke and Donaghey 2015; Riisgaard and Hammer 2011), and the various regulatory 'innovations' that have emerged to address these 'governance gaps' (Locke 2013; O'Rourke 2006). Recent studies have demonstrated that positive changes in conditions of work are realised when the interests of these 'new' and 'old' actors are aligned to improve labour standards (Berliner et al. 2015) and that private governance can best succeed when 'layered on' public governance (Locke 2013, p. 11). Indeed, a lot of intensive scholarship has focussed on the impact of the voluntary codes of conduct of TNCs on equity for workers (hours of work, wages etc.). Whilst more effective vertical private governance mechanisms incorporate the fundamental ILO Conventions and compliance with other forms of public governance, many are less specific and are weak in ensuring workers' voice, such as guaranteeing freedom of association and collective bargaining (Anner 2012). The overall conclusion is that these mechanisms are 'woefully inadequate' (Gereffi and Lee 2016, p. 29).

The critical role of consumers in mobilising pressure against TNCs to promote and protect decent work has also emerged as a particular area of interest (Donaghey et al. 2014; Riisgaard and Hammer 2011). These campaigns are most effective when they involve a broad coalition of actors (Berliner et al. 2015); however, workers are typically not involved in the establishment of multi-stakeholder mechanisms and may lack an opportunity to validate or comment on reports, or influence decision making processes (Egels-Zandén and Merk 2014). Thus, whilst these new social movements state their commitment to improved labour standards, they typically view workers as 'passive victims' that need to be helped by consumer campaigns (Tampe 2018). For example, Accenture (2013, p. 3) recommends 'interventions for key stakeholder groups, namely governments and corporations, to eliminate the [palm oil] industry's dependency on and exposure to slavery' but completely ignores the agency of labour. Rather the company appeals to those who are primarily responsible for the indecent work in the palm oil sector. Initiatives such as the Bangladesh Accord on Building and Fire Safety signed by two global union federations (GUFs) and over 200 multinationals, with the ILO as an independent chair, represents an innovate form of multi-stakeholder governance (Reinecke and Donaghey 2015); however, key actors such as the Bangladeshi government and smaller sub-contractors are not included in its governance arrangements, limiting its effectiveness.

Ultimately, much GPN employment is insecure and unprotected, falling well short of the objectives of the employment relationship (Budd 2004, p. 2). Whilst GPNs can create and bring organisational efficiency, they systematically fail to guarantee labour rights (Gereffi and Lee 2016). Figure 12.1 summarises the extent to which several mechanisms for global governance fulfil the objectives of voice, equity and efficiency. Free trade, as promoted through international finance institutions, emphasises efficiency above equity and voice (bottom-left corner of Figure 12.1). In a similar vein, the establishment of GPNs is also founded on the desire of TNCs to maximise efficiency and reduce costs. Corporate codes of conduct and Fairtrade certification maintain a balance between efficiency (through higher productivity from suppliers) and equity (through provisions on

Source: Adapted from Budd (2004, p. 6).

Figure 12.1   Objectives of the employment relationship and global governance

child labour, for example, although they typically exclude freedom of association). International institutions for providing employee voice include European Works Councils as well as transnational union activity through the establishment of International Framework Agreements (IFAs) (top of Figure 12.1). International labour standards established by the ILO typically combine an equity (restrictions on child and forced labour) and voice (tripartite consultation) mechanism rather than promote the demand for organisational efficiency. However, in the new economy, efficiency is strong, and equity and voice are weak, and this represents a major challenge for workers in GPNs. What is therefore needed is vertical regulation along these production networks (vertical public governance), providing tripartite (horizontal) actors at the national level with greater leverage to protect and promote decent work (Thomas and Turnbull 2018).

3. WORKERS IN CHAINS?

Since the early 1990s an extensive literature has evolved to help explain how the world economy is organised and governed and how relationships between actors have impacted the development and upgrading opportunities of regions, nation states, firms and (most importantly) labour. From a multi-disciplinary field of enquiry, two key theories have emerged, namely Global Value Chains (GVCs) and Global Production Networks (GPNs). Both have the same purpose, which is to provide researchers with the analytical tools to connect a multitude of actors even though they are geographically dispersed. Of importance here is the ability to understand how these chains/networks affect employment relations and *vice versa*.

The (early) GVC/GPN literature had very little to say about employment relations or labour as an 'active participant' of the global economy as opposed to a 'passive victim' of restructuring processes (Cumbers et al. 2008, p. 369). With relationships between firms at centre stage, 'labour [was] largely written out of the script' (Cumbers et al. 2008, p. 370). If labour did appear in the script, it was more often as a commodity (a cost to be controlled and flexibly deployed) rather than human beings with rights and entitlements. Indeed, theoretical approaches to employment relations and GVCs have often viewed workers as a 'static' category (Lakhani et al. 2013) with (private and inter-firm) governance relationships as a key determinant (Gereffi and Lee 2016). In other words, they paint a picture of a future of work rooted in soft norms, encouraging 'self-regulation' rather than hard law that demands compliance, where decent work for those workers engaged in GPNs is irreconcilable with corporate self-interest. However, this leaves little room for the consideration of alternatives. Whilst GVC theory offered important insights into the coordination of firms across national boundaries, it neglects institutional influences and labour agency. An understanding of GPNs, in contrast, embraces not only interaction between lead firms and suppliers, but also the extended range of (strategic) actors who contribute to influencing and shaping global production (e.g. national governments, multi-lateral organisations, national and international trade unions, and CSOs) (Barrientos et al. 2011, p. 321). The three main conceptual elements that 'drive' GPN research are value (to estimate where value is captured), power (how power is used in capturing this value) and embeddedness (the degree to which the network is territorially and consequently, socially and institutionally embedded) (Henderson et al. 2002). Within GPNs, the focus is on 'the way that different social actors interact in the process of value creation and capture and how this shapes geographical outcomes' (Cumbers et al. 2008, p. 371). Thus, the characteristics of 'GPN trade' – as 'trade in tasks' rather than simply 'trade in goods' – captures a multitude of relationships and actors (Nathan 2013).

Labour action has an important effect upon territorial decisions within and between countries, thus determining in part the geography of activities within a network (Coe and Jordhus-Lier 2011). Much has been written on the impact of globalisation on organised labour's ability to represent and bargain for its members. Whilst the practices of TNCs have put downward pressure on labour standards, there are also examples of new forms of governance to promote workers' rights, and of worker organisation. As Tilly (1995, p. 5) points out: 'if workers are to enjoy collective rights in the new world order, they will have to invent new strategies at the scale of international capital'. The response of trade unions to the proliferation of GPNs is best captured by the number (albeit small) of IFAs that have been signed in recent years with limited success (Niforou 2014) and national and global unions have played a key role in international forums tasked with dealing with the impact of production networks on the promotion and protection of decent work (Donaghey and Reinecke 2018; Thomas and Turnbull 2018). Whilst the potential of workers to exercise agency is uneven across GPNs (Coe and Hess 2013), these networks offer opportunities for workers to realise conditions of work (Rainnie et al. 2011). As Padmanabhan (2012, p. 988) demonstrates, 'organizing locally can, in fact, be an effective strategy for use in case of confrontation with social actors who are organized at the global and other extra-local scales'. Riisgaard and Hammer (2011) demonstrate that the scale of labour action and engagement by trade unions in 'power analyses' can identify the most effective location and method of strategic action, whilst Selwyn (2008) illustrates how just-in-time production used by TNCs is vulnerable to workers disrupting the production network by targeting specific 'choke points'. The importance of the GPN approach is the recognition that both labour agency and the impact of GPNs on labour is 'heavily shaped by local institutional and regulatory conditions, and so will vary considerably between regional economies: place matters, to a powerful degree, when it comes to labour' (Coe and Yeung 2015, p. 192).

Structural approaches analyse employment relations as the result of configurations between buyers and suppliers and argue that labour stand-ards are more likely to be followed when 'lead firms have more control and leverage over suppliers' (Lakhani et al. 2013, p. 462; see also Riisgaard and Hammer 2011). This however presupposes an inevitability of governance relationships based on commercial dynamics, with the focus on the lead firm as the ultimate source of value creation, which overlooks a whole host of other (non-commercial) strategic actors that can create and distribute value. Whilst the two leading conceptual frameworks in GVC research have been used effectively in employment relations research – Gereffi's (1994) producer/ buyer driven chains and Gereffi et al.'s (2005) fivefold inter-firm governance typology – these theoretical tools often suffer from a lack of explanatory power due to their static conception of governance and their neglect of territorial (horizontal) effects. As Lakhani et al. (2013, p. 466) admit, 'the GVC framework accounts for the characteristics that are likely to give rise to different patterns of GVC governance, absent other influences. If a pattern of governance does not fit the theory, then another factor may be at work'. Governance is always in contest with 'other influences' particularly when top-down private governance initiatives intersect with 'another factor', for example local organising campaigns (Ruwanpura 2016). In other words, inter-firm relationships are an important but not determining influence on employment relations, and the exact strength and nature of that influence are ultimately an empirical question. Relationships in GPNs are dynamic and emergent and the assumed certainty of future employment relations out-comes as a result of top-down dynamics obscures how workers might 'break free' of their chains. Here GPN theory is useful in placing labour action in the forefront of analysis and not secondary to institutional arrangements where alternative futures of work can be uncovered, which can potentially 'rebal-ance' the asymmetry of power inherent in all GVCs in favour of workers.

4. A FUTURE RESEARCH AGENDA FOR EMPLOYMENT RELATIONS AND GPNS

A future research agenda for employment relations should take into account the emergence of GPNs in three different but interrelated aspects: 1) Contestation; 2) Multi-scalarity; and 3) Voice.

4.1 Contestation

Most broadly, the term 'governance' refers to the explicit or implicit 'rules of the game'; however, without a global authority that has been able to define the 'floor' below which any participants in an international 'race-to-the-bottom' would be 'disqualified', these rules are often contested. Whilst the ILO was the original 'umpire' of the 'rules of the game' (Polanyi 1944), the goalposts have shifted with CSOs and TNCs trying to carve themselves a place at the 'labour governance table'. Take, for example, the clash between TNCs' search for lower costs via outsourcing and exploiting 'spaces of exception', the striving of trade unions for recognition and better conditions of work, and attempts by CSOs through their own 'rules of the game' to promote ethical accountability. In many sectors these relationships create an ongoing source of contest for labour governance (Alford et al. 2017) and, in the future, this contestation is likely to increase.

Whilst the governance of GPNs and its impact on the employment relationship can be viewed through the prism of both production and consumer relations (Donaghey and Reinecke 2018) this strand of research has primarily focussed on the alliances between consumers and workers and the complementarity of their actions (Donaghey et al. 2014; O'Rourke 2006). However, less attention has been paid to the negative impact of private power on labour power and the contested nature of labour governance with a greater focus on how workers: are 'resilient to' – get by; 'rework' – improve their conditions of work; and 'resist' – directly challenge capitalist social relations (Coe and Jordhus-Lier 2011, p. 216; Cumbers et al. 2008). For example, in the tea sector, the rise of various certification schemes established by TNCs has posed a significant threat to trade union organising by putting all tea producers on a 'level playing field' irrespective of their actual conditions of work (Thomas 2019). Future research should consider the various attempts to improve labour standards by both private and public actors, whether they complement, substitute or contest, with the ultimate test being whether it improves workers' voice and equity in the GPN. A key component of this future research agenda will be a recognition of the multi-scalar nature of labour governance.

4.2 Multi-scalarity

As noted above, many theories of employment relations are based at the level of the firm or comparisons between national institutional contexts. GPN analysis is an effective tool for exploring the multi-scalar linkages between global and local capital, national institutional actors, and workers who are societally and territorially embedded (Alford et al. 2017). These inter-linked scales provide an analytical tool for exploring the implications of the future of work on the employment relationship. The focus of future research should not be only on one scale but on the whole range of (strategic) relationships that exists, from the local to the global and the employment relations outcomes of these actions. A sole focus on the national or local level does not capture vertical work processes in particular sectors that are linked to GPNs and can create barriers to understanding and acknowledging the range of strategic actors and institutions that are involved in promoting and protecting decent work. At the same time a focus on the (re) regulation of labour standards at the global level often obscures the importance of local labour campaigns and their ability to alter the governance arrangements of GPNs from the bottom up. In other words, the emergence of GPNs has opened up new sites of bargaining, contestation and struggle for governance; this calls for theoretical perspectives that facilitate examination of new forms of multi-scalar labour agency.

To date, most research has focussed on North American and European lead firms outsourcing their production to low-cost developing country producers. However, GPNs are multi-directional. South–South and South–North trade is increasing, in particular in finished goods, and lead firms based in the global South have begun to play much more important roles in shaping the governance patterns of GPNs. Emerging economies within Asia, Latin America and Africa have become fast-growing producer and consumer end markets. Taking a multi-scalar approach helps unpack the connections between the activities of these new lead firms and their interaction with Northern lead firms, alternative governance actors (CSOs etc.), the national institutional context, and the individual and collective voice of workers. This is particularly important when analysing the labour agency of workers in many of these countries, who have limited recourse to more traditional forms of voice (Lakhani et al. 2013).

4.3   Voice

Even in contemporary accounts of the future of work it is assumed that if firms (primarily suppliers) can successfully move to higher value-added activities in GPNs then workers 'automatically' benefit through improvements in equity (wages and hours of work) (see ILO 2018, p. 3). There is, however, by now a sufficient consensus, both institutionally and academically, that this is not the case – economic upgrading (whereby enterprises move from low-efficiency to relatively high-efficiency activities) does not lead to social upgrading (equity and voice) in all cases (Barrientos et al. 2011). Ultimately, equity and voice – both collective and individual – are important objectives of the employment relationship in their own right even if they do not increase organisational efficiency (Budd 2004). Although equity and voice may clash with collective or individual responses, the more telling conflicts are between efficiency on the one hand, and equity and voice on the other. We do not expect all workers to receive the same material treatment (equity) throughout the world, but any improvements in labour governance should focus on giving workers, *inter alia*, a voice in wage setting to determine their 'living wage' and the right to negotiate working time, rest breaks etc. Therefore, a central aspect of any study of the future of work and GPNs should be the analysis of different forms of governance towards improving workers' voice, particularly as the participation of workers and trade unions is weak or lacking altogether in many of these mechanisms. In other words, focussing on agency shows how change in one part of the chain can impact another and seeks to reveal weak spots within the production network that workers can exploit, subsequently finding new allies and maximising their potential for voice (Quan 2008).

Here the case for a GPN driven approach to employment relations as opposed to GVC theory has been made. However, it is undoubtable that GVC theory has been useful to policymakers. After all, Gereffi et al. (2005, p. 82) preferred 'to create the simplest framework that generates results relevant to real-world outcomes'. This partly explains the significant uptake of this approach with international organisations. However, as noted above, the conceptualisation of a linear 'chain' connecting economic actors within the GVC model ignores the complexity of horizontal and vertical governance arrangements (Coe et al. 2008; Rainnie et al. 2011) 'as if the "invisible hand" of the market worked its magic to arrange supply chains' (Reinecke et al. 2018, p. 460). Thus, GVC theory applied uncritically assumes a rather narrow view of the future of work, one that has been used by international organisations who espouse the merits of GVC participation for national economies and the efficiency of firms with very little appreciation or understanding of the impact on social relations. It is in this domain that employment relations scholars have the opportunity to give a voice to the marginalised and form a counter-narrative to this future of work, informed by GPN theory that has a more nuanced view of the implications of engagement in production networks for workers' voice.

5. CONCLUSION: FUTURE OR FUTURES OF WORK FOR GLOBAL LABOUR GOVERNANCE?

The proliferation of GPNs and their impact on the world of work is an emerging field of scholarship. Although competitive pressures have always existed in some sectors, these pressures now transcend national boundaries and the state-based system of global labour governance has struggled to deal with, and adjust to, the expanding power of TNCs. The rise of GPNs has major implications for conventional understandings of employment relations, especially the effectiveness of existing forms of organisation and regulation. Labour governance is no longer the sole province of governments or trade unions and any contemporary account of employment relations should recognise the impact of all strategic actors at multiple scales and the contestation that occurs, with a much greater focus on the voice of workers. Enhanced dialogue between the GPN and employment relations literatures would therefore seem to offer benefits to both sides in understanding the future of work.

The predicted future of work may well not happen. Regardless of this, new ways must be found to bolster the position of labour in GPNs. The ILO's recent call for a Universal Labour Guarantee is a step in the right direction as it decouples access to labour rights from the (increasingly fissured) employment relationship and places emphasis on the need for the worker's voice in these networks (ILO 2019). In short, the fate of workers engaged in GPNs is not set in stone. The increasing proliferation of private governance by TNCs suggests a future of work rooted in voluntary, self-regulatory standards with labour issues being portrayed through consumers rather than workers and their representatives. Indeed, it could be argued that the current global labour governance 'regime' leaves very little room for organised labour. At a time when public governance and the power of workers is on the wane, alternatives are needed. One such alternative is the potential of a new international labour standard for decent work in global supply chains at the ILO (Thomas and Turnbull 2018), whereby a system of vertical public governance could be established that would encourage states to enforce international standards on other states and actors connected through GPNs. Another alternative template for labour governance is the Bangladesh Accord, which, for all its critique, is a prime example of transnational co-determination along the production network between representatives of labour and capital (Donaghey and Reinecke 2018). These initiatives, amongst others, indicate the prospects for enhancing voice in the context of the future of work.

Ultimately, there is work to be completed in ascertaining what the future of work will really look like for workers in GPNs as the claim of a singular future of work obscures the real alternatives that are already in motion. The futures of work are currently the subject of active debate and review, most notably at the ILO, and will inevitably play out in different ways in different countries, sectors and production networks. What is dangerous about presupposing one future of work is that it assumes one destination already set, depriving people of the agency to shape and resist it through organisation and regulation. If we consider multiple futures for workers in GPNs rather than a terminus it allows us to imagine a future that is not concluded and one in which activists, unions, academics, policymakers and others can identify and understand what they do and what they need to do to support the plight of the millions of workers engaged in GPNs.

NOTES

1. In this chapter I use the acronym 'GPN' to denote both the theory and the empirical phenomenon.
2. Go to: https://futuresofwork.co.uk/2018/09/05/editorial-from-the-future-of-work-to-futu res-of-work/ [accessed 10 October 2019].

REFERENCES

Accenture (2013), *Exploitative Labor Practices in the Global Palm Oil Industry*. Available at http://humanityunited.org/pdfs/Modern_Slavery_in_the_Palm_ Oil_Industry.pdf [accessed 8 April 2019].

Alford, M., S. Barrientos and M. Visser (2017), 'Multi–scalar labour agency in global production networks: contestation and crisis in the South African fruit sector', *Development and Change*, 48 (4), pp. 721–45.

Anner, M. (2012), 'Corporate social responsibility and freedom of association rights: the precarious quest for legitimacy and control in global supply chains', *Politics & Society*, 40 (4), pp. 609–44.

Barrientos, S., G. Gereffi and A. Rossi (2011), 'Economic and social upgrading in global production networks: a new paradigm for a changing world', *International Labour Review*, 150 (3–4), pp. 319–40.

Berliner, D., A. Greenleaf, M. Lake, M. Levi and J. Noveck (2015), *Labor Standards in International Supply Chains: Aligning Rights and Incentives*, Cheltenham, UK and Northampton, MA, USA: Edward Elgar Publishing.

Budd, J.W. (2004), *Achieving Decent Work by Giving Employment a Human Face*, Geneva: International Labour Office.

Coe, N. and M. Hess (2013), 'Global production networks, labour and development', *Geoforum*, 44, pp. 4–9.

Coe, N. and D. Jordhus-Lier (2011), 'Constrained agency? Re-evaluating the geographies of labour', *Progress in Human Geography*, 35 (2), pp. 211–33.

Coe, N. and H. Yeung (2015), *Global Production Networks: Theorizing Economic Development in an Interconnected World*, Oxford: Oxford University Press.

Coe, N., P. Dicken and M. Hess (2008), 'Global production networks: realizing the potential', *Journal of Economic Geography*, 8 (3), pp. 271–95.

Cumbers, A., C. Nativel and P. Routledge (2008), 'Labour agency and union positionalities in global production networks', *Journal of Economic Geography*, 8 (3), pp. 369–87.

Donaghey, J. and J. Reinecke (2018), 'When industrial democracy meets corporate social responsibility—a comparison of the Bangladesh Accord and Alliance as responses to the Rana Plaza disaster', *British Journal of Industrial Relations*, 56 (1), pp. 14–42.

Donaghey, J., J. Reinecke, C. Niforou and B. Lawson (2014), 'From employment relations to consumption relations: balancing labor governance in global supply chains', *Human Resource Management*, 53 (2), pp. 229–52.

Egels-Zandén, N. and J. Merk (2014), 'Private regulation and trade union rights: why codes of conduct have limited impact on trade union rights', *Journal of Business Ethics*, 123 (3), pp. 461–73.

Gereffi, G. (1994), 'The organization of buyer-driven global commodity chains: how US retailers shape overseas production networks', in G. Gereffi and M. Korzeniewicz (eds), *Commodity Chains and Global Capitalism*, Westport, CA: Praeger, pp. 93–122.

Gereffi, G. and J. Lee (2016), 'Economic and social upgrading in global value chains and industrial clusters: why governance matters', *Journal of Business Ethics*, 133 (1), pp. 25–38.

Gereffi, G., J. Humphrey and T. Sturgeon (2005), 'The governance of global value chains', *Review of International Political Economy*, 12 (1), pp. 78–104.

Henderson, J., P. Dicken, M. Hess, N. Coe and H. Yeung (2002), 'Global production networks and the analysis of economic development', *Review of International Political Economy*, 9 (3), pp. 436–64.

Herod, A., A. Rainnie and S. McGrath-Champ (2007), 'Working space: why incorporating the geographical is central to theorizing work and employment practices', *Work, Employment and Society*, 21 (2), pp. 247–64.

ILO (2014), *Trade Union Manual on Export Processing Zones*, Geneva: International Labour Office.

ILO (2015), *World Employment and Social Outlook 2015*, Geneva: International Labour Office.

ILO (2016), *Decent Work in Global Supply Chains*, Geneva: International Labour Organization.

ILO (2018), *Global Value Chains for an Inclusive and Sustainable Future*, Geneva: International Labour Organization.

ILO (2019), *Work For a Brighter Future: Global Commission on the Future of Work*, Geneva: International Labour Organization.

Lakhani, T., S. Kuruvilla and A. Avgar (2013), 'From the firm to the network: global value chains and employment relations theory', *British Journal of Industrial Relations*, 51 (3), pp. 440–72.

Levi, M., C. Adolph, D. Berliner, A. Erlich, A. Greenleaf, M. Lake and J. Noveck (2013), *Aligning Rights and Interests: Why, When and How to Uphold Labor Standards?*, Background paper for the World Development Report.

Lillie, N. (2010), 'Bringing the offshore ashore: transnational production, industrial relations and the reconfiguration of sovereignty', *International Studies Quarterly*, 54 (3), pp. 683–704.

Locke, R. (2013), *The Promise and Limits of Private Power: Promoting Labor Standards in a Global Economy*, Cambridge: Cambridge University Press.

Meardi, G. and P. Marginson (2014), 'Global labour governance: potential and limits of an emerging perspective', *Work, Employment and Society*, 28 (4), pp. 651–62.

Nathan, D. (2013), 'Industrial relations in a global production network', *Economic and Political Weekly*, 48 (30), pp. 29–33.

Niforou, C. (2014), 'International framework agreements and the democratic deficit of global labour governance', *Economic and Industrial Democracy*, 35 (2), pp. 367–86.

O'Rourke, D. (2006), 'Multi-stakeholder regulation: privatizing or socializing global labor standards?', *World Development*, 34 (5), pp. 899–918.

Padmanabhan, N. (2012), 'Globalisation lived locally: a labour geography perspective on control, conflict and response among workers in Kerala', *Antipode*, 44 (3), pp. 971–92.

Polanyi, K. (1944), *The Great Transformation: The Political and Economic Origins of Our Time*, Boston, MA: Beacon Press.

Quan, K. (2008), 'Use of global value chains by labor organizers', *Competition & Change*, 12 (1), pp. 89–104.

Rainnie, A., A. Herod and S. McGrath-Champ (2011), 'Review and positions: global production networks and labour', *Competition & Change*, 15 (2), pp. 155–69.

Reinecke, J. and J. Donaghey (2015), 'After Rana Plaza: building coalitional power for labour rights between unions and (consumption-based) social movement organisations', *Organization*, 22 (5), pp. 720–40.

Reinecke, J., J. Donaghey, A. Wilkinson and G. Wood (2018), 'Global supply chains and social relations at work: brokering across boundaries', *Human Relations*, 71 (4), pp. 459–80.

Riisgaard, L. and N. Hammer (2011), 'Prospects for labour in global value chains: labour standards in the cut flower and banana industries', *British Journal of Industrial Relations*, 49 (1), pp. 168–90.

Ruwanpura, K. (2016), 'Garments without guilt? Uneven labour geographies and ethical trading—Sri Lankan labour perspectives', *Journal of Economic Geography*, 16 (2), pp. 423–46.

Selwyn, B. (2008), 'Institutions, upgrading and development: evidence from North East Brazilian export horticulture', *Competition & Change*, 12 (4), pp. 377–96.

Standing, G. (2008), 'The ILO: an agency for globalization?', *Development and Change*, 39 (3), pp. 355–84.

Tampe, M. (2018), 'Leveraging the vertical: the contested dynamics of sustainability standards and labour in global production networks', *British Journal of Industrial Relations*, 56 (1), pp. 43–74.

Thomas, H. (2019), 'A "decent cuppa": worker power and consumer power in the Sri Lankan tea sector', *British Journal of Industrial Relations*. Online first, available at https://onlinelibrary.wiley.com/doi/full/10.1111/bjir.12489 [accessed 10 October 2019].

Thomas, H. and P. Turnbull (2018), 'From horizontal to vertical labour governance: the International Labour Organization (ILO) and decent work in global supply chains', *Human Relations*, 71 (4), pp. 536–59.

Tilly, C. (1995), 'Globalization threatens labor's rights', *International Labor and Working-Class History*, 47, pp. 1–23.

UNCTAD (2013), *World Investment Report 2013: Global Value-Chains, Investment and Trade for Development*, Geneva: United Nations Conference on Trade and Development.

Yeung, H. and N. Coe (2015), 'Toward a dynamic theory of global production networks', *Economic Geography*, 91 (1), pp. 29–58.

13. Navigating the future of work to build meaningful careers

Edwin Trevor-Roberts

INTRODUCTION

In 1909 Frank Parsons published a seminal article widely viewed as the birth of the careers field (Pope and Sveinsdottir, 2005). He proposed that, in order to have a good career, a person needed to do three things: first, understand themselves; second, understand what the labour market needed; and third, make a logical connection between the first two. Parsons' work laid the foundation for the career field for almost a century. Subsequent theorists explored the myriad of relationships between environmental and personal variables (Dawis and Lofquist, 1976; Holland, 1959; Holland, 1973). Career guidance and counselling focussed on identifying the traits, interests and skills of each individual and then matching them to an occupation where those traits were best suited.

While our understanding of careers today has evolved over the past century there remains an inherent assumption that careers are built in an environment of certainty, or at the very least, an individual will purposefully move toward certainty in their career. The future of careers, however, is predicated on uncertainty. The pace of change, whether it be technological, societal or organisational, will continue to accelerate. Individuals face uncertainty in the various structural options for their career such as boundaryless, portfolio, gig, traditional, or a combination of these. In addition, people can no longer expect clearly identifiable career paths mapped out by their organisation (De Cuyper *et al.*, 2011; McElroy and Weng, 2016) as organisations themselves explore new methods for producing value (Batt, 2018). In this sense, organisations may no longer be willing (or able) to offer certainty or even take much responsibility for an individual career. The focus of this chapter is how, in these circumstances, individuals make sense of, and craft, their careers.

It follows, then, that a successful career in the future will be one characterised by a person's ability to manage the uncertainties they experience. We should at this point clarify that the focus of this chapter is on professional workers, defined loosely as those involved in some form of knowledge work. Professional careers are particularly uncertain. The complexity (Burke and Cooper, 2004) and ability to 'customize' professionals' careers (Valcour *et al.*, 2007) result in a range of uncertainties that stem from the choices available to them. Knowledge obsolescence is a key concern as the useful lifespan of knowledge has been shortened by the exponential growth in accessible information and the rapidity by which it can be shared globally. This results in two additional uncertainties for professionals – *what* they should learn next and *how* they should learn it. The very role of occupations and professions is itself under threat. No longer is work clearly delineated along boundaries such as 'engineering' or 'accounting'. Instead, professionals contribute by weaving together skills and expertise from multiple disciplines in order to adapt to the changing context of the organisations or clients they work with. Finally, professionals face a variety of alternative employment arrangements due to the way in which clients are found and work is secured. Temporary, contract and gig work are increasingly common, challenging the notion of a full time role within an organisation (De Cuyper *et al.*, 2011; Guest *et al.*, 2006).

The purpose of this chapter is to explore what a career will look like in the future. I follow Arthur and Rousseau's definition of career as 'a person's unfolding sequence of work related activities over time' (Arthur and Rousseau, 1996a, p. 30). In the future of work, how will these activities unfold and what will be most important to individuals? Exploring what motivates people in the future has implications for organisational behaviour, organisational development and leadership. The chapter starts with a reconceptualisation of careers as subjective sense-making processes that are enacted within an environment of uncertainty. I then offer five fundamental questions that may motivate people to pursue work-related activities in the future.

RECONCEPTUALISING CAREERS

The future of work requires a reconceptualisation of careers that provides flexibility for the unknown changes that will impact on people's working lives in the decades ahead. The speed at which the nature of work is changing is unlikely to abate – if anything it will continue to accelerate (see Barley *et al.*, 2017) – suggesting that the future of careers lies not in exploring the specificity of context, but rather providing deeper, more relevant insights to help people live a meaningful life in a constantly changing environment.

Managing our own careers in an evolving employee relations environment, however, requires us to be active agents in our working life rather than experiencing the passivity many enjoyed when organisations managed our careers for us. No longer do our careers instantly 'make sense', especially as external markers of objective career success, such as pay and status, become increasingly diffuse (Weick, 1996). Take, for example, the increasing permeability of career boundaries. Traditional boundaries of employment are no longer certain (Arthur and Rousseau, 1996b; Donnelly, 2009) and new forms of career structure are required to meet new methods through which organisations create economic value. The concept of the boundaryless career was created to define those careers that unfold beyond a single employment setting (Sullivan and Arthur, 2006). Researchers have focussed on boundaries or, more accurately, the permeability of boundaries such as geographic (Inkson, 2003; Lazarova, 2003; Stahl *et al.*, 2002), occupational (Boh *et al.*, 2001; Jackson, 1996; Tolbert, 1996), organisational (Gunz *et al.*, 2000) and role (Kramer, 1994; Sullivan, 1999).

Careers in the future require individuals to make sense of their disparate work-related experiences in order to provide coherence to their career. Such a process necessitates a shift to internal self-generated guides of success. Broadly termed the 'subjective career' (Barley, 1989) this perspective focusses on a person's internal experience and interpretation of work-related events (Arthur *et al.*, 2005; Khapova *et al.*, 2007). An example of a pivot in the career field toward more integrative approaches is that of Savickas and his colleagues (2009), who formulated *life design* as a lifelong, holistic and contextual framework for counselling interventions to answer the question, '*how may individuals best design their own lives in the human society in which they live?*' (p. 241, original emphasis). The theory was developed to address the crisis in the 'fundamental assumption of predictability based on stability' and 'personal characteristics and secure jobs in bounded organisations' (p. 240) – in other words, the future of a career in an uncertain world.

THE FUTURE OF CAREERS

A successful career in a future of work characterised by uncertainty requires a different approach from the twentieth century when careers were predicated on stability (Trevor-Roberts, 2006). An expansionary view of careers is required; one that integrates, and makes sense of, the complex interdependency of factors and experiences across a person's working life. Those with successful careers in the future will adapt to changes, respond quickly when necessary, and proactively seek opportunities to further develop their skills and expertise. Such individuals will have a network of strong relationships that they continuously draw upon while helping others.

In this future of careers, organisations may respond to these trends by focussing on creating a place within which individuals can derive a sense of meaningfulness and success in their work while at the same time balancing the inherent tension of flexibility and achieving economic outputs. This will require organisations to think differently about how they design work to tap into people's intrinsic motivation (Ryan and Deci, 2000). Moreover, organisations will create a sense of community where people feel like they belong, to counter the historical trend of reducing work to (almost) meaningless activities in order to gain efficiencies of scale and scope.

To understand what this future of careers looks like, we need to ask different questions to move beyond the historical narrative of work as merely a factor of production. Instead, proposed here is a human-design approach centred upon the individual and their relationship to work. To assist in this task I draw on a line of philosophical inquiry into the nature of human action and motivation. The philosopher Kenneth Burke (1945) was particularly interested in what motivates people to take action. Through his interest in language and the narrative construction of reality he created what he called a 'dramaturgical pentad' as a framework with which to understand action. I draw on Burke's pentad to offer five questions through which to explore the future of careers. These are: (1) Who are my people? (2) What is my contribution? (3) Where is my place in this world? (4) How do I adapt to constant change? (5) How do I find meaningful work?

Who Are My People?

Belonging to a group is a fundamental human need (Baumeister and Vohs, 2002). The relational approach to careers (Hall and Associates, 1996) emphasises the importance of relationships and affiliative behaviour highlighting the social processes inherent in enacting a career. Traditionally the workplace or organisation provided people with a stable cohort with whom they could identify (Ashforth *et al.*, 2008). However, the centrality of the organisation to provide a sense of belonging has diminished as new organisational forms emerge, impacting on how work is structured. The term 'boundaryless' careers (Gunz *et al.*, 2000) was coined to explain how individuals move across, through and between organisational, occupational and geographic boundaries. In this more diffuse world people look for alternative collectives to which they can feel a sense of belonging. Examples include occupations (Kunda *et al.*, 2002), professions (Allen, 2011; Pratt *et al.*, 2006), communities (Parker and Arthur, 2000; Parker *et al.*, 2004) or organisations (Ashforth *et al.*, 2008). Identification with a collective helps define one's self: 'the perception of oneness or belongingness to some human aggregate' (Ashforth and Mael, 1989, p. 21). However, forming an identity is a complex and dynamic process that is inherently uncertain (Brocklehurst, 2003; Sveningsson and Alvesson, 2003). Identities are not formed in isolation but are influenced by a range of factors such as societal mores (Gergen and Gergen, 1983; Giddens, 1991), cognitive schemas (Bruner, 1986), work flexibility (Grote and Raeder, 2009), psychosocial tasks of exploration and commitment (Blustein *et al.*, 1989), and emotions (Law *et al.*, 2002; Dutton *et al.*, 2010).

The challenge for individuals is how to find a sense of belonging as collective boundaries continue to change (Susskind and Susskind, 2015). Occupations, for example, provide a major source of belonging for individuals, especially those with specific rules for joining and enforced continuous professional development (Freidson, 2001). The purported benefits of belonging to an occupation include market shelter, occupational closure and access to knowledge (Allen, 2011). Yet, occupations are changing. On the one hand, the gradual diffusion of collectives' boundaries may continue as the nature of work changes, making it increasingly difficult to clearly delineate where one occupation finishes and another begins (Reed, 2007). Another perspective sees a 'rebirth' of professions as a distinct and important form of work (Freidson, 2001).

As organisational, occupational and geographic boundaries continue their trend to permeability, individuals will increasingly move in, through and out of groups as their work activities flux and change. Forming a cohesive identity from multiple disparate sources is an uncertain process (Grote and Raeder, 2009; Allen, 2011) and the future of careers will require individuals to rapidly negotiate and re-negotiate a sense of identity (Ibarra and Barbulescu, 2010; Ibarra and Petriglieri, 2010). Research is nascent in this area although Grote and Raeder's (2009) study identified four different types of identity, each representing different patterns of identity formation, career success and preferences for work flexibility.

One possible strategy that individuals may employ in the future is to create their own 'tribe' to which they can derive a sense of belonging. Parker and her colleagues (2004) coined the term 'career communities' defined as 'self-organizing member-defined social structures through which [individuals] draw career support' (Parker and Arthur, 2000, p. 494). Ten different communities were identified: company; industrial; occupational; regional; ideological; project; alumni; support; family; and virtual. Across these communities lies the additional opportunity for individuals to connect with a number of people who, when combined, provide a sense of belonging.

As markers of belonging to a collective become increasingly diffuse, individuals need alternative methods to feel a sense of belonging. For example, the closer the link between a person's identity and work, the greater will be their difficulty in coping with a period of unemployment.

It is more effective for people's identity to be based on personal capacities and attitudes rather than on a traditional working relationship, which may be subject to change at any time (Kossen and McIlveen, 2017; Amundson, 1994; Hall and Associates, 1996). Identification with a person's career is increasingly important as 'occupations transcend any given organisation' (Ashforth *et al.*, 2008, p. 352).

What Is My Contribution?

A central issue for people to navigate in their career is what they should seek to do; that is, what job or tasks should they be looking to undertake. From an organisational perspective, the impact of job design on individual motivation has strong empirical support (Humphrey *et al.*, 2007). For example, poor work design results in negative outcomes, such as boredom or anxiety, affects individual motivation to perform an assigned job (Kass *et al.*, 2001), while excessive job demands may lead to psychological 'burnout' (Van den Broeck *et al.*, 2008).

At the individual level, helping people figure out what they want to do is the very basis of the career counselling field. However, knowing 'what' to do in one's career is increasingly uncertain (Trevor-Roberts, 2006) as rapid changes in knowledge, automation and globalisation have shortened the span of time for which skills and knowledge remain relevant (McKercher and Mosco, 2007; Pazy, 1990). The direct impact on individuals is that the time available to master new knowledge has decreased, meaning that people need the ability to rapidly acquire new skills and knowledge. Hall (2002) describes this process as *learning cycles*, arguing that a career is a succession of mini-stages of learning. Each learning cycle consists of a period of exploration or trial of new skills followed by a period of mastery of the new work area. Each learning cycle may be less than five years so the ability to learn becomes, arguably, more important than the content itself.

Another reason why continuous learning is important is that we are living longer. A child born in a Western country today has more than a 50% chance of living to be over 105 (Gratton and Scott, 2016). This has significant consequences for the structure of a person's career across their lifespan. With a longer working life individuals will likely go through multiple stages of work with each stage involving a different type of work. Similar to Hall (2002), Gratton describes how these stages will be preceded by the acquisition of different skills and a period of transition to secure work in a new arena. Gratton's argument for different learning stages stems not from knowledge obsolescence but from a pragmatic argument of finances. The longer we live, the more we need to earn to sustain our livelihood. The default retirement age of 65 simply doesn't allow enough working time to generate sufficient wealth to lead a 100-year life. So, what we do in our career – the jobs we hold and activities we undertake – will evolve through several distinct stages.

Moreover, it may become increasingly difficult for organisations to clearly delineate tasks and activities into neat packages of work called 'jobs'. The work that people will be required to do in the future will be a rapid and constant negotiation and re-negotiation of tasks and activities to solve the imminent needs or challenges of the organisation rather than a pre-determined set of activities labelled as a 'job'. This represents a shift from a focus on the *outputs* that employees produce to the *outcomes* that they achieve. Examples are seen in the rise of the gig economy (see Healy and Pekarek, this volume) where contract workers are paid for a specific outcome. For example, online platforms allow independent professionals to bid for pieces of work across a whole range of professional domains such as graphic design, editing or finance. While the trend is toward greater flexibility in how organisations produce value and for employees preferring flexibility, it is unlikely that the construct of a 'job' will disappear as it remains central to our social psyche and industrial relations system. Moreover, the balance of power between employers and employees will continue to flux in the future of work, driven, in part, by organisations subcontracting out non-core activities to focus primarily on its stable core of workers (Thompson, 2003). Careers in the future of work will see greater variability in how 'job' is both defined and enacted, requiring increased flexibility and adaptation from individuals.

Where Is My Place in This World?

The workplace in the future of work will no longer offer the same level of security and stability that it has in the past. Changes in organisational structures and the way in which they produce goods and services result in workplaces that feel increasingly fragmented. Consequently individuals feel less that they 'belong' (Ashforth *et al.*, 2008) to their organisation, and that it no longer affords them with a sense of place. Take, for example, the importance of the physical environment in which people work (Sander, 2017) and the backlash against hot-desking as people vie to work at the same desk each day instead of moving around. Human behaviour is a function of the interaction between the employee and their environment (Lewin, 1951), yet scant attention has been paid to the importance of place in careers.

The concept of place is central in other domains of research. The sociologist Richard Florida (2008) argues that cities have their own unique personality that attracts certain types of people. A combination of the physical presence of the city with the social, institutional and governmental support structures creates a unique feeling or vibe of each city. Individuals are attracted to certain places that mirror their personalities and worldview. The importance of the physical environment has been central to the lives of Aboriginal people of many countries who define themselves and make decisions based on their connection to a place (McCormick *et al.*, 2003). Sociologists have long explored the concatenation of factors that create social capital in a particular location. Bourdieu's (1984) classic theory of society argues strongly for the importance of the environment or context. Societies, says Bourdieu, are constructed through behavioural patterns and processes of individuals called *habitus* resulting in social capital that are accumulated over time. This social capital is created and competed for in *fields* – various social and institutional arenas in which people act. A field may be a network, structure or set of relationships housed in various forms such as intellectual, religious, educational or organisational. For example, a person may behave differently because of norms associated with the particular field they are in, such as when with old school friends, in a mosque, at a university or at work. In essence, what Bourdieu and other sociologists argue is that the context within which a person undertakes their work creates a particular sense of place because of the inherent norms and assumptions they contain. In our careers, we gravitate toward workplaces where we feel comfortable.

Yet in a future of work where careers will increasingly become boundary-less, the role of place becomes more complex and fragmented. While organisations will continue to provide a sense of place for full-time employees, this is not the case for many others. Finding a sense of place as a contingent worker (e.g. portfolio, gig or contract) becomes important to feeling they have a successful and meaningful career. Burke (1945) introduces a useful concept of a *container* in his treatise on what drives human motivation. He says that, for every act we undertake, such as work, there is a scene or place in which it is undertaken, in other words there is a thing that *contains* the action: 'to tell what a thing is, you place it in terms of something else. This idea of locating, or placing, is implicit in our very word for definition itself: to *define,* or *determine* a thing, is to mark its boundaries' (Burke, 1945, p. 24, original emphasis). For example, we may define ourselves as a nurse because we belong to a profession – a place – that brings together others who do similar work. Thus our work*place* too, be it a hospital or aged care home, reinforces how we define ourselves as the physical environment comes to represent the work that we do.

In the future of careers, organisations will no longer provide a sense of place for all people. It will be up to individuals to craft for themselves what a sense of place is. They may draw upon their geographical location, occupation or, most likely, craft a sense of place from the unique 'field' in which they inhabit consisting of all the various institutional and organisational connections they have in all domains of their life (see Parker *et al.*, 2004). This is difficult and ambiguous work and we don't yet fully understand all the processes. However, it is important as the consequence of not having a sense of place is marginalisation and disillusionment (Sennett, 1998).

How Do I Adapt to Constant Change?

The prevailing career advice throughout the twentieth century was to find an occupation that matched your talents and interests (e.g. Holland, 1985) and then work hard to progress within your chosen field. This was an appropriate strategy when the labour market was relatively stable. A key question for careers in the future of work is, how will individuals cope with increasing uncertainty? An interpretive study of the role of uncertainty in professionals' careers found that people had different notions of what uncertainty meant to them (Trevor-Roberts *et al.*, 2019). The meaning ascribed to career uncertainty ranged in a continuum from being something negative through to being something positive. The interviewees were found to display different career behaviours (e.g. decision making, search for career success, career structure) depending on how they viewed the role of uncertainty in their career.

Being able to adapt one's career behaviour in the face of constant change is a critical competency for the future of work. Career adaptability is defined as 'an individual's readiness and resources for coping with current and imminent vocational development tasks, occupational transitions, and personal traumas' (Savickas, 2005, p. 51). With this in mind Tim Hall calls adaptability a *metacompetency* (Hall, 1996), meaning that mastery of this will allow one to master many other specific skills. At the heart of adaptability in the future of work is a mindset. We need to let go of the myth that there is one job, one occupation, one ideal career state in the future that we are striving toward. A rigid focus on pursuing one discrete career outcome opens up the very real threat of what will happen if that ideal state is no longer needed by society. It is easy in hindsight to look back and see the jobs of the past that no longer exist. A successful career in the future requires people to actively pursue multiple possibilities simultaneously, by imagining multiple possibilities of who *we could be* at the same time (Ibarra and Barbulescu, 2010). Adaptability in the future of work requires individuals to form, maintain and revise their identities. Guichard (2009) argues that the career field has shifted in focus from choosing a vocation to *self-construction* or forming an identity.

Career adaptability, however, requires that our working identity not be based exclusively on those aspects of work that are likely to change, such as a job or type of employment relationship. Instead, it is more effective for people's identity to be based on personal capacities and attitudes than on a traditional working relationship, which may be subject to change at any time (Amundson, 1994; McArdle *et al.*, 2007). A poignant example is found in a longitudinal study of two professional golfers by David Carless and Kitrina Douglas (2009). One golfer told a consistent story across the years about being an elite athlete resulting in a one-dimensional identity that, when faced with withdrawal from the sport, caused considerable difficulty and trauma. The other golfer crafted a more complex narrative involving elite performance but also other discovery-orientated stories. Her multi-dimensional self was a major contributor to her positive and success-ful withdrawal from tournament golf. This study highlights how work is a major influence on a person's identity (Blustein *et al.*, 1989), and is particu-larly evident during periods of unemployment when a rapid renegotiation of identity occurs (Amundson, 1994). The closer the link between a per-son's identity and work, the greater will be their difficulty in coping with the unemployment period, suggesting that identification with a person's career (as opposed to a job) is increasingly important (Ashforth *et al.*, 2008).

Forming an identity is complex. Guichard (2009) suggests that identity is crafted through *subjective identity forms* that are 'sets of ways of being, acting and interacting in relation to a certain view of oneself in a given context' (p. 253). For example, a person may view him- or herself as an entrepreneur and so may behave in a way perceived as suitable for such an occupation. These subjective identify forms allow us to hold multiple identities depending on the context we are in.

The process of enacting a career, also termed identity work (Ibarra and Barbulescu, 2010; Ibarra, 2003; Pratt *et al.*, 2006; Sveningsson and Alvesson, 2003) involves activities people undertake to craft, maintain or strengthen their identities. Identity work can be undertaken through a variety of strategies including experimenting with possible selves (Ibarra, 1999, 2003), learning about the nature of the work undertaken by a person (Pratt *et al.*, 2006), and rhetorical techniques such as self-narratives and accounts (Bruner, 1997; McAdams, 1999) An example of a strategy that highlights the uncertainty of identity enactment is 'identity play', defined as 'the crafting and provisional trial of immature (namely, still unelabo-rated) possible selves' (Ibarra and Petriglieri, 2010, p. 13). Experimentation, playfulness and exploration characterises identity play, and is full of uncer-tainty as people experiment with possibilities for future selves without the historical markers that provide social validation for current identities.

How Do I Find Meaningful Work?

Workforce values have shifted over the past few decades toward a desire for more enriched work (Myers and Sadaghiani, 2010; Winograd and Hais, 2011). The seminal *hierarchy of needs* created by Abraham Maslow (1954) calls this 'self-actualisation' or the pursuit of deeper questions about meaning and purpose once a person's basic needs are met. Maslow's work focussed on a person's whole life and highlights the importance of meaning in life more broadly. Meaning in life is 'the extent to which people comprehend, make sense of, or see significance in their lives, accompanied by the degree to which they perceive themselves to have a purpose, mission, or overarching aim in life' (Steger, 2009, p. 682). Victor Frankl (1984) concluded from his time in the concentration camps of World War II that a person's search for meaning is the primary motivation in life. Living a meaningful life (as opposed to a pleasant life or a good life) provides the highest level of fulfilment and happiness (Seligman, 2002). Meaning allows people to achieve a sense of self-worth and to identify and direct energy to what matters most (Steger, 2009).

With work playing such a major part in people's life, it is not surprising that people seek a sense of meaning from their work. This, however, presents two challenges: (1) how do individuals identify what meaningful work is to them? and (2) how do organisations make explicit the meaning-making opportunities inherent in the activities undertaken? Successful careers in the future will have these questions answered. That is, individuals will be able to articulate what meaningful work looks like to them and organisations will be able to connect the tasks and activities of employees to the broader purpose of the organisation (Bailey *et al.*, 2017).

There are four main sources of meaning in work: the self, other people, the work context and spiritual life (Rosso *et al.*, 2010). The self, or more accurately, a person's self-concept is the thoughts and feelings that a person has about themselves which continuously changes in response to experiences (Ashforth and Mael, 1989). A person's self-concept contributes to meaningfulness at work through values, motivation and orientation to work. Inherent in a person's self-concept are the values that they hold. Values play a pivotal role in shaping the meanings that people make of their work. If an individual feels like their values are being compromised at their workplace (Brown, 2002) then the sense of meaningfulness they derive from work will decrease and they will likely change their employment situation. The relationship between values and work will continue to play an important role in the future. Another well-documented process through which individuals experience meaningfulness in their work is when they are intrinsically motivated, defined as the expected congruence between a person's self-concept and a particular activity (Ryan and Deci, 2000). Known as self-determination theory, people are most motivated when they experience autonomy, competence and relatedness in their work activities. Since the popularising of these concepts, individuals have increasingly come to expect that their jobs will be designed in such a way that they experience these three elements. Organisations need to increasingly pay attention to how they design jobs and the flow of work through an organisation to allow for people to be engaged with their work (Bakker and Demerouti, 2008). Finally, people derive meaning from their work depending on how central work is to that person compared with other domains in their life such as family, community, sport, religion etc. (Brown, 1996). For some people work plays the central part of their life and the mere act of working provides a sense of meaning. For others, work is simply a means to an end where work is the money-making activity that allows them to undertake more meaningful activities outside work.

The second source through which people experience meaning at work is through their relationships and interactions with others. There is an old cliché that people join companies and leave managers; however, this can be extended to leaving co-workers, clients, suppliers or any people they interact with on a regular basis. Humans have an inherent need to belong and people identify with, and feel part of, the organisations they work for (Ashforth *et al.*, 2008). Organisations that foster this special sense of 'us' and 'we' (Haslam, 2004) provide greater opportunities for individuals to derive a sense of meaning from being part of their organisation. This can be seen in particular with organisations founded to address a social cause as employees can feel part of not just an organisation but a 'movement' all working together for a common good. Moreover, leaders play a critical role in influencing the meaning of work. Leaders help to communicate the purpose of the organisation and help people understand how their work contributes to the greater good, thus influencing perceptions of the meaning of their work.

The work context itself is the third source from which people derive meaning from their work. Research conducted by Amy Wrzesniewski and her colleagues (in Berg *et al.*, 2010; Wrzesniewski and Dutton, 2001) found that people constantly re-design the relational and task boundaries of their job in order to shape the meaning of their work. This process is called 'job crafting' and highlights the role of individual agency in the pursuit of meaning at work through the subtle altering of *how* a job is completed. This research is important as organisations are likely to remain a feature in the future of work and, by default, so will 'jobs'. While certain performance parameters are required for organisations to achieve their objectives, it is likely that employees will retain leeway to craft their work to experience a greater sense of meaning. There remains a risk that the 'virtuous cycle' described above – where the employer provides more freedom for job crafting and the employee reciprocates with improved outcomes – may cycle the opposite way. If employers take advantage of technology innovations to increase monitoring and evaluation of work (which decreases autonomy and therefore job satisfaction), employees may correspondingly adjust their effort downwards.

The final source of meaning at work is from spirituality. The past few decades has seen an increasing interest in secular practices in the workplace taking the form of mindfulness training, reflective leadership and wellbeing. In the careers literature Hall and Chandler (2005) argue that the greatest meaning a person can derive from work is when a career comprises a calling. Calling means 'a course of action in pursuit of prosocial intentions embodying the convergence of a person's sense of what he or she would like to do, should do, and actually does' (Elangovan *et al.*, 2010, p. 430). At these times a person feels that her work is her purpose in life driven by the psychological engagement with the meaning of work. When individuals hold a deep spiritual conviction they perceive work from this spiritual perspective and work is likely to take on a deeper sense of meaningfulness and purpose. There is a downside to seeing work as a calling, however, and this is expressed through a sense of being 'bound' to the work (Bunderson and Thompson, 2009). Nonetheless, it is likely that careers of the future will increasingly contain explicit connection to spirituality as dialogue in our society matures around spiritual and religious concepts.

CONCLUSION

There remains one constant amidst all the uncertainties about the future of work – work is an important domain in a person's life. Through the work that we do across the course of our career, we have the unique opportunity to explore our potential, to learn and grow, and to make a contribution to others. On the one hand, the future of work provides new opportunities for individuals to craft their career in different ways through new and emerging employment relationships, and by working across traditional boundaries. On the other hand, if the future is bright for careers, it is also up to each person to create their unique career story amidst evolving and increasing uncertainty. Given inherent future uncertainty, the five questions offered in this chapter are intended to provide a lens through which to explore both future career challenges and opportunities.

REFERENCES

Allen, B.C. (2011) 'The role of professional identity commitment in understanding the relationship between casual employment and perceptions of career success', *Career Development International*, 16(2), pp. 195–216.

Amundson, N.E. (1994) 'Negotiating identity during unemployment', *Journal of Employment Counseling*, 31, pp. 98–104.

Arthur, M.B. and D.M. Rousseau (1996a) 'A career lexicon for the 21st century', *Academy of Management Executive*, 10(4), pp. 28–39.

Arthur, M.B. and D.M. Rousseau (eds) (1996b) *The Boundaryless Career: A New Employment Principle for a New Organizational Era*. New York, NY: Oxford University Press.

Arthur, M.B., S.N. Khapova and C.P.M. Wilderom (2005) 'Career success in a boundaryless career world', *Journal of Organizational Behavior*, 26(2), pp. 177–202.

Ashforth, B.E. and F. Mael (1989) 'Social identity theory and the organization', *Academy of Management Review*, 14(1), pp. 20–39.

Ashforth, B.E., S.H. Harrison and K.G. Corley (2008) 'Identification in organizations: an examination of four fundamental questions', *Journal of Management*, 34(3), pp. 325–374.

Bailey, C., A. Madden, K. Alfes, A. Shantz and E. Soane (2017) 'The mismanaged soul: existential labor and the erosion of meaningful work', *Human Resource Management Review*, 27(3), pp. 416–430.

Bakker, A.B. and E. Demerouti (2008) 'Towards a model of work engagement', *Career Development International*, 13(3), pp. 209–223.

Barley, S.R. (1989) 'Careers, identities, and institutions: the legacy of the Chicago School of Sociology', in M.B. Arthur, D.T. Hall and B.S. Lawrence (eds) *Handbook of Career Theory*. Cambridge: Cambridge University Press, pp. 41–65.

Barley, S.R., B.A. Bechky and F.J. Milliken (2017) 'The changing nature of work: careers, identities, and work lives in the 21st century', *Academy of Management Discoveries*, 3(2), pp. 111–115.

Batt, R. (2018) 'The financial model of the firm, the "future of work", and employment relations', in A. Wilkinson, T. Dundon, J. Donaghey and A. Colvin (eds) *The Routledge Companion to Employment Relations*. London: Routledge, Taylor & Francis Group, pp. 465–479.

Baumeister, R.F. and K.D. Vohs (2002) 'The Pursuit of Meaningfulness in Life', in C.R. Snyder and S.J. Lopez (eds) *Handbook of Positive Psychology*. 1st edn. New York, NY: Oxford University Press, pp. 608–619.

Berg, J.M., A. Wrzesniewski and J.E. Dutton (2010) 'Perceiving and responding to challenges in job crafting at different ranks: when proactivity requires adaptivity', *Journal of Organizational Behavior*, 31(2/3), pp. 158–186.

Blustein, D.L., L.E. Devenis and B.A. Kidney (1989) 'Relationship between the identity formation process and career development', *Journal of Counseling Psychology*, 36(2), pp. 196–202.

Boh, W.F., S. Slaughter and S. Ang (2001) 'Is information technology a "boundaryless" profession? A sequence analysis of the career histories of IT professionals from 1979–1998', *Academy of Management Proceedings*, pp. A1–A6.

Bourdieu, P. (1984) *Distinction: A Social Critique of the Judgement of Taste*. London and Melbourne: Routledge & Kegan Paul.

Brocklehurst, M. (2003) 'Careers, identity and boundaries'. Paper presented at Academy of Management Annual Meeting, Seattle, WA, USA.

Brown, D. (2002) 'The role of work values and cultural values in occupational choice, satisfaction, and success: a theoretical statement', in D. Brown and Associates (eds) *Career Choice and Development.* 4th edn. San Francisco, CA: Jossey-Bass, pp. 465–510.

Brown, S.P. (1996) 'A meta-analysis and review of organizational research on job involvement', *Psychological Bulletin,* 120(2), pp. 235–255.

Bruner, J. (1986) *Actual Minds, Possible Worlds.* Cambridge, MA: Harvard University Press.

Bruner, J. (1997) 'A narrative model of self-construction', in J.G. Snodgrass and R.L. Thompson (eds) *The Self across Psychology: Self-recognition, Self-awareness, and the Self Concept.* New York, NY: New York Academy of Sciences, pp. 144–161.

Bunderson, J.S. and J.A. Thompson (2009) 'The call of the wild: zookeepers, callings, and the double-edged sword of deeply meaningful work', *Administrative Science Quarterly,* 54(1), pp. 32–57.

Burke, K. (1945) *A Grammar of Motives.* New York, NY: Prentice-Hall.

Burke, R.J. and Cary L. Cooper (2004) *Leading in Turbulent Times: Managing in the New World of Work,* Malden, MA and Oxford: Blackwell.

Carless, D. and K. Douglas (2009) ' "We haven't got a seat on the bus for you" or "All the seats are mine": narratives and career transition in professional golf', *Qualitative Research in Sport and Exercise,* 1(1), pp. 51–66.

Dawis, R.V. and L.H. Lofquist (1976) 'Personality style and the process of work adjustment', *Journal of Counseling Psychology,* 23(1), pp. 55–59.

De Cuyper, N., H. De Witte and H. Van Emmerik (2011) 'Temporary employment: costs and benefits for (the careers of) employees and organizations', *Career Development International,* 16(2), pp. 104–113.

Donnelly, R. (2009) 'Career behavior in the knowledge economy: experiences and perceptions of career mobility among management and IT consultants in the UK and the USA', *Journal of Vocational Behavior,* 75(3), pp. 319–328.

Dutton, J.E., L.M. Roberts and J. Bednar (2010) 'Pathways for positive identity construction at work: four types of positive identity and the building of social resources', *Academy of Management Review,* 35(2), pp. 265–293.

Elangovan, A.R., C.C. Pinder and M. McLean (2010) 'Callings and organizational behavior', *Journal of Vocational Behavior,* 76(3), pp. 428–440.

Florida, R. (2008) *Who's Your City? How the Creative Economy is Making Where to Live the Most Important Decision of Your Life.* Toronto, ON: Random House.

Frankl, V.E. (1984) *Man's Search for Meaning.* 3rd edn. New York, NY: Pocket Books.

Freidson, E. (2001) *Professionalism: The Third Logic.* Chicago, IL: University of Chicago Press.

Gergen, K.J. and M.M. Gergen (1983) 'Narratives of the self', in T.R. Sarbin and K.E. Scheibe (eds) *Studies in Social Identity.* New York, NY: Praeger, pp. 254–273.

Giddens, A. (1991) *Modernity and Self-identity: Self and Society in the Late Modern Age.* Stanford, CA: Stanford University Press.

Gratton, L. and A. Scott (2016) *The 100-Year Life.* London: Bloomsbury.

Grote, G. and S. Raeder (2009) 'Careers and identity in flexible working: do flexible identities fare better?', *Human Relations,* 62(2), pp. 219–244.

Guest, D.E., P. Oakley, M. Clinton and A. Budjanovcanin (2006) 'Free or precarious? A comparison of the attitudes of workers in flexible and traditional employ-
ment contracts', *Human Resource Management Review*, 16(2), pp. 107–124.
Guichard, J. (2009) 'Self-constructing', *Journal of Vocational Behavior*, 75(3), pp.
251–258.
Gunz, H.P., M.G. Evans and R.M. Jalland (2000) 'Career boundaries in a "bound-
aryless" world', in M.A. Peiperl, M.B. Arthur, R. Goffee and T. Morris (eds)
Career Frontiers: New Conceptions in Working Lives. Oxford: Oxford University
Press, pp. 24–53.
Hall, D.T. (1996) 'Protean careers of the 21st century', *The Academy of Management
Executive (1993–2005)*, 10(4), pp. 8–16.
Hall, D.T. (2002) *Careers In and Out of Organizations: Foundations for Organizational
Science*. Thousand Oaks, CA: Sage Publications.
Hall, D.T. and Associates (1996) *The Career is Dead – Long Live the Career: A
Relational Approach to Careers*. San Francisco, CA: Jossey-Bass.
Hall, D.T. and D.E. Chandler (2005) 'Psychological success: when the career is a
calling', *Journal of Organizational Behavior*, 26(2), pp. 155–176.
Haslam, S.A. (2004) *Psychology in Organizations: The Social Identity Approach*.
2nd edn. London: SAGE.
Holland, J.L. (1959) 'A theory of vocational choice', *Journal of Counseling
Psychology*, 6(1), pp. 35–45.
Holland, J.L. (1973) *Making Vocational Choices: A Theory of Careers*. Englewood
Cliffs, NJ: Prentice Hall.
Holland, J.L. (1985) *Making Vocational Choices: A Theory of Vocational
Personalities and Work Environment*. 2nd edn. Odessa, FL: Psychological
Assessment Resources Inc.
Humphrey, S.E., J.D. Nahrgang and F.P. Morgeson (2007) 'Integrating motiva-
tional, social, and contextual work design features: a meta-analytic summary
and theoretical extension of the work design literature', *Journal of Applied
Psychology*, 92(5), pp. 1332–1356.
Ibarra, H. (1999) 'Provisional selves: experimenting with image and identity in
professional adaptation', *Administrative Science Quarterly*, 44(4), pp. 764–791.
Ibarra, H. (2003) *Working Identity*. Cambridge, MA: Harvard Business School.
Ibarra, H. and R. Barbulescu (2010) 'Identity as narrative: prevalence, effective-
ness, and consequences of narrative identity work in macro work role transi-
tions', *Academy of Management Review*, 35(1), pp. 135–154.
Ibarra, H. and J.L. Petriglieri (2010) 'Identity work and play', *Journal of
Organizational Change Management*, 23(1), pp. 10–25.
Inkson, K. (2003) 'International career self-management: theory and empirical
evidence symposium'. Paper presented at Academy of Management, Seattle,
WA, USA.
Jackson, C. (1996) 'Managing and developing a boundaryless career: lessons from
dance and drama', *European Journal of Work & Organizational Psychology*, 5(4),
pp. 617–628.
Kass, S.J., S.J. Vodanovitch and A. Callender (2001) 'State-trait boredom: rela-
tionship to absenteeism, tenure and job satisfaction', *Journal of Business and
Psychology*, 16(2), pp. 317–327.
Khapova, S.N., M.B. Arthur and C.P. Wilderom (2007) 'The subjective career in
the knowledge economy', in H.P. Gunz and M. Peiperl (eds) *Handbook of Career
Studies*. Thousand Oaks, CA: Sage Publications, pp. 114–130.

Kossen, C. and P. McIlveen (2017) 'Unemployment from the perspective of the psychology of working', *Journal of Career Development*, 45(5), pp. 474–488.

Kramer, M.W. (1994) 'Uncertainty reduction during job transitions: an exploratory study of the communication experiences of newcomers and transferees', *Management Communication Quarterly*, 7(4), pp. 384–412.

Kunda, G., S.R. Barley and J. Evans (2002) 'Why do contractors contract? The experience of highly skilled technical professionals in a contingent labor market', *Industrial & Labor Relations Review*, 55(2), pp. 234–261.

Law, B., F. Meijers and G. Wijers (2002) 'New perspectives on career and identity in the contemporary world', *British Journal of Guidance & Counselling*, 30(4), pp. 431–449.

Lazarova, M. (2003) 'Global careers: considerations for a boundaryless world'. Paper presented at Academy of Management, Seattle, WA, USA.

Lewin, K. (1951) 'Field theory in social science: selected theoretical papers', *The American Journal of Sociology*, 57(1), pp. 86–87.

Maslow, A.H. (1954) *Motivation and Personality*. New York, NY: Harper and Row.

McAdams, D.P. (1999) 'Personal narratives and the life story', in L. Pervin and O. John (eds) *Handbook of Personality: Theory and Research*. 2nd edn. New York: Guilford Press, pp. 242–262.

McArdle, S., L. Waters, J.P. Briscoe and D.T. Hall (2007) 'Employability during unemployment: adaptability, career identity and human and social capital', *Journal of Vocational Behavior*, 71(2), pp. 247–264.

McCormick, R., N. Amundson and G. Poehnell (2003) *Guiding Circles: An Aboriginal Guide to Finding Career Paths*. Vancouver, BC: Ergon Communications.

McElroy, J.C. and Q. Weng (2016) 'The connections between careers and organizations in the new career era', *Journal of Career Development*, 43(1), pp. 3–10.

McKercher, C. and V. Mosco (2007) *Knowledge Workers in the Information Society*. Lanham, MD: Lexington Books.

Myers, K.K. and K. Sadaghiani (2010) 'Millennials in the workplace: a communication perspective on millennials' organizational relationships and performance', *Journal of Business and Psychology*, 25(2), pp. 225–238.

Parker, P. and M.B. Arthur (2000) 'Careers, organizing, and community', in M.A. Peiperl, M.B. Arthur, R. Goffee and T. Morris (eds) *Career Frontiers: New Conceptions of Working Lives*. New York, NY: Oxford University Press, pp. 99–122.

Parker, P., M.B. Arthur and K. Inkson (2004) 'Career communities: a preliminary exploration of member-defined career support structures', *Journal of Organizational Behavior*, 25(4), pp. 489–514.

Pazy, A. (1990) 'The threat of professional obsolescence: how do professionals at different career stages experience it and cope with it?', *Human Resource Management*, 29, pp. 251–269.

Pope, M. and M. Sveinsdottir (2005) 'Frank, we hardly knew ye: the very personal side of Frank Parsons', *Journal of Counseling & Development*, 83(1), pp. 105–115.

Pratt, M.G., K.W. Rockmann and J.B. Kaufmann (2006) 'Constructing professional identity: the role of work and identity learning cycles in the customization of identity among medical residents', *Academy of Management Journal*, 49(2), pp. 235–262.

Reed, M.I. (2007) 'Engineers of human souls, faceless technocrats, or merchants of morality? Changing professional forms and identities in the face of the neoliberal challenge', in A. Pinnington, T. Campbell and R. Macklin (eds) *Human*

Resource Management: Ethics and Employment. Oxford: Oxford University Press, pp. 171–189.

Rosso, B.D., K.H. Dekas and A. Wrzesniewski (2010) 'On the meaning of work: a theoretical integration and review', *Research in Organizational Behaviour*, 30, pp. 91–127.

Ryan, R.M. and E.L. Deci (2000) 'Self-determination theory and the facilitation of intrinsic motivation, social development, and well-being', *American Psychologist*, 55(1), pp. 68–78.

Sander, E.J. (2017) 'Responses to the physical work environment: focus, sense of beauty and connectedness'. Available via https://research-repository.griffith.edu.au/handle/10072/370650 (accessed 10 October 2019).

Savickas, M.L. (2005) 'The theory and practice of career construction', in S.D. Brown and R. Lent (eds) *Career Development and Counseling: Putting Theory and Research to Work*. Hoboken, NJ: John Wiley, pp. 43–70.

Savickas, M.L., L. Nota, J. Rossier, J.-P. Dauwalder, M.E. Duarte, J. Guichard, S. Soresi, R. Van Esbroeck and A.E.M. van Vianen (2009) 'Life designing: a paradigm for career construction in the 21st century', *Journal of Vocational Behavior*, 75(3), pp. 239–250.

Seligman, M. (2002) *Authentic Happiness: Using the New Positive Psychology to Realize Your Potential for Lasting Fulfillment*. Milsons Point, NSW: Random House.

Sennett, R. (1998) *The Corrosion of Character*. New York, NY: W. W. Norton & Company.

Stahl, G.K., E.L. Miller and R.L. Tung (2002) 'Toward the boundaryless career: a closer look at the expatriate career concept and the perceived implications of an international assignment', *Journal of World Business*, 37(3), pp. 216–227.

Steger, M.F. (2009) 'Meaning in life', in S.J. Lopez (ed.) *Handbook of Positive Psychology*. 2nd edn. New York, NY: Oxford University Press, pp. 679–688.

Sullivan, S. and M. Arthur (2006) 'The evolution of the boundaryless career concept: examining physical and psychological mobility', *Journal of Vocational Behavior*, 69(1), pp. 19–29.

Sullivan, S.E. (1999) 'The changing nature of careers: a review and research agenda', *Journal of Management*, 25(3), pp. 457–484.

Susskind, R. and D. Susskind (2015) *The Future of the Professions: How Technology will Transform the Work of Human Experts*. New York, NY: Oxford University Press.

Sveningsson, S. and M. Alvesson (2003) 'Managing managerial identities: organizational fragmentation, discourse and identity struggle', *Human Relations*, 56(10), pp. 1163–1193.

Thompson, P. (2003) 'Disconnected capitalism: or why employers can't keep their side of the bargain', *Work, Employment and Society*, 17(2), pp. 359–378.

Tolbert, P.S. (1996) 'Occupations, organizations, and boundaryless careers', in M.B. Arthur and D.M. Rousseau (eds) *The Boundaryless Career: A New Employment Principle for a New Organizational Era*. New York: Oxford University Press, pp. 331–349.

Trevor-Roberts, E. (2006) 'Are you sure? The role of uncertainty in career', *Journal of Employment Counseling*, 43(3), pp. 98–116.

Trevor-Roberts, E., P. Parker and J. Sandberg (2019) 'How uncertainty affects career behaviour: a narrative approach', *Australian Journal of Management*, 44(1), pp. 50–69.

Valcour, M., L. Bailyn and M.A. Quijada (2007) 'Customized careers', in H.P. Gunz and M. Peiperl (eds) *Handbook of Career Studies*. Thousand Oaks, CA: Sage Publications, pp. 188–210.

Van den Broeck, A., M. Vansteenkiste, H. De Witte and W. Lens (2008) 'Explaining the relationships between job characteristics, burnout, and engagement: the role of basic psychological need satisfaction', *Work and Stress*, 22(3), pp. 277–294.

Weick, K.E. (1996) 'Enactment and the boundaryless career: organizing as we work', in M.B. Arthur and D.M. Rousseau (eds) *The Boundaryless Career: A New Employment Principle for a New Organizational Era*. New York, NY: Oxford University Press, pp. 40–57.

Winograd, M. and M.D. Hais (2011) *Millennial Momentum: How a New Generation is Remaking America*. New Brunswick, NJ: Rutgers University Press.

Wrzesniewski, A. and J.E. Dutton (2001) 'Crafting a job: revisioning employees as active crafters of their work', *Academy of Management Review*, 26(2), pp. 179–201.

14. The future of employee engagement: the challenge of separating old wine from new bottles

Bruce E. Kaufman, Michael Barry, Adrian Wilkinson and Rafael Gomez

INTRODUCTION

Forecasting the future of a management practice is particularly challenging because many practices cycle in and out as a combination of a generic idea overlain with new rationale, improved implementation, and different terminology. For example, industrial democracy, human relations, Japanese management, employee participation, and employee empowerment were all big topics at various points over the twentieth century, enjoyed a heyday of popularity, and then faded from sight as interest waned and attention shifted to the next business problem and heralded new solution.

Some of the chapter topics in this volume on the future of work are relatively free of this conundrum: for example, the gig economy is obviously a new technological development, while meaningful work has been discussed by philosophers and theologians for centuries. A reading of the current literature on employee engagement almost unanimously indicates it is a new idea and management practice, originating in the 1990s and described by one author (Bryne 2015, p. 22) as still "in its infancy." If this is the case, a forecast of the future of employee engagement has little of a past trend line to anchor the analysis and must instead focus on the new elements and forces in the business situation that have spawned the idea, the extent to which they are transient or long-term developments, and the degree to which employee engagement adds significant business value that helps separate fad from staying power. On the other hand, to the degree employee engagement is the proverbial "old wine in new bottle," it has a recorded history that provides a helpful baseline trajectory for making a forecast into the future, albeit with need to still factor in changing conditions and developments.

Before these short-run/transient and long-run/permanent dimensions of employee engagement can be sorted and weighed, it is first necessary to define the concept. Accordingly, the next section of this chapter provides a review of alternative engagement definitions and conceptualizations in prominent studies. In the second section, we provide two short vignettes from the historical literature, which collectively indicate engagement has a large generic, old wine component – a finding that suggests the future of engagement is partly known by studying its past. Working out an informed, on-target forecast of the future of employee engagement is also facilitated by consideration of recent empirical patterns and trends in engagement, which we briefly present in the third section. In the fourth and final section, several published models of employee engagement drivers and moderators are introduced, contextual insights from historical and empirical sections are added, and the package is used to derive a best-estimate forecast of both the time–series trend and cross-section pattern of national-level measures of employee engagement over the next one and two decades. The approach taken in this chapter to the future of work is novel, therefore, in its greater analytical, model-driven orientation.

WHAT IS EMPLOYEE ENGAGEMENT?

The first requisite for an evaluation and forecast of employee engagement (EE) is definition and conceptualization of the construct. A summary review of the EE literature reveals more than usual diversity on this matter.

The concept of employee engagement is almost universally attributed to William Kahn (1990), professor of organizational behavior (Schaufeli and Bakker 2010, p. 12; Guest, 2014, p. 142). He proposes that engagement, as a generic behavioral concept, is part of a continuum with full disengagement at one end and full engagement at the other. He (Kahn) says of engagement, "People can use varying degrees of their selves, physically, cognitively, and emotionally, in the roles they perform" (1990, p. 692). He describes the behavioral dualism contained in the engagement/disengagement concepts (E/D hereafter) as a coupling–attaching of the self to a role in the former case and uncoupling–detaching in the latter. An alternative dualism is approach–withdrawal behavior.

E/D behavior, Kahn states, applies to all human roles, such as student, spouse, soldier, employee, and executive. In this regard, Kahn does not discuss *employee* engagement per se but engagement across life roles. He argues E/D behavior arises from a psychological process that is largely coterminous with motivation but gains a unique identity as a holistic combination of body, mind, and heart. Also, Kahn represents motivation as an internal psychological state and process while engagement is externally visible actions and behaviors in role performance.

Kahn's paper and engagement concept might have quickly disappeared if academic uptake had been the decisive factor. However, the concept was independently picked up and applied to employees by management consultants and transformed into a hugely popular and influential line of research and practice. The pioneer was the Gallup organization. Backed by an extensive research program of company interviews, data from thousands of organizations across numerous countries, and sophisticated statistical analysis, Gallup rolled out in the late 1990s its Q^{12} employee engagement survey.

Gallup (2018) defines an engaged employee as "those who are involved in, enthusiastic about, and committed to their work and workplace." The organization's engagement survey quickly garnered national media attention, particularly because its finding that only one third of employees are engaged quickly set off alarm bells in executive suites. The media publicity and burgeoning consulting business for Gallup spurred other management/ HR consulting firms to develop their own engagement surveys, although with differentiated methodologies, definitions, constructs, models, and measures.

The university research community was slow to embrace the engagement wave and, as late as 2006, Saks (p. 600) observed, "There is a surprising dearth of research on employee engagement in the academic literature." Over the next decade, however, engagement research boomed with hundreds of journal articles and many new definitions, models, and measures. This literature is too vast to survey, but chapters from a handbook provide an accurate snapshot.

In an introductory chapter to *Handbook of Employee Engagement*, Albrecht (2010, p. 4) tells readers, "Common to many definitions . . . is the idea that engagement is a positive work-related psychological state (reflected in words like enthusiasm, energy, passion and vigor) and that engagement is also a motivational state reflected in a genuine willingness to invest focused effort toward organizational goals and success." He continues, "Perhaps the most widely cited definition of engagement is that offered by Schaufeli et al. (2002, p. 74), who defined engagement as 'a positive, fulfilling, work-related state of mind that is characterized by vigor, dedication, and absorption'." Albrecht explains that Schaufeli and colleagues operationalized their engagement construct into a seventeen-item questionnaire, the Utrecht Work Engagement Scale, which has emerged as the academic version of Gallup's Q^{12}. The seventeen items are drivers or indicators of their three central components of engagement: vigor (e.g., "At my work, I feel that I am bursting with energy"), dedication (e.g., "I find the work that I do full of meaning and purpose"), and absorption (e.g., "Time flies when I'm working").

The academics and consultants do not see eye to eye on employee engagement (Truss et al., 2014), perhaps inevitably given their different agendas and success criteria. Bakker and Leiter (2010), for example, chide the consultants for pouring a dozen or more traditional concepts, such as affective commitment, involvement, and job satisfaction, into a large pot, adding their proprietary secret sauce, stirring the mix, packaging it with a veneer of science and eye-catching success stories, and marketing the product as a sure-fire tonic to pep up the workforce. They say that this approach "fail[s] to capture the distinct value added by the new concept of work engagement. Hence, the way practitioners conceptualize engagement comes close to putting old wine in new bottles" (p. 182). People on the consulting side (e.g., Fleck and Inceoglu, 2010), however, chide the academics for an over-emphasis on individual-level psychological theorization of engagement, neglect of situational context and environmental forces, and lack of relevance and application to practitioners.

The subject of employee engagement has a noticeable but largely unquestioned managerialist purpose and cast. Schaufeli and Bakker (2010), for example, observe that the principal reason companies, consulting firms, and management researchers are investing huge sums of money, organizational resources, and time into understanding employee engagement is the strong evidence that a more engaged workforce leads to positive outcomes for firms. As they summarize, "The message for organizations is clear: increasing work engagement pays off" (p. 11), such as in higher productivity, lower turnover, increased profitability, and competitive advantage in the market. Less examined and critically questioned is the effect of high engagement on employees, their families, and the community/society (Keenoy, 2014).

Engaged employees often report very positive feelings and satisfying experiences, such as charged-up enthusiasm, high job satisfaction, and personal gratification from extraordinary accomplishment (Halbesleben, 2010). On the other side of the scale, however, are potential dark sides for the employee, such as workaholism, stress, burnout, and family neglect.

THE EMPLOYEE ENGAGEMENT CONSTRUCT: NEW DISCOVERY OR REINVENTED–REPACKAGED IDEA?

Some writers on employee engagement conclude the voluminous and still ongoing debate over definition of the concept is neither productive nor necessary. Purcell (2012, p. 13) summarizes, for example, "I don't think it matters that employee engagement is a term capable of many shades of meaning. At its heart are employees' feelings, beliefs and attitudes concerning their job, their co-workers, the customers, their manager, and concerning the organization as a whole and especially the senior management team." He continues, "We know that if employees believe that the organization and its management, at the local and top levels, provide support to them as a person, a person with feelings and beliefs about fairness and wanting some development, they are likely to respond with cooperative behaviors of benefit to the firm."

Purcell's position is attractive because it sweeps aside discordant definitional nitpicking and gets to the core of the engagement idea. However, the question then arises of how it is possible that such a seemingly straightforward, managerially important concept lay undiscovered until the early 1990s, when Kahn first published a journal article on it and Gallup devised an empirical measure and started doing engagement surveys.

Investigation quickly reveals that Kahn is, in fact, not the first person to discover the engagement concept. Two short snapshot accounts demonstrate the point and further clarify and develop the engagement construct (with key words italicized for emphasis) in ways that usefully go beyond Purcell's one-sentence sketch. The sources/authors are, respectively, Adam Smith (1723–1790) and John Commons (1862–1945).

Adam Smith devotes several chapters in *Wealth of Nations* (1776[1937]) to firms, management, and labor. He also at several places uses the words *engaged* and *engaging*. One of the most famous passages in the book is, "It is not from the benevolence of the butcher, the brewer, or the baker, that we expect our dinner, but from their regard to their own self-interest" (p. 14). For a poverty-stricken person, however, Smith notes directly above this passage that, when "he has no other means of *engaging* them to act according to his inclinations," the only remaining option is to "endeavor . . . to obtain their *goodwill*" (p. 14). The word Smith uses most often to capture the engagement idea is *industrious*, while he uses the word *indolent* for disengagement (i.e., E/D is industrious/indolent). In another passage, Smith observes that the opportunity for a worker to make good wages, do interesting and meaningful work, and get ahead in life, "*animates him to exert that strength to the utmost* [and] . . . we shall always find the workman more *active, diligent, and expeditious*" (p. 81, all emphases added).

Smith also notes that at some point more engagement becomes harmful to the employee. He observes that, when workers "are liberally paid by the piece, [they] are very apt to over-work themselves, and to ruin their health and constitution in a few years" (p. 82).

John Commons was an early twentieth-century labor economist and co-founder of the American fields of employment/industrial relations and personnel/human resource management (Kaufman, 2008). He explains in *Industrial Goodwill* (1919, and noting Smith's use of the goodwill term) that American industry in the two decades before World War I was being torn apart by capital–labor hostility, violent mass strikes, and spread of radical trade unions and anarchist–socialist political movements. When the US entered the war in 1917, patriotism and unity of purpose swept the land, capital and labor quickly transitioned from enemies to partners, and both sides mobilized all their energies and resources to defeat the German enemy.

When companies saw how much workers could increase production when aroused by patriotism and common purpose, they sought to recreate this spirit by shifting to an early-1920s version of what today is called a high-commitment/high-performance work system (HPWS; see Paauwe et al., 2013), but which Commons in the terminology of his day labeled a *goodwill* employment system. Goodwill, Commons states, is an attitude built from workplace justice, reciprocity, participation, joint interests, and mutual gain, which for the worker (1919, p. 20) *"enlists his whole soul and all his energies in the thing he is doing*. It is that unknown factor pervading the business as a whole . . . which the French give the name, *l'esprit de corps.*" He goes on to say (p. 25) that, "goodwill is coming to be an *intangible asset of business more valuable than the tangible properties* [because] it brings larger profits and lifts the employer somewhat above the level of competing employers by giving him a more productive labor force than theirs in proportion to the wages paid."

To summarize, neither of these two people use the term "employee engagement." However, when Smith describes how hope for a better life "animates him to exert that strength to the utmost" and Commons observes how goodwill and a common purpose "enlists his whole soul and all his energies in the thing he is doing," they surely grasped the essentials of the engagement idea. In this respect, our understanding of engagement fundamentals seems to have advanced very little from then to now – per Kahn's observation twenty years after his pioneer article that "many of us have different understandings of what engagement is . . . except that it involves people working hard and caring about what they are doing" (2010, p. 20).

When engagement is framed in this simple, transparent way, the core of the construct seems a clear case of a very old wine with a long-term but cyclic demand. Since the early 1990s, modern academics and consultants have entrepreneurially reformulated, repackaged, and rebranded it into a variety of more complex, powerful, and science-guided blends. Even if the substance of the new version is not much different or improved, it has nonetheless been successfully positioned and sold as a newly pioneered, high-powered twenty-first-century employee energy drink. In turn, the future of employee engagement would be easy to predict if the new version was indeed a successful across-the-board boost to working hard and caring about the job and company. However, since the latest surveys find only 30–40 percent of employees say they feel actively engaged considerable room for change exists on both the upside and downside, and predicting the direction of change in engagement takes on greater scientific challenge and practical usefulness (Gomez et al., 2019).

EMPIRICAL CONTEXT FOR ASSESSING THE FUTURE OF EMPLOYEE ENGAGEMENT

The historical record provides one source of valuable context and data points for thinking out the likely trend of employee engagement in the years ahead. In this section additional context is provided by brief review of empirical patterns in employee engagement. The guiding supposition is that patterns of employee engagement witnessed today are likely to significantly shape the patterns ten and twenty years from now.

The evidence examined is the cross-section pattern in reported engagement levels for the four countries of Australia, Canada, United Kingdom (UK), and United States (US). The authors of this chapter recently completed a large-scale survey aimed at measuring and assessing the state of the employment relationship (ER) and human resource (HR) management function within and across these four countries with data obtained from a nationally representative sample of, respectively, managers and employees (for more details, see Wilkinson et al., 2018; Kaufman et al., 2018; Gomez et al., 2019). The survey is called the *State of the Workplace Employment Relations Survey* (SWERS) and the data were collected in early 2016.

Since the purpose of the survey is to provide a comprehensive data checklist on all aspects of work, employment, and human resource management in companies, space was available to include only one question on employee engagement. The managers were asked to rate on a 1–7 scale (1 = lowest, 7 = highest) the level of employee engagement (EE) for the largest group of core employees for which they had reasonable knowledge, such as at a company, division, or enterprise level. Since employees are typically knowledgeable of a smaller part of the company, they were instructed to rate engagement for employees for which they had reasonable familiarity at the enterprise, department, or work unit level. In the manager survey, the engagement statement reads: *"My company/organization's employees are fully engaged in their work and give 100%."* In the employee survey, the statement was slightly rephrased to ensure the employee understood engagement covers all the mind, body, and heart dimensions. It reads: *"Employees at my unit/workplace give all of their hearts, minds, and efforts."*

A numerical summary of the responses, including survey average, is shown in tabular form in Table 14.1.

A number of interesting findings emerge from the data. For example, there is striking similarity across the countries. One interpretation is that within each country's ER/HR system is a common employee engagement subsystem or module, such as researchers postulate in theoretical models of engagement and draw in box–arrow diagrams. This subsystem contains a universalist core set of engagement determinants, drivers, mediating mechanisms, and cause–effect relations that through a X(Z) → EE process generate a relatively common pattern of workforce engagement levels. The common pattern across countries comes from a strong main effect in the equation (the X drivers) but with some cross-country differences in distributions due to heterogeneity in national-level contextual and contingent factors (as discussed above). Among these factors, included in the Z variable, are industry composition, workforce demographics, cultural norms, employment law regimes, and union density, which modify the X effect.

Employee engagement is an interesting and worthwhile topic in its own right, but, nonetheless, what companies and researchers *really* care about is EE's effect on organizational performance (P). This form of the engagement equation, therefore, is X(Z) → EE → P. SWERS collected data on measures of organizational performance but establishing the existence and nature of an EE → P connection requires sophisticated statistical analysis that we have not completed and which is beyond the scope of this chapter. Nonetheless, the SWERS data reveal that the dispersion in EE scores *within* countries is much larger than the dispersion *across* countries. To the degree EE confers competitive advantage, firms within a country appear to have more scope and opportunity to use it to surpass rivals than do rival nations in global competition.

However, if the quantitative size of the EE → P relationship is significant, even small differences across countries can make a big difference in international competition. The SWERS data in Table 14.1 reveal that the US is in the top position among the four countries; the country in the bottom position is less clear but overall looks to be the UK. The US/UK divergence in manager scores is 5.63 vs. 5.28 and 4.68 vs. 4.49 for employees. The largest source of disparity is in the manager responses where 29 percent of American managers marked the highest score (7) versus 15 percent of British managers. Other engagement surveys also find that, on average, EE scores are higher in North America than in Europe (Aon Hewitt, 2018).

Another finding from SWERS is that managers and employees have significantly different workplace experiences and perceptions, with managers giving much higher ratings than employees. The mean engagement score for managers is 5.63 but falls for employees by nearly a full point to 4.68.

Table 14.1   Mean and distribution of engagement scores, four countries

	Manager survey			Employee survey		
	Frequency	Percent	Cumulative	Frequency	Percent	Cumulative
United States						
1 – Very Strongly Disagree	6	1.2	1.2	88	4.29	4.29
2	5	1	2.2	99	4.83	9.12
3	20	3.99	6.19	167	8.15	17.27
4 – Neutral	54	10.78	16.97	557	27.17	44.44
5	111	22.16	39.13	495	24.15	68.59
6	161	32.14	71.27	413	20.15	88.74
7 – Very Strongly Agree	144	28.74	100	231	11.27	100
Total	501	100		2,050	100	
Mean	5.63			4.68		
United Kingdom						
1 – Very Strongly Disagree	4	0.96	0.96	81	3.95	3.95
2	6	1.45	2.41	108	5.27	9.22
3	25	6.02	8.43	225	10.97	20.19
4 – Neutral	62	14.94	23.37	618	30.13	50.32
5	116	27.95	51.32	507	24.72	75.04
6	140	33.73	85.05	356	17.36	92.40
7 – Very Strongly Agree	62	14.94	100	156	7.61	100
Total	415	100		2,051	100	
Mean	5.28			4.49		

231

Table 14.1 (continued)

	Manager survey			Employee survey		
	Frequency	Percent	Cumulative	Frequency	Percent	Cumulative
Australia						
1 – Very Strongly Disagree	6	1.5	1.5	56	2.8	2.8
2	10	2.5	4	86	4.3	7.10
3	27	6.75	10.75	159	7.94	15.04
4 – Neutral	67	16.75	27.5	582	29.07	44.11
5	99	24.75	52.25	548	27.37	71.48
6	118	29.5	81.75	395	19.73	91.21
7 – Very Strongly Agree	73	18.25	100	176	8.79	100
Total	400	100		2,002	100	
Mean	5.22			4.68		
Canada						
1 – Very Strongly Disagree	0	0	0	44	4	4
2	4	2	2	60	5.45	9.45
3	10	5	7	99	9	18.45
4 – Neutral	22	11	18	335	30.45	48.90
5	60	30	48	284	25.82	74.72
6	70	35	83	191	17.36	92.08
7 – Very Strongly Agree	34	17	100	87	7.91	100
Total	200	100		1,100	100	
Mean	5.42			4.52		

Note: Percent and cumulative totals have been rounded to 100 percent for United States and United Kingdom (both manager survey and employee survey) and for Canada (employee survey).
For managers the statement read was: "My company/organization's employees are fully engaged in their work and give 100 per cent." For employees the following statement was read: "Employees at my unit/workplace give all of their hearts, minds, and efforts." Both groups were asked to respond using a 7 point agree/disagree scale with these statements.

232

The difference is large enough to change the evaluation from "engaged" to "disengaged." The fact that managers and employees have different perspectives on breadth and depth of engagement in their workplaces is not surprising. However, the fact the divergence is quite large and it is the employees – the ones actually delivering the engagement – who give the lower grade is a warning signal.

BRINGING IT ALL TOGETHER: ASSESSING THE FUTURE TREND IN EMPLOYEE ENGAGEMENT

Predicting the future trend in engagement requires three things. The first is a fleshed-out model of employee engagement of the generic $X(Z) \rightarrow EE$ type described in the previous section, where the X vector contains the drivers of engagement. The second is a forecast of the direction of change of the driver variables, ΔX, which then leads to predicted ΔEE. The predicted ΔEE is the change in the mean value of engagement across firms in the frequency distribution, measured on the SWERS 1–7 scale. The third requirement is forecast of changes in important moderator variables in the Z vector and mediator variables in the transmission mechanism symbolized by the arrow.

These three inputs, along with incorporation of qualitative, hard-to-measure factors and application of good judgment in working out the final answer, can then be used, speaking at a conceptual level, to generate estimates of the trend in EE over the forecast period (done in Kaufman, 2015, for employee voice). Starting with the current-period measured engagement level as anchor point, the trend line can be extended forward to, say, 2030, by plotting the annual forecasted value of the aggregate engagement measure. With more disaggregated analysis, and again speaking at the conceptual level, the overall engagement score can be decomposed into rank–order categories, such as the Gallup three-way classification of low, middle, and high engagement. The end product is the hallmark of a science – that is, ability to develop and use knowledge, tools, data, and human judgment to make a ceteris-paribus prediction of what will happen to the overall level and compositional pattern of employee engagement over the next one or two decades.

We canvassed the academic, consulting, and business book literatures for theoretical models of the employee engagement process suitable as a framework for forecasting future macro-level trends. At the start of our search, we looked for models that are formally represented in a diagram, such as box–arrow or flow-chart form. Many models of this type were found in the academic research literature but proved unsuitable for making a macro-level forecast. The major reason is that many of the academic researchers, often trained in psychology, theorize the determinants of employee engagement at an individual micro level using a plethora of hard-to-measure and -generalize psychological variables, constructs, and theories (e.g., see the ten chapters in the handbook by Albrecht, 2010, on "key drivers").

As one illustrative example, an oft-used theoretical framework in the academic engagement literature is the job demands-resources (JD-R) model (Hakanen and Roodt, 2010). It posits that an individual's propensity to exhibit engaged behavior is a joint function of challenging demands for performance from the organization coupled with high supply of both personal and organization-provided resources to successfully accomplish the task. A diagram model of engagement based on the JD-R framework is presented by Bakker (2010, p. 240). The level of analysis is the individual employee and nearly every driver variable in the three categories of job demands, job resources, and personal resources is an unobservable psychological construct. Examples, respectively, are work pressure and emotional demands, autonomy and social support, and resilience and self-esteem. The model is insightful for identifying a slice of drivers of engagement at the individual and small group level but is too fine-grained and internal to the person and workplace to provide a useful framework for forecasting macro trends.

Major management and HR consulting firms have also crafted EE models and they typically are presented at the organization level, which is more useful for forecasting purposes. We searched among them for good representations of driver (X) variables and selected three models from, respectively, Bersin (2019), Aon Hewitt (2018), and Voice Project (2019).

The Bersin and Aon-Hewitt models have six drivers and the Voice Project model has five. We add one more study on engagement drivers even though it did not contain a diagram-type model. John Purcell, a leading academic researcher in Britain, has done considerable work on engagement and identifies seven strategic drivers (Purcell, 2014). They are: employee trust in management, satisfaction with work and the job, involvement in decision-making at work, climate of relationships between management and employees, satisfaction with pay, job challenge, and sense of achievement from work.

The labels given to the drivers differ across models, but at a generic content level they have many similarities. We synthesize them to the following seven categories with examples of important attributes:

Organizational Identity: Purpose Driven, Inspiring Mission, People Values, Stakeholder.
Senior Leadership: Capable, Trusted, Involved, Visionary, Team Leader.
Front-Line Managers: Collaborative, Capable, Clear and Open Communication, Fair and Respectful.

Nature of the Work: Meaningful, Autonomy, Participative, Team Oriented, Appealing Conditions.

Culture: Mutualism, Learning and Development, Equitable, Open to Diversity and Innovation.

Organizational Practices: Attract and Develop Talent, Training and Promotion Opportunities, Attractive Pay and Benefits, Involvement and Voice.

Organizational Support: Work/Family Balance, Up-to-date Technology, Needed Quantity/Quality of Resources, Quality of Work Life.

The assumption in these studies is that more of each of these seven drivers, per the $X(Z) \rightarrow$ EE causal equation, leads to higher employee engagement in the workplace (ceteris paribus). A term now coming into vogue is "the employee experience" (IBM Analytics, 2017), to summarize the composite effect of these EE drivers. In keeping with a systems perspective, the drivers need to be balanced, combined, and adjusted to take into account complementarities and synergies among them and, also, contingency moderators with the external environment and other organizational subsystems. The parallel assumption is that fewer of these drivers individually and collectively, and less quality of fit and synergy, leads to a decline in workplace employee engagement. Crucial to engagement success, however, is dedicated executive leadership as without it the other drivers are far less effective and often erode over time. Likewise, it is not practices per se that fuel sustained high-level employee engagement but an engagement culture supported by leaders and practices (Robinson and Gifford, 2014; Bersin, 2015; Gallup, 2018).

For forecasting purposes, we need to determine whether these drivers are likely to expand, remain the same, or contract over the next decade. Ideally, we also need to know the relative importance of each driver and the structure of the complementarities and synergies among them and across organizational subsystems, particularly if some drivers expand but others contract.

Unfortunately, at this point most of the EE literature goes silent. The academic research literature is too fine-grained, psychological, and methods driven to offer much insight into future trends in macro-level engagement/disengagement. Consulting reports and practitioner-authored engagement books are somewhat more helpful, since they are organization-level focused, but for the most part they deal with the here-and-now issues of implementing engagement programs and the likely outcomes and benefits. Among the few exceptions found, the most in-depth and helpful is *The Future of Engagement Thought Piece Collection* (Robinson and Gifford, 2014). The report is sponsored by the Institute for Employment Studies

(IES) and Chartered Institute of Personnel and Development (CIPD) in the UK and composed of short thought pieces by leading academics and practitioners.

An earlier part of this chapter described the historical roots and evolution of the engagement concept, partly to establish that, while the terminology may change over time and across countries, the basic EE idea is generic and long standing. The bearing of this for the present section is that it establishes engagement is not a here-today-and-gone-tomorrow fad but an enduring phenomenon and strived-for objective of organizations and organizational leaders both past and present. The trend of engagement for the next decade, therefore, is likely to be anchored on a fairly solid past trend line. Also to be expected is modest-sized cyclical movements around the trend line associated with ups and downs in employment, unemployment, wage growth, and other such situational factors.

Our confidence in the generic, long-enduring nature of the engagement phenomenon is reinforced by the observation of CIPD chief executive Peter Cheese at the beginning of the IES/CIPD report. He observes,

> What is certainly true is that the motivation and alignment of people to a common cause, to contribute more of themselves, to support each other, are important principles of any successful endeavor and as old as the hills – from rousing Shakespearean speeches on the battlefield, to the ancient pursuit of team sports . . .. The language of employee engagement may be new, but really it is a time-old tension: transactional and controlling Taylorist management versus leadership that emphasizes purpose and values, and supports employees to perform. (Robinson and Gifford, 2014, pp. 6–7)

We suggest there are a number of specific plus/minus factors and developments likely to impact EE levels over the next decade.

On the plus side, for example, are these items: ongoing IT revolution that facilitates decentralization of management, improved team coordination, upskilling of jobs, and work flexibility; spread of employee use of social media with increased exposure and accountability of management practices/treatment; continuing competitive pressure on companies to get more contribution and loyalty from employees; intangible human-related assets becoming a progressively larger source of revenues, competitive advantage, and capitalized value; increased public pressure on companies for social responsibility practices; growing proportion of the workforce composed of millennials/Gen Y who have increased expectations of collaboration and career development; and expanding management focus on creating a positive employee experience, mutualist win-together culture, and closer alignment of employee goals and cultural values with the mission and strategy of the business.

On the negative side are other items. Examples include: downsizing and restructuring have increased the work load and responsibilities of managers and they cannot focus on EE; CEO compensation/stock packages incent them toward short-term investments and away from long-term EE initiatives; erosion of internal labor markets and development systems erode employee security, career advancement paths, and company loyalty; CEO and executive pay is skyrocketing while nonsupervisory employee real hourly pay is largely stagnant and benefit costs are shifted to employees; the corporate message that going forward employees need to take responsibility for their training and careers saps engagement; and decline of unions and threat of unions reduces pressure on companies to take into account employees' interests and wellbeing.

These diverse plus and minus situational factors and developments are informative but difficult to weigh and synthesize into an up, down, or remains-the-same forecast. We can get a nudge closer to an overall assessment, however, through a different route. This route is suggested in the IES/CIPD report. One of the commentators, Martin Reddington, observes,

> An emerging view is that engagement needs to be characterized as transformational with organizations spending 90 per cent of their engagement effort "post-survey" and focusing on building an environment which truly energizes people, inspires them to give their best, and aligns their efforts with the needs of the business. (Robinson and Gifford, 2014, p. 27)

The key word here is "transformational," which links back to the earlier quotation from Cheese regarding the inherent tension between the Taylorist command–control approach to management (aka Theory X, per McGregor, 1960) and a participative–commitment approach (aka Theory Y) built on socio-technical work redesign principles and a mutualist stakeholder governance system (Walton, 1985). Broadly viewed, the seven drivers of engagement listed above are part of a larger system of organizational design and management known in the 1980s as a transformed high-commitment or high-involvement approach (Beer et al., 1984; Lawler, 1986) and today most often referred to as an HPWS or high-performance work system (Huselid, 1995; Appelbaum et al., 2000; Paauwe et al., 2013). From this perspective, a supplemental way to capture the likely EE trend in the years ahead is to forecast the trend in proportion of employees working in HPWS organizations.

Statistical evidence on the proportion of the workforce across countries employed in transformed HPWS workplaces is quite meager. For the US, for example, one study (Osterman, 2000) estimated that in the 1990s over 40 percent of workplaces had introduced at least several HPWS-type practices but, on the other side, another study estimated that less than five percent had implemented the entire package (Blasi and Kruse, 2006). With regard to the UK (CIPD, 2014), data indicate slow but steady increase in HPWS practices up to the World Financial Crisis of 2008, with perhaps 30 percent of workplaces having adopted a substantial portion, albeit more so in the public sector. The extent of HPWS practices then declined with the downturn in the economy but started to slowly expand again in 2012. However, conclusions about whether a workplace qualifies as an HPWS based on a count of practices is problematic, for as suggested earlier, practices by themselves do not ensure management has been able to successfully create the mutualist, unity of interest, goodwill form of team spirit that is the core attitudinal driver of superior performance.

Another complication is that what influences the future trend in engagement is not the current density *level* of HPWS workplaces but the plus/ minus direction of *change*. A large body of quantitative research literature explores the beneficial outcomes of HPWS adoption, but little examines the antecedent drivers of HPWS adoption across companies and countries. We are left, therefore, to largely rely on informed judgment.

Our expectation is that, in advanced, relatively neoliberal economies (e.g., the four in the SWERS survey), the trend growth in the proportion of the workforce employed in transformed HPWS workplaces is at best likely to be marginally positive and more probably roughly zero or even negative. Work system transformation started in the 1970s in the manufacturing sector and is still most associated with manufacturing workplaces yet the manufacturing sector in most advanced countries is a relatively small and steadily shrinking share of employment (e.g., more than 100,000 manufacturing plants have closed in the US since 1980). An offsetting factor is that HPWS-type employment systems have successfully diffused into other capital- and knowledge-intensive economic sectors, such as high-tech development companies, airlines, financial institutions, consulting firms, and public sector organizations. Weighing on the other side, however, is that transformed high-performance systems are infrequently found in several of the most rapidly growing sectors, such as retail, services, lodging, restaurants, and small start-up enterprises.

An important contingency that affects the expansion versus contraction trend of high-engagement HPWS workplaces is the rate of economic growth over the next decade. If national economies continuously and rapidly grow over the next ten years, companies will have the profits and productivity incentives to upgrade their work design and people management systems toward the HPWS model. Since this model incorporates the seven drivers of engagement identified above, macro-level employee engagement levels should trend upward. On the other hand, as economic growth slows so does HPWS adoption and when growth turns negative in a recession then few HPWS workplaces are built and a much larger number shrink or close. A corollary factor is that a strong HR culture and function in companies also promotes effective HPWS and employee engagement practices and HR's influence also waxes in a full-employment economy and wanes in a high-unemployment economy (see Cushen, this volume, in relation to HRM under financialization).

Other macro-level developments are also important drivers of the engagement trend. An important example is financialization. In the American context, financialization of business started in the 1980s, has steadily advanced, and without legislative action is likely to continue. Financialization refers to the growing focus in business on making money through short-term trading and financial asset investment rather than long-term product innovation and investment in physical, human, and intellectual capital. One consequence of financialization is a trend from stakeholder governance and strategy to shareholder governance and strategy; a second consequence is a shift away from long-lived investments in plant, equipment, workforce development, and R&D and toward shorter-term cost reductions, financial investments, and merger/acquisition plays. As an independent EE driver, and as it works indirectly through the HPWS channel, greater financialization has on balance a clear negative influence on the projected engagement trend. European and Asian companies may have the advantage in this area since their national economies and business systems are less free-market, neoliberal, and finance driven and thus provide an economic environment more encouraging to the longer-lived types of physical/human capital investments that are conducive to a high-engagement workplace.

Another macro-level trend affecting employee engagement is shifts in the occupational and educational composition of the workforce. People in white-collar jobs, for example, report higher average levels of engagement than people in blue-collar jobs, as do college graduates relative to high-school graduates (Truss et al., 2014; Bryne, 2015). These factors on balance favor a rising engagement trend.

Other macro-level contextual and driver factors can be cited, but at this point the general outline is established. Some underlying trends, such as greater IT connectivity, white-collar share of employment, and transformed socio-technical work systems promote engagement, while others, such as expanding financialization, low-wage service sector, and shrinkage of the manufacturing base, reduce engagement levels.

All of these factors affect the direction of the EE trend line, but recent research also finds that, to determine the ultimate outcome, one also has to know how company CEOs and top leadership teams react to them. A research study by IBM Analytics (2017) finds, for example, that fully 70

percent of the variation in EE experience is attributable to strategic decisions and actions of company managers. As has been visible for decades,
many CEOs and companies say employees are their most valuable asset,
but far fewer consistently and credibly walk the talk. If levels of employee
engagement are to significantly increase over the next decade, the start
point will be with a broad range of CEOs who articulate a stakeholder/
HPWS form of people-led business strategy, drive the strategy throughout
the company and into the fabric of the culture, make large and visible
investments in the people-led strategy, and ensure the psychological contract is consistently honored or revised only after genuine employee participation and voice.

It is not obvious, once all the rhetoric is stripped away, that the underlying drivers are in place on the company side to spur such a people-led, high-
road, HPWS movement on a significant scale (Osterman, 2018). Similarly,
employees are only willing to make a major investment of their minds,
bodies, and hearts in the success of their companies if they have long-term
job security and trust the organization will reciprocate with proportional
investment in things that matter to them, such as well-paying jobs with
interesting work, career development, and meaningful voice and participation. The conundrum is these employee perquisites raise and rigidify direct
short-run labor cost which many companies seek to avoid and also require
managers to share more of their time, power, resources, and decision
making which many resist (Stewart et al., 2017).

Our conclusion, therefore, is that the overall level of EE may rise somewhat in the next decade as a larger share of the economy's jobs shifts to
more intrinsically motivating and meaningful professional, technical, creative, and knowledge occupations, but, for the rest of the workforce and
for the reasons outlined above, simply maintaining the current level of
employee engagement is likely to be a challenge. Should the current decade-
long economic expansion end, say from trade wars, over-speculation in
stocks/real estate, or stagnant growth in household income and purchasing power, the engagement outlook for people in the lower half of the job
hierarchy correspondingly deteriorates.

CONCLUSION

The future of work topic examined in this chapter is employee engagement.
While many thousands of articles, reports, and books have been written
on engagement in the last thirty years, and many box–arrow causal models
drawn and explained, very few studies have taken these ideas and tools and
used them to analyze the future direction of a workplace outcome, such as

EE. The engagement level of employees over the next decade, for example, may follow a steady upward trend, remain roughly constant, decrease along a negative trend line, or cycle up and down, and it is a value-added function of scientific research to provide an informed prediction.

In this chapter we have adopted an analytic, model-driven approach to predicting the future direction of employee engagement. This approach, encouraged by Boxall, Purcell, and Wright (2008) as a method to strengthen the scientific credibility and contribution of management research, will not appeal to all readers and, as with other approaches, has strengths and weaknesses. It does provide, however, a systematic framework for thinking about EE as a dependent variable, the independent driver variables that cause it to change, important contextual and moderator variables that condition main effects, the nature of the cause–effect mediating process and key variables in it, and the entire bundle as an interdependent system. An important part of the scientific project is to develop logical cause–effect explanations of human behavior patterns, express them as theories, translate the theories into operational models, and use the models to deduce hypotheses and predictions. Even if our predictions of the future course of EE prove greatly inaccurate, the exercise nonetheless makes a methods/tool contribution through the development and application of an analytical modeling framework and a theoretical/empirical contribution by clarifying the nature of the engagement construct and identifying not only variables that belong in an engagement model but also those that don't.

In ending, it needs to be said that all of the predictions -- or call them guestimates – offered here are made with the proviso of ceteris paribus. Many aspects of the economic and political situation may greatly change in years ahead in ways that no one can anticipate, with large repercussions for companies, employees, workplace attitudes and relations, and behaviors such as EE. A model can predict an outcome within a given situational context, but change the situation, such as a global financial crisis, and we all enter uncharted territory.

NOTE

The authors acknowledge financial support from the ARC (DP140100194), SSHRC (435-2015-0801), and the Innovation Resource Center for Human Resources (IRC4HR).

REFERENCES

Albrecht, S. (2010). "Employee engagement: 10 key questions for research and practice." In S. Albrecht (Ed.), *Handbook of Employee Engagement: Perspectives, Issues, Research and Practice* (pp. 3–19). Cheltenham, UK and Northampton, MA, USA: Edward Elgar Publishing.

Aon Hewitt. (2018). *2018 Trends in Global Employee Engagement*, at https://www.aon.com/2018-global-employee-engagement-trends/index.html (accessed October 13, 2019).

Appelbaum, E., T. Bailey, P. Berg, and A. Kalleberg (2000). *Manufacturing Advantage: Why High-Performance Systems Pay Off*. Ithaca, NY: ILR Press.

Bakker, A. (2010). "Engagement and 'job crafting': engaged employees create their own great place to work." In S. Albrecht (Ed.), *Handbook of Employee Engagement: Perspectives, Issues, Research and Practice* (pp. 229–44). Cheltenham, UK and Northampton, MA, USA: Edward Elgar Publishing.

Bakker, A. and M. Leiter (2010). *Work Engagement: A Handbook of Essential Theory and Research*. New York, NY: Psychology Press.

Beer, M., P. Spector, P. Lawrence, D. Mills, and R. Walton (1984). *Managing Human Assets*. Boston, MA: Harvard Business School Press.

Bersin, J. (2015). "Becoming irresistible: a new model for employee engagement." *Deloitte Review*, 16 at https://www2.deloitte.com/insights/us/en/deloitte-review/issue-16/employee-engagement-strategies.html (accessed October 13, 2019).

Bersin, Josh (2019). "Employee engagement 3.0 – from feedback to action," at https://joshbersin.com/2019/04/employee-engagement-3-0-from-feedback-to-action/ (accessed October 13, 2019).

Blasi, J. and D. Kruse (2006). "U.S. high-performance work practices at century's end." *Industrial Relations*, 45(4), pp. 457–78.

Boxall, P., J. Purcell, and P. Wright (2008). *Oxford Handbook of Human Resource Management*. Oxford: Oxford University Press.

Bryne, Z. (2015). *Understanding Employee Engagement*. New York, NY: Routledge.

Chartered Institute for Personnel and Development (CIPD). (2014). *Megatrends: Are UK Organizations Getting Better at Managing Their People?* London: CIPD.

Commons, J. (1919). *Industrial Goodwill*. New York, NY: McGraw-Hill.

Fleck, S. and I. Inceoglu (2010). "A comprehensive framework for understanding and predicting engagement." In S. Albrecht (Ed.), *Handbook of Employee Engagement: Perspectives, Issues, Research and Practice* (pp. 31–42). Cheltenham, UK and Northampton, MA, USA: Edward Elgar Publishing.

Gallup Organization. (2018). *Employee Engagement on the Rise in the U.S.*, at https://news.gallup.com/poll/241649/employee-engagement-rise.aspx (accessed October 13, 2019).

Guest, D. (2014). "Employee engagement: a skeptical analysis." *Journal of Organizational Effectiveness: People and Performance*, 1(2), pp. 141–56.

Gomez, R., Barry, M., Bryson, A., Kaufman, B., Lomas, G. and Wilkinson, A. (2019), "The "good workplace": The role of joint consultative committees, unions and HR policies in employee ratings of workplaces in Britain", Vol. 2 No. 1, pp. 60-90. https://doi.org/10.1108/JPEO-09-2018-0024

Hakanen, J. and G. Roodt (2010). "Using the job demands–resources model to predict engagement: analyzing a conceptual model." In A. Bakker and M. Leiter (Eds.), *Work Engagement: A Handbook of Essential Theory and Research* (pp. 85–101). New York, NY: Psychology Press.

Halbesleben, J. (2010). "A meta-analysis of work engagement: relationships with burnout, demands, resources, and consequences." In A. Bakker and M. Leiter (Eds.), *Work Engagement: A Handbook of Essential Theory and Research* (pp. 102–17). New York, NY: Psychology Press.

Huselid, M. (1995). "The impact of human resource management practices on turnover, productivity, and corporate financial performance." *Academy of Management Journal*, 38(3), pp. 635–72.

IBM Analytics. (2017). *The Employee Experience Index*, at https://www.ibm.com/downloads/cas/JDMXPMBM (accessed October 13, 2019).

Kahn, W. (1990). "Psychological conditions of personal engagement and disengagement at work." *Academy of Management Journal*, 33(4), pp. 692–724.

Kahn, W. (2010). "The essence of engagement: lessons from the field." In S. Albrecht (Ed.), *Handbook of Employee Engagement: Perspectives, Issues, Research and Practice* (pp. 20–30). Cheltenham, UK and Northampton, MA, USA: Edward Elgar Publishing.

Kaufman, B. (2008). *Managing the Human Factor: The Early Years of Human Resource Management in American Industry*. Ithaca, NY: Cornell University Press.

Kaufman, B. (2015). "The future of employee voice in the USA: Predictions from an employment relations model of voice." In S. Johnstone and P. Ackers (Eds.), (pp. 278-99). Oxford: Oxford University Press.

Kaufman, B., M. Barry, R. Gomez, and A. Wilkinson (2018). "Evaluating the state of the employment relationship: a balanced scorecard approach built on Mackenzie King's model of an Industrial Relations system." *Relations Industrielles* [Industrial Relations], 74(4), pp. 664–701.

Keenoy, T. (2014). "Engagement: the murmuration of objects?" In C. Truss, R. Delbridge, K. Alfes, A. Shantz, and E. Soane (Eds.), *Employee Engagement in Theory and Practice* (pp. 197–220). London: Routledge.

Lawler, E. (1986). *High-Involvement Management*. San Francisco, CA: Jossey-Bass.

McGregor, D. (1960). *The Human Side of Enterprise*. New York, NY: Harper.

Osterman, P. (2000). "Work reorganization in an era of restructuring: trends in diffusion and effects on employee welfare." *Industrial and Labor Relations Review*, 53(2), pp. 179–96.

Osterman, P. (2018). "In search of the high road: meaning and evidence." *Industrial and Labor Relations Review*, 71(1), pp. 3–34.

Paauwe, J., D. Guest, and P. Wright (2013). *HRM & Performance: Achievements and Challenges*. New York, NY: Wiley.

Purcell, J. (2012). "The limits and possibilities of employee engagement." Warwick Papers in Industrial Relations, No. 96. Coventry: Warwick University.

Purcell, John. (2014). "Time to focus on employee voice as a prime antecedent of employee engagement: rediscovering the black box." In D. Robinson and J. Gifford (Eds.), *The Future of Engagement Thought Piece Collection* (pp. 21–27). Brighton: Institute for Employment Studies.

Robinson, D. and J. Gifford (2014). *The Future of Engagement Thought Piece Collection*. Brighton: Institute for Employment Studies.

Saks, A. (2006). "Antecedents and consequences of employee engagement." *Journal of Managerial Psychology*, 21, pp. 600–619.

Schaufeli, W. and A. Bakker (2010). "Defining and measuring work engagement: bringing clarity to the concept." In A. Bakker and M. Leiter (Eds.), *Work*

Engagement: A Handbook of Essential Theory and Research (pp. 10–24). New York, NY: Psychology Press.

Schaufeli, W., M. Salanova, and A. Bakker (2002). "The measurement of engagement and burnout: a two sample confirmatory factor analytic approach." *Journal of Happiness Studies*, 3, 71–92.

Smith, Adam. (1776[1937]). *An Inquiry into the Nature and Causes of the Wealth of Nations*. New York, NY: Random House.

Stewart, G., S. Astrove, C. Reeves, E. Crawford, and S. Solimeo (2017). "Those with the most find it hardest to share: exploring resistance to the implementation of team-based empowerment." *Academy of Management Journal*, 60(6), pp. 2266–93.

Truss, C., R. Delbridge, K. Alfes, A. Shantz, and E. Soane (2014). *Employee Engagement in Theory and Practice*. London: Routledge.

Voice Project. (2019). At https://www.voiceproject.com/surveys/employee_engagement (accessed October 13, 2019).

Walton, R. (1985). "Toward a strategy of eliciting employee commitment based on policies of mutuality." In R. Walton and P. Lawrence (Eds.), *HRM Trends & Challenges* (pp. 35–68). Boston, MA: Harvard Business School Press.

Wilkinson, A., M. Barry, R. Gomez, and B. Kaufman (2018). "Taking the pulse at work: an employment relations scorecard for Australia." *Journal of Industrial Relations*, 60(2), pp. 145–75.

Index